Penzance
THE BIOGRAPHY

MICHAEL SAGAR-FENTON

AMBERLEY

About the Author

Michael Sagar-Fenton was born in Penzance and educated at Humphry Davy School. He has been involved in many strands of Penzance life: as a school governor, director of the Golowan Festival, assistant director of Stage-Struck Youth Theatre Co., trustee of the Acorn Theatre, chair of the Ritz Community Centre Trust, and press officer of the Penlee Lifeboat, among others.

His published books include *Penlee – The Loss of a Lifeboat*, *The 'Rosebud' and the Newlyn Clearances*, *Serpentine*, *The History of St Michael's Mount* and a novel, *True Colours*.

He was made a Bard of the Cornish Gorsedd in 2005 with the title *'Carer Geryow'* (*'Lover of Words'*).

First published 2015

Amberley Publishing
The Hill, Stroud
Gloucestershire, GL5 4EP

www.amberley-books.com

Copyright © Michael Sagar-Fenton, 2015

British Library Cataloguing in Publication Data.
A catalogue record for this book is available from the British Library.

ISBN 978 1 4456 4263 5 (print)
ISBN 978 1 4456 4273 4 (ebook)

Typesetting and Origination by Amberley Publishing.
Printed in the UK.

Contents

	About the Author	2
	Preface	4
	Introduction	5
1	Beginnings	7
2	The Haven	11
3	The Celts	14
4	Hut Villages	18
5	What the Romans Did	21
6	More Saints in Cornwall	24
7	'History' Begins	28
8	One Town	32
9	Penzance	36
10	Plague	40
11	Growth	43
12	Tudor Days	48
13	Rebellion	56
14	Spanish Fire	63
15	Taking Stock	71
16	Incorporation	78
17	Consolidation	83
18	Civil War	91
19	Recovery	100
20	Sinners	113
21	'... Even in this Place'	120
22	Steam	124
23	Local Difficulties	128
24	Isolation	132
25	Down the Mine	135
26	The Montpellier of England	140
27	Humphry Davy	145
28	Expansion	150
29	'Ye Gods, Is This Penzance!'	158
30	Guides	168
31	High Noon	178
32	Holding On	183
33	The Early Twentieth Century	188
34	The Hungry Years	194
35	War and Peace	199
36	'Modern' Times	207
37	A New Century	217
	Bibliography	221
	Index	223

Preface

This is the ongoing story of a Cornish town. It has been assembled from the written sources listed in the bibliography, and, in its later stages, my own memory. It is as accurate as I have been able to make it, though I apologise at the outset for any errors or omissions.

It follows the work of many celebrated predecessors, in particular Mr P. A. S. Pool's *History of Penzance*, and also Frank Halliday's superb *History of Cornwall*, along with many other diligent scholars and observers.

I have tried to keep its focus on Penzance, though I have diverged into the surrounding areas on which its fortunes depended, and into Cornwall's and England's history for a wider context where it seemed appropriate. I have no evidence, for example, that anyone from Penzance followed An Gof's Cornish Rebellion, the Prayer Book Rebellion or Hopton's Cornish Army in the Civil War, but I cannot imagine that they would not have been present.

I thank all those who have helped me in this project: Penlee House Gallery and Museum; Morrab Library, Linda Collins and Martin Nixon for photographs; Jenny Dearlove and the Penwith Local History Group; my good friend Simon Turney for his merciless work on the text.

Writing the history of my home town has been an adventure I wouldn't have missed, and I thank Amberley Publishing for giving me this opportunity.

Michael Sagar-Fenton
January 2015

Introduction

'The first thing you notice about Penzance', said comedian Mark Steel in his BBC Radio 4 profile of the town, 'is that it's miles away...'

So true. Most visitors arrive from the east at the dog-end of a long and strenuous journey. Many will have turned off to other Cornish destinations on the way, but some travel wearily on, through traffic jams or enduring the last few stale hours in a railway carriage, until Mount's Bay spreads out in front of them. Why?

Penzance does not fall into any particular category. Other towns are more celebrated, more picturesque or more obviously appealing. Yet large numbers of visitors come back to Penzance and district year after year, some so enchanted that they put down roots here.

Many have come to Penzance only because it gives them access to somewhere else. Guidebook after guidebook extols Penzance as somewhere to go and then to leave at once in search of more iconic destinations. As a railway terminus and ferry-port for the Isles of Scilly, it may offer no more than a brief transit.

However, this is not the whole picture. It's no accident that so many of the town's sons and daughters stay there despite the dearth of career opportunities, or come back home as soon as their life's journey allows. The tangible warmth of the town centre, the wide haven of the harbour, the vista from the promenade on a calm morning, the lifting of the heart for returning travellers as their car or train rounds the last curve to open out the broad embrace of the bay: St Michaels' Mount – extraordinarily lovely in any light, Cudden Point away to the east, Penzer Point to the west, and sleeping under the western hills at the Bay's heart, Penzance.

1

Beginnings

'The Borough of Penzance has little or no history of importance...'
Ward Lock & Co.'s *Guide to Penzance*, 1913

Geologists tell us that the basic shape of Cornwall was formed 3 million years ago; an outpouring of molten rock formed a massive, single foundation stone that was 75 km deep and stretched, unbroken, from Dartmoor to the Isles of Scilly. It pushed up a series of jagged granite peaks, once mightily higher than today, including Bodmin Moor and the West Penwith massif, worn down to softer contours by time and weather. It is the giant geological feature known as the Cornubian Batholith.

To witness human settlements, one then has to wind the clock forward almost all the way, ignoring the eruptions and inundations, the advances and retreats of the ice, the rise and fall of both sea and land, the tectonic dance of the super-continents, and pause at 4000 BC. By then, the English Channel had fully formed, separating Britain from the continent, and the shape of a recognisable Cornwall emerged. Except for the right angle of the Lizard, which arrived from a different geological source, Cornwall is a wedge pointing directly south-west, offering the least resistance to the prevailing winds. It receives the first and worst of whatever comes across the ocean – millennia of gales, sheeting rain, violent storms and huge waves. The journey to the extreme west is still an expedition into the wild.

In a bad storm the salt spray drives over the county from one coast to another, and the sound of its roar fills the air. On kinder days, even those nowhere near the coast can feel the sea's moisture softening the air and see the extra clarity of the light. Surrounding the peninsula with a natural constancy of temperature, the sea wraps around Cornwall, taking the edge off the hot weather and raising low temperatures to an equable minimum, banishing ice and snow to a few short winter weeks, if at all. Cornwall's history came first from the sea.

Its other legacy was hidden from sight, one that meant almost nothing in 4000 BC but came to dominate its industry, prosperity and the fate of those who lived here in later generations.

Cornwall is a geological marvel, a jigsaw with few mineral formations extending more than a dozen miles in any direction. Many people think Cornwall's geology is entirely made up of granite. It certainly sits on a giant lump of it, but the changes over the last 3 million years, including a period of almost complete submersion, added many different varieties of surface material. To detail them all would require another book, but they include large areas of Devonian slate, china clay, various breccias and schists, some sandstone and shale, and other smaller deposits. Most significantly, as the granite cooled down numerous deep cracks appeared, as they do in a loaf of bread. Into these cracks – or 'dykes' as they are known – flowed metals that were still in a molten state. These filled up the cracks, cooled and solidified to form lodes of tin, copper, lead, small quantities of silver and gold and even uranium.

The early civilisations of the Mediterranean and the Far East discovered an alloy called bronze; a workable but durable material, fit for the making of complex tools, weapons, containers and even beautiful works of art. It was crucial to human advancement and gave its name to a whole age of development, lasting around 5,000 years. Bronze consists mostly of copper, but copper was too soft to be useful until it was stiffened with 10–20 per cent of another metal, with the most successful alloy being the combination of copper and tin. The developing world depended on a supply of tin for bronze and is many uses.

It was never Cornwall's part in history to conquer and occupy other territories. A society relying on simple, hard-won subsistence, far from any centre of human activity, might have been its natural fate until the age of travel and leisure. However, Cornwall held a reservoir of essential minerals beneath its surface so wide and rich that the outside world soon come to know of it. Tin was comparatively rare in continental Europe, and so prospectors travelled far and wide in search of it; they took to their boats and extended their search overseas. Their major discovery was Ireland, where they found not only large deposits of copper but an even greater treasure – gold. On one unrecorded day they came to shore between the wide arms of Lizard and Land's End, and landed in Mount's Bay.

The first visitors may have come across from Brittany or have been gradually prospecting down the coast of England. They were possibly en route to Ireland, looking to find an alternative route to the passage of Land's End, whose seas, contrary winds, tides, reefs and shoals have been a terror to sailors from the earliest times. Their boats were large by local standards, containing a crew to handle the oars and leather sail, navigators, skilled metal-workers who would recognise what they were looking for, as well as provisions, gifts of bronze and jewellery to exchange, and some light weapons. The boats would have been mainly open, made of wood and leather with a covered canopy at the rear, navigated by the sun and stars and mapping coasts as it went. Their original port of departure may have been the Aegean or some other port in the Mediterranean or North Africa. Rumours of Cornish tin might already have percolated along the south coast of England and directed their quest, or perhaps a serious shortage drove them to venture at random, far into the dangerous western seas.

Watching their progress into the bay was a race of people who were settling from nomadic wandering to the risky venture of making permanent settlements. Their Neolithic ancestors were descended from European tribes who had settled in small communities across southern England before the Channel turned it into an island. As the climate allowed, they had moved further south and west.

To the more advanced civilisations of southern Europe, British tribes were less developed, less socially organised and far less skilled in the finer work of construction, manufacturing, art and warfare. However, their lives and preoccupations were not so dissimilar to our own. They lived in communities, built habitable dwellings, knew how to make a living for themselves and their families from the resources available and had a definite individual culture, of which we have dramatic evidence.

Most of the physical remains of their lives have gone with the millennia, including the disappearance of all organic material, leaving only the stories that can be told in stone. These include the traces of early village hut circles and a few stone tools and weapons. Towering above these are the huge structures past communities made to honour their dead. We cannot tell if these were intended for individuals or members of a dynasty, as any clues have been obliterated by thousands of years of curiosity and looting. The only remains are the tombs themselves. Originally covered by high earth mounds, these massive granite chambers still astonish us with their scale and technology, their engineering and the sheer force required to build them. Only a well-organised and confident culture could have directed the crowds of labourers and their overseers, their housing, feeding and discipline, but even more the sophistication to imagine such tombs and carry their designs to completion. Like present-day cathedrals, these structures reigned over the landscape to awe onlookers with their silent meditation upon death, the afterworld and the journey of the spirit.

The lower ground, anywhere out of the scouring wind, would have been covered in forests and scrubland, so they placed their tombs closest to the sky on hilltops along the central spine of West Penwith. Many more were built on the single island that later became the Isles of Scilly, which founded the legend of Lyonesse, the graveyard of heroes beyond the setting sun.

Nearby, on the higher slopes, single gigantic menhirs and stone circles survive. The most complete circles are found at Boleigh, near Lamorna; the Merry Maidens; Boscawen-Un near Tregonebris, with its inclined central menhir, and at Tregeseal below the spectacular granite outcrop of Carn Kenidjack. Some are close to underground chambers known as Fougous. These precise structures have significance we can only guess at. Over 4,000 years ago, twenty centuries before Christ, the early settlers found the time, energy and skill to sanctify their beliefs with buildings that would stand as long as the landscape itself endured.

2

The Haven

On a more domestic level, settlements began on the coast as well as the hills. Hoards of limpet and mussel shells have been found in Cornwall and Scilly. Fish bones show that the settlers' diet featured a large variety of familiar fish – conger, wrasse, pollock, bass, ling and turbot among others. These settlers had boats, probably small one-man coracle-like fishing craft that were tethered to the shore by a line. Free ranging by ship was not yet part of their lives. They would have seen passing ships, inquisitive explorers not yet ready to land, and had perhaps even encountered them in a tentative way. However, a foreign ship would one day make its way towards shore in a way that showed a determination to land.

Excluding the muddy beaches, the bay offered three realistic possibilities as ports of call. One was Mousehole, a deep cleft in the sheltered cliffs of the eastern side, cut by a stream and protected by an offshore island. Further to the east was a more intriguing prospect, the bare tidal island of St Michael's Mount, then no more than a stub of granite, closer to the coastline than it is now. It is likely that local settlers found this unusual feature useful as a lookout and as a place where boats could be easily loaded and floated off with no need of a jetty. However, the first visitors may have had misgivings about the nature of their welcome and preferred to anchor rather than commit themselves to stranding on a beach, in case the locals decided to attack.

In the innermost part of the bay was a third prominent feature. A large spur of rock sloped down in a single sweep from the higher hills and formed a short peninsula jutting into the bay, eventually diving under the waves, where it continued to feature as a reef for some distance. Close to the waterline, a further small reef jutted out at an angle towards the east. The main spur had a steep face below which was calm water, a tiny bay within a bay that was sheltered from the prevailing winds and close to a shoreline, where small skiffs could land but allowing a quick escape if necessary. There, protected by this headland, was an ideal anchorage.

Spits of land of this type are not uncommon in Cornwall and very common in the Isles of Scilly – shale-covered slopes punctuated by large boulders, bare lichen-covered rocks on the exposed tops with clumps of grass and vegetation taking advantage of the many fissures in the sides, solid rock walls, grey on the weather side and dark on the lee, perhaps a cave or two, the slope gentling out where it neared the sea and changing to the tidal zone where barnacles and other creatures abounded, then the seaweed and the deep sea.

The bones of Penzance are still there under its modern skin. Following the spur down towards the water is Chapel Street, still a windy thoroughfare. At its lower end, the slope steepens and then widens out to a small plain, with Quay Street on the east and Green Street to the west, ending at the solid bulk of the Barbican, the lowest point practical for a permanent building. The spur then descends to the Battery Rocks, under and beside the Jubilee Pool, where the angle leads eastward, hidden under the first two stages of the South Quay. The main feature continues as an underwater reef in a south-eastward direction as far as the final peak of rock on which now stands the warning beacon of the Gear Pole.

Buttressed against the west side of this granite neck, a beach was formed and inland a gently sloping area of arable land once known as the Western Green (hence Green Street). In contrast, the east side was an almost vertical cliff for much of its length, gradually angling to a steep rise where Jennings Street and New Town Lane now run, until finally flattening out near to where the railway station stands. A short beach emerged as it neared this point, though much of the present development there is on land that was reclaimed later. Above the coast was open country.

When the first traders penetrated the interior of West Penwith, their prospecting dreams would have come true. There were large quantities of tin lying on the surface that were easy to recover. Some of the tin lodes had been washed over by rain and streams over the millennia to form a thick layer of mineral silt at lower levels, ready to be dug up and separated by 'streaming'. This involved simple agitation in water, washing away the lighter silt and collecting the heavier minerals in suitable containers ready to be refined into a relatively pure metal. This ore would have been carried by hand in leather sacks down the slopes of the bay towards the most promising loading point. Once peaceful trading relations had been established, this would not have been at the rocky peninsula but the shores of St Michael's Mount, with its easy access at low tide, straight on to the boats. However, in bad weather, the ships would have been dangerously exposed near the Mount and would have run eastward to take shelter either in 'Gwavas Lake' south of Newlyn, or in the lee of the haven's cliffs. Faint pathways would have been drawn on the virgin territory: from Penzance up to the tin grounds of Madron and St Just, and back again, bypassing the headland directly to the Mount.

As traders came more frequently, they would have wished to combine journeys to Cornwall and Ireland. Avoiding the maritime graveyard of Land's End was so vital that they chose to land on one side of the Cornish peninsula, cross the hinterland, and set off again from the other. Regular routes across the peninsula were established. One led from Fowey to Padstow, a long overland journey for heavy loads but flanked by two safe river anchorages. A shorter journey led over the neck of land from St Michael's Mount to Hayle, a highway for caravans of men and later mules, returning with panniers of copper and gold, some in a raw state and some already fashioned by Irish craftsmen into beautiful ornaments, one or two of which were lost on the way until discovered in modern times.

The Neolithic culture, the cult of elaborate graves, stone circles and standing stones around West Penwith, had gradually faded away, and life in West Cornwall was already connected to the wider world by 1500 BC. Due to new finds elsewhere in Europe, the mineral trade slowed to a steady routine. The climate then took a kinder turn, so, despite this setback, more groups of families began to settle, experimenting with year-round agriculture as well as what the country could provide. West Cornwall was a remote community of small self-sufficient tribal groups of no particular interest to the wider world. Technical advances elsewhere had little impact on them, and Cornwall slept, free of invasion or war for around 500 years, the longest period of peace in its history.

Then, in the space of a generation, came the Celts.

3

The Celts

Many people still think of Celts as Cornwall's original residents, but they first began to appear less than 3,000 years ago, as incomers and invaders like any other. They were a mixed group of tribes and people, some short and dark, some tall and fair, pushed out of their territories in France and Western Germany by a settled and expanding local population. At first they were just a few refugees, but towards 700 BC they crossed the Channel in huge numbers, occupying villages in southern England. These probably put up a fight, but the Celts were schooled in battle and far better armed with bronze swords, spears and shields, some beautifully worked, while the villagers had no more experience of warfare than the occasional local dispute. The Celts took over much of southern England, coming gradually to Cornwall by land. At the same time, they were occupying what became the other Brythonic Celtic nations of Brittany and Wales.

With them came not only advances in the arts of war but greater expertise in agriculture, husbandry, weaving and boat-building. The disturbances and skirmishes of central Europe made carrying goods overland dangerous and sea-trading was once again more attractive, especially with the development of the first true ocean-going sailing ships. The traffic from Brittany to Ireland via the Cornish land crossings flourished, and not all of the trade bypassed West Cornwall. The invasion of Cornwall was mostly on these peaceable lines. Tin was in high demand. The first true excavations began, shallow surface scrapes as they were, and the ore was no longer transported in its natural state but smelted into solid blocks close to the workings. The faint moorland trails became established tracks as pack animals took the strain, and some of the trails probably became the roads we follow today. It became worthwhile to create small year-round communities to serve the trade, some on the uplands near the tin streams, some nearer the coast to cope with storage and shipping, and some providing domestic and agricultural support.

Unlike their predecessors, the busy Celts had little time for the culture of the dead, preferring to cremate them and pack their ashes into modest urns. To them, the stone circles and mighty megaliths, already nearly 2,000 years old, were alien and deeply mystical. Their Gods were more practical; the sun, the trees, the elements, augury and superstition and ceremonies of the living, though also including the powerful force of sacrifice conducted by the priesthood of Druids.

It was the time of the founding of the great empires: Greek, Persian and the beginnings of the Roman. Cornwall could not rival these standards of civilisation, but was part of the emerging northern European world, eager to share their cultural and technological advances.

One of the most important of these arrived with a new wave of Celtic invaders around 500 BC, who introduced the first iron tools. Cornwall had almost no deposits of iron, and these imports brought a whole new range of possibilities. Before then, cutting down trees and hewing timber was extremely slow and laborious work. Iron enabled a huge improvement in the clearing of land for planting, ploughing, hoeing, building, and not least mining. Iron could not compare to bronze in finer work, and the Iron Age added an extra capacity to the Bronze Age rather than replacing it. The demand for tin remained steady. It was the lifeblood that kept West Cornwall in the circulation of European trade.

It is around this time that the first recorded snapshot of life in West Cornwall appears, and it has a certain shock value for those who imagine Cornish residents of the time as primitive. The Greek geographer Pytheas made a long voyage sometime between 400–300 BC, principally in search of amber, and toured the south coast of Britain. There is a tinge of surprise in his own account, as recounted many years later by the Roman historian Diodorus Siculus, on finding:

The inhabitants of that part of Britain which is called Belerion are very fond of strangers, and from their intercourse with foreign merchants are civilised in their manner of life. They prepare the tin, working very carefully the earth in which it is produced. The ground is rocky but contains earthy veins, the produce of which is ground down, smelted, and purified. They beat the metal into masses shaped like knuckle-bones [*astragali*] and carry it off to a certain island off Britain named Ictis. During the ebb of the tide the intervening space is left dry and they carry over to the island tin in abundance in their wagons... Here then the merchants buy the tin from the natives and carry it over to Gaul, and after travelling overland for about thirty days they finally bring their loads on horses to the mouth of the Rhone.

Historians have enjoyed attempting to identify the whereabouts of Ictis and to disprove the claims of others, but it is hard to imagine it being anywhere but St Michael's Mount. Sea levels may have changed and land masses sunk, but the presence of a tidal island so close to a rich tin-field is surely unique. It paints a picture of a peaceful and organised hive of industry with a well-prepared product smelted into convenient units for transport, a sizable labour force of waggoners and porters, and a reasonable level of prosperity onshore. A working social hierarchy with established settlements, skilled metalworkers and farmers to supply their needs living in their hillside 'rounds' is suggested by such a description. There is a calming note in the description of Ictis, a society in harmony with itself and the outside world in which the arts of war were unpractised and unnecessary.

However, soon after Pytheas' departure, the reality of the international warfare that was afflicting Europe came to Cornwall with dramatic suddenness. Another tribe of Celts, known from their origins in Switzerland as 'La Tene' Celts, began to pour across the Channel. They were aggressive and well-armed and soon took charge of most of southern Britain. Cornwall was not forgotten. The La Tene were accustomed to harrying and robbing those transporting goods, including tin, in their long journeys across Europe, but they resolved to do better and capture these mineral riches at the source.

Cornwall had no reserves of iron to make weapons and could not counter the iron-tipped spears or broadswords of the invaders. However, they put up a determined resistance, retreating from coastal dwellings and small communities to gather in large, more protective groups in fortified camps on the higher hills. The sea had lost its innocence, no longer the highway for the explorer, trader or friend but as dangerous as any forest from which marauding strangers could be revealed by the light of morning, where a sail could as easily bring bloodshed and sudden death as trade and prosperity. It was many, many centuries before that threat ceased to be a source of anxiety to all who lived within reach of the coast.

Such resistance as there was could not last long. Those who survived the invasion were enslaved, and the new Celtic overlords, anticipating other potential invaders, put the countryside on a more warlike footing. They took over the small native hill forts and transformed some of them into massive strongholds with two or three defensive rings of stone ramparts, a large central area of dwellings, animal pens and wells – everything needed to withstand a siege. They naturally chose the highest points with the best visibility and occupied the chain of hills on the West Penwith plateau; Castle-an-Dinas above Ludgvan; Bartinney and Caer Bran near Sancreed in the centre; Chapel Carn Brea with its panoramic outlook at the western end; and most magnificent of all, Chun Castle on the moors above Morvah. What the builders of Chun Castle made of Chun Quoit – just a couple of hundred yards away but already two millennia old – can only be imagined, but it would have been as great a source of wonder to them as it is to us, and they were superstitious enough to let it sleep on its hillside.

On a smaller scale, overlooking Mount's Bay, was the fortress of Lescudjack Castle.

4

Hut Villages

This impressive feature, sloping down sharply to the south and east and more gently into the inner landscape, was an ideal defensive redoubt. If the sea was now a place of fear, there was no better outpost from which to observe it, to gather in the populace and send a warning beacon to other similar 'castles'. In times of tension the surrounding communities would take shelter behind its walls. It's easy to imagine those engaged in shipping or fishing leaving their families in the fort in the morning, and at the end of the day climbing up the long hill, through the earthen ramparts to the gates of the armed stockade, to gather again inside before a curfew in the early days of the La Tene invasions.

Lescudjack Castle is an enclosure of around 3 acres, towering over the eastern approach of Penzance above Chyandour. It is best appreciated from the end of the South Pier, where its strategic position is easiest to see. Antiquarians gave it almost none of the attention lavished on other historic 'castles' and it was largely ignored by the townspeople, most of whom were unaware of its presence or significance. Houses were built on its perimeter, and part of the central circle within the ancient ramparts was given over to allotments. However, in recent years its importance has finally been recognised. It was purchased for the town in 2004, and an annual celebration of the Winter Solstice known as Montol now takes place within its bounds.

Within a few generations, the relations between the La Tene overlords and the native occupants softened and merged to a more mutual community. However, the fortifications remained vital to their well-being. Upheavals in central Europe and the expansion of the various warring empires led to the displacement of many other tribes who were forced to fight for territory in the west of France and Brittany. By around 200 BC many of these took ship and became pirates, roaming the Channel, landing swiftly with ruthless violence and carrying off whatever they could steal. All around the coasts of Cornwall and Brittany natural headlands were enclosed and fortified as defensive retreats. The shelter of Lescudjack became more important than ever, a vital link in the little settlement's survival.

Between such alarms the influence of iron as a substitute for bronze was making profound changes. With iron came ploughshares strong enough to be drawn by oxen, axes for clearing woodland, saws to hasten the building of dwellings or boats, and for the first time a means of shaping the granite of the landscape itself, the first meaningful working of stone. This led to the building of more complex stone dwellings and courtyards, as well as the ability to revolutionise the extraction of tin as mines were dug into the solid rock.

Many of the courtyard villages survive, some built on the former sites of wooden buildings. They were built over a wide length of time, perhaps abandoned for a while then re-inhabited, most showing signs of alteration and improvement over a long period. The best preserved hut villages in Penwith are those at Porthmeor, now hidden by bushes in farmland near Morvah; Carn Euny near Sancreed with its magnificent underground Fougou; and, most celebrated of all, the complex at Chysauster above Gulval. The villages are clearly peacetime developments, lower down the hills than the 'castles', on land cleared of trees and capable of cultivation. Shorn of roofs, fireplaces, domestic details, implements, animals and the business of the families who lived there, they seem bleak and primitive. However, generations of Cornish people found them comfortable and convenient enough to make their homes in.

West Cornwall's climate may have been more moderate at the time, but people still wonder why their forebears chose such windswept and exposed places to live. It was partly because life far from the sea was considerably less risky, partly because most of the lower, more fertile land was still covered in thick forest, and partly because they needed to be defensive positions with a clear view over their surroundings, enclosed by a wooden palisade that kept domestic animals in and intruders and thieves out. However, these communities were eventually abandoned when better alternatives became available for exactly those reasons of exposure to the weather and poverty of land. There is evidence of a temporary period of worsening climate that would have made the uplands even more inhospitable. No doubt the more successful villages, those still lived in now, began in just the same way and no doubt beneath many of them courtyard villages, like Chysauster, once existed. The rest remain as they were left in the last few years BC.

By the first days of the Christian era, the three foundations of Cornwall's wealth – tin, fish and farming – were established. Central England was well populated and, as the first skirmishing Romans discovered, well protected, but it was made up of warring tribes interrupted by constant intrusions from the Continent. Great river ports like London and Liverpool were still villages on muddy estuaries and there were no great inland cities. Further north, the country became increasingly wild up to the constantly permeable border with the fierce Scots. The Cornish, together with many of the Venetii tribes of Brittany who had crossed over to their cousins' lands as refugees, were as secure and civilised as anywhere in mainland Britain.

5

What the Romans Did

Despite their profound effect on the island of Brittania, the Romans left Cornwall mostly to its own devices. Unlike other invaders with their lightning strikes by sea, the Romans made most of their conquests the hard way, overland, consolidating their control and leaving garrisons behind to cover their supply chains as they slowly advanced. They would have been aware of Cornwall's existence since it was one of the few places in Britain with an international reputation. However, their westward advance over England petered out at Exeter. No doubt they sent scouts further west who would have reported on the bleak miles of Dartmoor and Bodmin Moor, a testing and expensive landscape to march over in what might be hostile country, requiring a huge investment of resources to keep a thin line of supply open. They came to the conclusion that invasion would not be worth the trouble. Instead, having made sure that a British revolt from the west was unlikely, they opened a small amount of trade with the Cornish and otherwise left them in peace. They had also discovered a new supply of tin in Spain and so had no special need at first of Cornwall's most valuable export.

Safe from the South West, having fortified the Welsh borders and built a wall against the Scots, the Romans painstakingly proceeded to conquer and pacify the rest of England. The social and physical advances they imported with them were a cultural leap for the islanders – paved roads, fine houses, cities, bridges, ports, water supplies, wine, and for the first time a unified order of governance. Britain quickly grew up to imitate the lifestyle of its Mediterranean masters, and was within a few generations enjoying something of the same standard of living, if not their climate.

Left out of this national civilising process were the western margins into which the Celts had fled and stubbornly defended, the newly defined Celtic Fringes. Cornwall, so recently the forerunner in civilisation and prosperity, became at least to the eyes of Roman Britain an irrelevant backwater, a stony projection they could happily live without. Indeed, for many years of Roman occupation the history of Cornwall is static and dark. The main part of Britain was fully assimilated into the Roman Empire. Britons were proud to describe themselves as Roman citizens, and the divide between them and the Cornish had never been wider.

Over time, a greater amount of interaction began to take place. Tin gained value again as overseas tin became scarce, and several excavated hoards of Roman coins, including one in Marazion Marsh – not to mention one at Caerhays containing some 2,500 coins – speak of lively business relations. Cornish communities began to consolidate into larger units. With the strength of iron tools, men could begin to dominate their environment instead of being confined within its limits. They cut paths, cleared woodland, enclosed fields with stone walls and created more ambitious communities. Agriculture became a practical way of life rather than a struggle for subsistence. The population started to expand. Communities were in contact with each other and, cut off from the Roman east, Cornwall together with West Devon began to think of itself as an entity.

Penzance harbour, by now fitted with wooden jetties, also grew as a dwelling place of its own. A little further up the hill, better protected from sudden skirmishes from the sea, a few dwellings set themselves up beside the old crossways where the outgoing trails to the tin fields crossed the road back to St Michael's Mount.

Penzance's chief rival for local sea traffic was Mousehole. It was no more than a steep cleft, but it provided a rough shore of shingle on to which boats could be hauled above high water and the bonus of protection from the island from which it took its original name, Porth Enys (Island Port). Tucked under the eastern hill, it could watch the south-westerly gales go roaring past though, like Penzance, it was exposed when the gale turned south-easterly. Mousehole developed as a major fishing port, which it continued to be until living memory.

A few Romans (very few) moved west into the pacified country. One or two Roman villa remains have been found, though often in its history Cornwall adopted up-country fashions long after they were new. It is quite possible that Roman styles were simply imitated by wealthy local traders. Meanwhile, the native Cornish population was building fully seaworthy boats to extend their reach, delving deeper into the ground, growing new crops and gaining a more stable social order in their own Celtic style. Celtic cousins still crossed over the Hayle–Marazion portage, bringing trade, innovations and news, but under the benevolent Roman shadow Cornwall had space and peace in which to grow.

This happy state lasted some 300 years, from around AD 50–350. In that time the Roman Empire reached its zenith, became gross with its own excesses and started to fracture.

Cornwall felt little of these pressures. Another revival of the tin trade occurred in the latter years of this period when Barbarians overran the Iberian tin-fields and the Romans had greater need to come west for tin. But the threats to their European empire and to Rome itself meant more and more of its troops were called back to defend them, reducing their garrisons in their furthest-flung colonies. Cornwall did not rise, having never been invaded, but all along the southern and eastern coasts of Britain skirmishing tribes started to gnaw at the formerly impregnable Roman defences and found them surprisingly vulnerable. It was a slow and painful process, the death by inches of a once majestic creature, but the momentum was unstoppable and the outcome could only end in chaos.

By then, another revolution was already under way, one that would prove more durable and profound than any of Rome's achievements. Out of sight of all but a few, the life and death of a Jewish preacher started a belief system that began to resonate with the masses, despite all attempts by Romans and Jews alike to snuff it out. At the height of Roman civilisation, while Cornish settlers were still constructing villages like Chysauster, Christianity was stuttering into flame.

6

More Saints in Cornwall

The rise of Christianity is one of the greatest phenomena the world has ever seen. The Disciples of Christ managed to spread their influence throughout the Middle East and eventually into the heart of Rome itself. From there Christianity reached out to the whole Roman Empire and around the world. Its path into Cornwall was a roundabout route via Ireland, which had not just embraced Christianity as enthusiastically as its own Celtic gods but put its own unique Celtic gloss on it. It was this Celtic Christianity arriving by sea, not the orthodox Roman style, which influenced Cornwall, supported by the traditional cross-fertilisation from Ireland to Wales, Wales to Cornwall, and Cornwall to Brittany.

The legends of the saints are typical of the romantic Celtic imagination. These were mainly individual preachers who established little chapels and set themselves the task of converting the Cornish. Many were no more than rough shelters near a site already believed to possess some magic, like a hilltop, an island, a stream, or especially a spring or well. Some tales tell of battles between Christians and established local chieftains, clearly later in the process when Christians were becoming a sect to be reckoned with. Apart from their names, little evidence is left of the coming of the saints. Often altered and corrupted, these remain the names of many Cornish villages and towns today, so many that it was said that there were 'more saints in Cornwall than there are in heaven'. Lacking authentic stories of their own, it was several centuries afterwards that others made up legends for them, thoroughly enjoyable tales of ridiculous means of transport and eye-popping miracles, happily regardless of time – as the supposed 'discovery' of tin by Cornwall's patron saint St Piran, which had already been extracted in Cornwall for 2,000 years.

The hermit cells turned into small meeting houses for year-round assemblies, made of wood or stone (the earliest surviving church is that of St Piran at Perranporth dating from around AD 600, which has been recently restored). Further buildings rose, fell and rose again until the congregation either abandoned them or they became the parish churches we still have. The strict division between Christian religion and other ancient beliefs came later and the Celtic tribes worshipped their local saints almost as freely as Christ. At some point, the villagers around the promontory of Penzance would have chosen for themselves a particular saint as a protective patron.

To the east, the country was being torn apart from its Roman unity to a battleground of rival invaders. Picts and Scots were crowding down from the north, Germanic tribes invaded the coastline on the east and south, and for the first time the name that would inspire terror along every coast, the Vikings, had begun their depredations. None of these took particular interest in the rocky west, but instead fought over the rich farmlands and forests of central Britain. Having lost its main customer for tin, Cornwall shrank back to a subsistence economy of farming and fishing. The Celtic fringes were a nation apart and glad to be so, though battles with the Saxon invaders raged as close as Somerset, Dorset, and East Devon.

The Saxons gained most of the country and settled down. Their warlike reputation was eventually modified by the arrival in 597 of St Augustine, who managed to convert them to a new Roman Empire of Christianity. This was ratified by the Synod of Whitby in 664, which unified the various Saxon churches into one. With the exception, as so often, of Cornwall, Dumnonia, as the Romans called it, remained a place apart. It already had its own Christian bishops, based at St Germans, its own monks, friaries and parishes, an entirely separate hierarchy of Christian worship.

In the struggle to unify England as a state under a single king, the Saxons finally turned their attention towards the west. By 710 they had reached as far as Exeter, though the Saxons, like the Romans, paused before tackling the bare western moors. Cornwall's time finally came in 814 when Egbert marched his troops through Cornwall from one end to the other, the first general to do so. The Cornish even attempted an alliance with the Vikings to stop them, but they were no match for the battle-hardened Saxons. Their last stand was at the hamlet of Boleigh, west of Lamorna, in the shadow of the ancient standing stones, the Piper and the Fiddler.

Cornwall was absorbed into Wessex. The Saxons were used to forcing Christianity on remote tribes they conquered, but this time they were met, to their surprise, with the news that Cornwall had been Christian for several hundred years longer than their invaders and even had their own clergy. Egbert wisely left them to it, though he imposed his administrative rule, the feudal system, on the Cornish, appointing English governors and reducing local chieftains to a more manageable status as lords of their manors. He also brought the English language, though its progress from east to west of Cornwall was to take several centuries.

Cornwall made its peace with its new overlords and was eventually glad of their protection as wave after wave of Vikings assailed the coastline. The county had little to tempt them but they were ubiquitous, sailing in large and well-organised fleets, expert in navigation and warfare, terrifying in battle and utterly merciless. Having devastated a place they would wait for a year or two until it was reconstructed before paying another visit. If they could find nothing else of value they would be satisfied to carry off as many men, women and children as they could to sell as slaves. There was no other defence than flight to the interior once their sails were sighted, and the burning of local villages was an inevitable consequence of their landings.

At some point in this uneasy period, the Christian inhabitants of the little port in Mount's Bay erected their first building to commemorate their faith, somewhere on the lower slopes of the hill above the harbour. It was built as a place of worship for those ashore and prominently placed to give comfort to homecoming sailors as they entered the bay. It was almost certainly dedicated from the first to St Anthony. They christened the cape from the Cornish 'Pen Sans', the Holy Headland.

Several small communities radiated from Pen Sans. Lescudjack Castle was still in use and would have been one of the defended strongholds during the Saxon invasion. There may have been a monastery in the area between the Western Green and Newlyn still known as the Mennaye, 'monastery' in Cornish. Most significant of all was the growing settlement at the crossing a couple of hundred yards up the hill from the port. Like most crossroads, it became a meeting place and a market, a focus for the community. It probably already existed as a Celtic village, but it was clearly well established as a separate entity from the port below by the time of the Saxons. As such, it became part of a manor granted to a Saxon overlord. His name – the first written name we have in connection with Penzance – was later noted in the Domesday Book as Alward or Alvard, and the manor in question Alwardtun, Alward's town. It's quite likely that Alward never set foot in his manor, but his name has come down the centuries as Alverton – still the name of streets, houses, a housing estate and a school today.

Saxon England consolidated its grip and eventually imposed its own Christian organisation on Cornwall, dividing the larger Celtic parishes into those we have today. Wherever possible, these centred on existing Celtic foundations. However, by 1043 the old Cornish bishopric of St Germans had been abolished. Cornwall became part of the diocese of Sherborne, Crediton and finally Exeter, in which it remained until 1876. By 1100, the parish division was mostly achieved. Penzance was flanked on one side by Gulval and on the other by Paul, but neither of the two settlements in between was chosen as a parish. Instead, they were both incorporated under the Parish of Madron, 2 miles into the interior.

Madron lies on the hills above Mount's Bay and commands a good view of it. It had been chosen as a sacred site by the Celts probably because of the 'holy' well on its outskirts and became a church early in the Christian era. Despite its proximity to the tin fields, Madron never grew into anything bigger than a rural village. Nonetheless, much of its prosperity came from Penzance. Local churches had been sustained from the beginning by gifts of food and other goods from the faithful, and as Christianity grew this converted into a compulsory tithe, a donation of a tenth of each household's resources, in kind or in cash. Like many settlements that were remote from their mother parish, Penzance chafed under this agreement, but it was subject to the laws of the Church and had no choice.

Cornwall settled down under the Saxon rule as it had under its Celtic chiefs, going about its ordinary business, slowly increasing in population, trade and sophistication. Then came the date known to every schoolchild – 1066.

7

'History' Begins

Faithful as usual to the regime they were under, the Cornish took up arms to resist the Norman invasion, marching across the border to support a local Saxon stronghold at Exeter and giving way only gradually, skirmish by skirmish. It was not until 1072 that the whole of Saxon England had resigned itself to Norman rule.

The Normans were themselves of Viking origin but had nothing in common with their forebears' smash-and-grab mentality. They were expert in the minutiae of governance, the painstaking division of their spoils into governable units, the ability to oversee them, keep them in order, and of course tax them as thoroughly as possible. The prime example of this is the Domesday Book, an inventory of the proceeds of their invasion and an estimate of how much tax could be exacted from each part of their new kingdom. Although Penzance did not feature, except for a reference to the Manor of Alwardtun, it gives an invaluable portrait of a country that had been little recorded since the departure of the Romans 500 years prior. The balance of farming, the arable 'hides' (units of around 120 acres), even the number of goats were faithfully set down along with the woodland, so vital for building ships and dwellings. It also counts Cornwall's population for the first time at around 20,000.

Four manors in West Cornwall are mentioned in the Domesday Book: Alverton, Lanisley (Gulval), Ludgvan and Truthwall. All told, the Manor of Alwardtun boasted seventy-one households, made up of villagers, smallholders and serfs, and was relatively large by Cornish standards. With these went extensive ploughland, pasture and meadow, supporting 9 cattle, 4 pigs, 100 sheep and various poultry, powered by an unnamed number of oxen and one hard-working horse.

William I's half-brother Robert, Count of Mortain, had provided 120 ships for the invasion fleet and fought at his side at the Battle of Hastings. His reward was a generous grant of lands and their income. The greater part of this bequest was the whole of Cornwall, of which he was created earl, though he soon returned to Normandy and spent little time in his Cornish earldom.

He did however make a gift of St Michael's Mount to the matching French Benedictine monastery of Mont St Michel. The Mount had long been the home of monks and a departing place for English pilgrims en route for Santiago de Compostela. In 495, a local fishing boat reported a timely vision of St Michael the Archangel standing on one of its rocky outcrops, which was officially recognised and promoted the Mount itself to a holy shrine and place of pilgrimage. It was a most lucrative piece of good fortune as pilgrims brought plenty of business and donations to the shrine with them. Robert bequeathed its monastery half a hide of land (around 60 acres) to support it and also the right for the shore-based community opposite to hold a Thursday market – in Cornish 'Margas Yow' – from which derived its old name of 'Market Jew'. A later market nearby was called 'Marghas Byghan', or 'Little Market' which eventually changed to 'Marazion'. Despite the obvious connotations of the names, neither of them had any connection with Jewry.

Alward's manor was granted to Robert with all the rest and remained in the possession of the earldom until 1230. Robert also built the spectacular castle at Launceston, not to protect Cornwall from eastern invaders but to keep the Cornish within their borders and under control.

The crown passed down from William to his son, Henry I. When both of Henry's sons drowned in the White Ship disaster he tried to secure the succession of his daughter Matilda as England's queen. However, Henry's nephew Stephen, Count of Boulogne, saw an opportunity. Backed by those who were unwilling to see England ruled by a woman, Stephen took a ship and landed in England, somewhere where he was sure he would not be observed. This was at Sennen Cove, to the certain astonishment of the local inhabitants. He was not the last potential monarch to come by that route, or to march to battle through Penzance's marketplace.

A brutal civil war ensued between the supporters of Stephen and Matilda, and Cornwall was heavily involved when Reginald, an illegitimate son of Henry I, became its earl. Reginald and Fitz Richard, his father-in-law and lieutenant of Cornwall, enlisted their Cornish peasants in Matilda's cause. It was a great burden on the unwarlike Cornish for whom such political struggles meant little more than submission to one feudal overlord or another. However, it forced Stephen to lead his army into Cornwall, capturing castle after castle and costing the lives of many of the Cornish conscripts. It was a pointless quarrel. Stephen regained Cornwall and the throne, but died six years afterwards. The country passed down to Matilda's son, Henry II, leaving Reginald once more in charge of Cornwall.

Despite these disturbances, life in Cornwall was becoming more settled and far better organised. Some communities had grown into small towns with an identity and status, a hierarchy of self-government and annual activities and traditions. The regulation of trading became necessary to solve local clashes and conflicts. Shops only existed in cities and most trading was carried out in open markets in town centres, so the Normans busied themselves in appointing specific days of the week for each town's markets, and days of the year for fairs.

Another preoccupation of the orderly Normans was the administration of the many national laws they were introducing. They created county courts and assizes to replace the more haphazard forms of Saxon justice that had existed before then. Local disputes were still resolved by manorial courts, and for more serious crimes judicial circuits were set up around which travelling justices would attend, though the Cornish assizes were held no closer than Launceston.

One area of regulation in particular applied to the tin industry. The Saxons had recognised tinners as a class, excusing them from the regular feudal responsibilities and granting them the right of 'bounding'. This allowed them to search for tin on any piece of suitable land and work it within the bounds marked by the turfs they lifted, subject to paying the landlord one-fifteenth of whatever he produced. The rights of stanneries in Cornwall and south Devon already existed, and in 1197 King John appointed a warden of the stanneries who produced an official charter that recorded and confirmed ancient privileges:

> Digging tin and turfs for smelting it, at all times freely and peaceably and without hindrance from any man, everywhere in moors and in the fees of bishops, abbots and counts, of buying faggots to smelt the tin without waste of forest, and of diverting streams for their works, just as by ancient usage they have been wont to do.

Tinners were distinguished by being answerable only to their warden, subject only to stannary courts, and with their own regime of taxation instead of manorial dues. Naturally, this privilege led to a huge increase in their numbers, enough to annoy the manorial lords. It was confirmed as part of the Magna Carta that they had first call on their subjects' service, tinners or not. This was overturned in turn by Henry III and many tinners' privileges stand, in theory at least, until this day. The increase in their numbers led to a leap in Cornwall's production, rising from 70 tons when the warden was first appointed to 600 tons by 1214, benefitting in turn the increasing shipping and the allied trades in Penzance.

Penzance was still effectively two communities. The higher settlement was clearly more convenient in terms of space and scope for its still-unofficial markets. It already had its own elegant market cross, a magnificent granite column that moved around Penzance several times in its long history and still stands in Penlee Park. The village began to rise to the same level of significance as the port. The thoroughfare between them became busier and the two elements – three including the church town of Madron – formed a highway in a straight line. Though they were physically close, they remained separate in character.

The working of a port was a messy business of hard physical labour in difficult surroundings, with depots of goods and all the paraphernalia of shipping, its noise and smell, and an itinerant population of tough sailors. Penzance's port was exposed to the weather, especially the odd south-easterly gale, against which it had no defences. Up the hill the circumstances were far more orderly. This part was mainly inhabited by a fixed population of local people, some comparatively wealthy, with a great variety of trades and occupations and a visible social order. It was there that the administrative centre naturally took root, and from there that links with other towns were formed. The relationship of the two was similar to other places in Cornwall, where a single community might consist of a port and a separate village, often a church town, higher up the hill away from the perils of the coast, for example Sennen and Sennen Cove, Mullion and Mullion harbour, and even closer at hand, Paul and Mousehole.

Penzance's port and marketplace were too close to be isolated from each other but just too far apart to form a cohesive whole, something which has bedevilled the town ever since. The distinction in names slowly faded away. In 1284, on an obscure assize roll, we first find an official record of the existence of a place with almost 3,000 years of history already behind it – 'Pensans'.

8

One Town

The first recorded mention of Pensans comes in the report of a lurid murder. Apparently,

> James clericus and Ralph the servant of Ralph the Monk of St Michael's Mount and Nicholas de Pensans fought with each other, such that James struck Nicholas in the stomach with a knife from which he died...

By then, the earldom of Cornwall had been passed by Henry III to his younger brother, Richard, and the manor of Alverton was sold by him to a private owner, Henry Le Tyes, in 1230. It remained in the hands of their family for the next 100 years.

Pensans, the holy headland, had by now supported a chapel for many years. No one now knows when it began, where exactly it was, or how many times it was rebuilt, but by Henry Le Tyes' time it was quite substantial. References written by antiquarians in the 1800s describe a stone building in a sad state of disrepair, which had fallen into use as a fish cellar and later a pigsty. One account describes the ruins of a building 30 feet long and 15 feet wide, entered from the direction of the sea, with a small niche containing a granite statue, possibly of St Anthony. The statue has a saint's face on one side and a Madonna on the other and was dated, by Professor Charles Thomas, as early twelfth century. It was ripped out of the building with considerable damage, and used as a building stone to form part of a wall until recognised and rescued in the 1850s. It was then placed in the churchyard of St Mary's church, where it can still be seen. The gardens which now stand below the spot are known as St Anthony's Gardens.

The road to Madron was long, steep and arduous even in fine weather, most unwelcoming in winter, and as Penzance grew it was soon agitating for a proper chapel of its own. Progress was made when, as a chantry roll records,

The chapel of Our Lady founded by Sir Henry Tyes, Knight, Lord of the Manor of Alverton, who gave £4 issuing out of the said lands and profits of the Manor for a priest to celebrate there.

This is the first mention of a chapel dedicated to St Mary. A chantry is a private chapel that is funded by a family who could afford to build it and pay a priest to say a daily Mass for the saving of their relatives' souls. This soon proved provident for the last Sir Henry. He fought for the revolutionaries against Edward II in one of the many insurrections of that troubled reign, and was executed for treason in 1322, along with his brother-in law, Warin De Lisle. Sir Henry's will describes a chapel in which Mass is celebrated daily by no less a person than the prior of St Michael's Mount – presumably weather permitting – and if the Lord Le Tyes himself was present, by the rector of Madron. After Sir Henry's death, the chantry was opened up to the people of Penzance as a chapel of ease. The road between the port and the town took the name, 'Our Lady Street', later Chapel Street.

The manor was seized once more by the Crown, the customary punishment for treason. In 1327, Sir Henry Le Tyes' sister, the widow of Warin De Lisle, sued to have the manor returned, with herself as its lord. Alice De Lisle is Penzance's first heroine, and a movement exists today to have her name celebrated in some permanent memorial as the true 'founder' of the town.

Alverton was certainly worth having back. When taken by the Crown in 1322, the assessment of the manor describes a property consisting of a manor house and garden, 200 acres of plough, meadow, pasture, unenclosed land and moorland. The community had risen to 220 households, including 29 who were significantly described as burgesses, urban tenants, a sign of the town's improving status. Eight fishing boats paid for the privilege of plying their trade from Pensans and also paid rent for the sheds that were essential to their trade. Turbary – the permission to cut turfs for fires – was another regular source of manorial income. There were also three water mills belonging to the manor whose importance grew considerably over the subsequent years. In total, the manor's annual income (in cash) was reckoned at the handsome sum of £68 3s 6½d.

The manor included Mousehole, which together with Paul had become a considerable settlement in its own right. It seems to have been run somewhat independently by Roger de Constantine, a clerk of Richard, Earl of Cornwall. He was also appointed parish priest of Paul and made a very comfortable living from these dual offices. In 1266, the Earl granted him permission to hold a three-day fair at Paul and the following year a Thursday market in Mousehole, making it one of the most important settlements in Mount's Bay. By 1327, sixteen fishing boats paid rent there.

Newlyn had started as a minor collection of huts and sheds, and by 1327 had only eight registered taxpayers and was still considered separate from the two other settlements of Tolcarne on the Penzance side of the river and Jackford on the other.

How Lady Alice persuaded the King to give up the manor is not clear, especially as it was undergoing a rapid rise in value. In five years, the number of Pensans boats had risen to thirteen, the turbary income had doubled and other rents were increasing accordingly.

Alice was born and raised in Cornwall and married Warin de Lisle in 1310, moving to his family seat at Kingston Lisle in Oxfordshire (formerly Berkshire) and bearing him five children. After Warin's execution, Kingston Lisle was also seized by the Crown, leaving her with her five children, mourning a brother and a husband, out of favour with the King and effectively homeless.

However, the King had other matters to worry about. By 1327, Queen Isabella with her lover Roger Mortimer had crossed over from France with an invading army and Edward II's power was slipping away. Anxious possibly to curry favour wherever he could, Edward granted Alice's petition in February 1327. By September of that year, he had been defeated, taken, and murdered in Berkeley Castle. At the age of forty, Alice became lord of the manor of Alverton and a wealthy woman.

After moving back to Cornwall, she consolidated her position and concentrated much of her efforts on the establishment of Pensans as the chief town of the district. Its main rivals were Marazion and Mousehole, but while Marazion had its market, it still mainly served as the landward station of the Mount. Mousehole was in her own manor, but clearly appreciated Pensans' more strategic location and its potential for growth (as well as being her own home).

Pensans had neither market nor fair to its name. Fairs were particularly significant, originally market days for a wider community where traders from the countryside and other towns gathered together, selling produce, livestock, horses, equipment, clothing, and later even their own labour. They began as one-day events, but some of the more popular ones extended for several days or even a week, a crucial part of the annual calendar. The crowds would be in a mood to spend and naturally attracted fringe entertainers, buskers, tumblers, bear-baiters, fire-eaters, magicians, musicians and plain beggars, as well as thieves and pick-pockets. They were a much loved public holiday for the town in question. They would have begun informally, as local customs and needs had dictated, but the right to hold a fair became a defining factor in a town's status and a vital element in its prosperity. These rights were much coveted and even fought over.

Edward III proved amenable, and on 25 April 1332 the following proclamation would have been declaimed in Pensans and surrounding towns:

The King to the Archbishops and others greeting.

Know that we of our special grace have given and have confirmed by this our Charter to our beloved Alice who was wife of Warin de Insula [de Lisle] that she and her heirs may have for ever one market every week on Wednesday at her manor of Pensans in the County of Cornwall and one fair there every year lasting for seven days namely on the Eve and Day of St Peter ad Vincula [31 July–1 August] and for five days following.

And one other fair every year at her manor of Mosehole in the said County lasting for seven days namely the Eve and Day of St Bartholomew the Apostle [23–24 August] and for five days following.

Provided that the market and those fairs be not to the damage of neighbouring markets and fairs.

Wherefore we wish and firmly command for us and our heirs that the said Alice and her heirs may have for ever the said market and fairs at her said manors with all liberties and free customs belonging to such markets and fairs as aforesaid.

Among the other details of this crucial text, it confirms that Alverton as a name for the town was beginning to fall out of use and that the two wings of the town would carry the name of Pensans into the future.

9

Penzance

Penzance was now firmly on the map. It now traces its foundation to the Royal Charter of 1614, but the grant in 1332 of a weekly market and an annual seven-day fair was the defining moment. Its straggling history acquired a firmly based future as a market town and trading centre, which would see it through good days and bad. It now stood equally among other Cornish towns, its fair part of the county's annual calendar, its market a magnet for traders around the peninsula that was soon destined to be far more popular than Mousehole's. With tin as its backbone, agriculture all around, and fishing and other port traffic below, it was at last a viable town rather than just part of a manor.

Lady de Lisle continued to show her mettle as a determined and far-seeing woman. In 1334, she applied for and was granted a licence to exhume the remains of her husband and her brother, and to have them reburied with honour in the old Le Tyes family chantry at Chilton Foliat in Wiltshire. In 1336, she was granted a licence to plant a new wood of 200 acres at Kingston Lisle. There is no record that she married again and she lived until 1347 when she was buried alongside her husband. Her estates were inherited by her son Gerald, 1st Baron de Lisle.

The eastern parts of Cornwall were entering into a new era of prosperity, fuelled by a prominent middle class. Guildhalls were being built and towns were sending members to parliament. Truro, Penryn, Lostwithiel, Fowey and Launceston were joining Bodmin as the county's principal towns. Edward III had devised the Duchy of Cornwall to take the place of the former earldom, and granted it to his son Edward, the Black Prince. It subsequently became the automatic inheritance of the heir to the throne, raising Cornwall's status even higher.

Progress in the west was far slower. With the exception of Helston, the land west of Truro was still regarded as a backwater, steeped in the ways of the past, still conversing exclusively in Cornish and of little interest to those enjoying a growing sense of pride in their own improving standards of living. However, it still had tin.

Tin was now in increasing demand throughout Europe, for the making of church bells, pewter and the art of tinplating, among other uses. The 'bounding' rights of the tinners were further complicated by the establishment of the duchy with its own stakes in the outcome. Much tin working was still done by individual prospectors who marked out their stakes and gave them each a name. Hamilton Jenkin mentions such curiosities as 'Clear Diamond, Little Dagger, Down Dribble, North Goodluck, Higher-Recover-the-Fault, Merry Between, Parc Buggens' and many others, each containing the gambler's dream of a single man and his family. Once he had managed by the strength of his arm to strike a worthwhile quantity of tin, he had to begin to share it with those who had never seen a shovel – the manorial lord, the Duchy, and all those connected with the coinage.

Coinage was the means by which the smelted and purified tin was assessed, firstly for quality in case base materials had intruded, and secondly for taxation. The 'coin' was simply the French for 'corner', where a corner of each ingot was cut off and tested. This was fine in theory, but was made greatly more difficult by the division of Cornwall into only four stannaries, based in Liskeard, Lostwithiel, Truro and, closest to Penwith, Helston. The royal assessors called at each in turn, and all tin to be sold had to be carried laboriously to the coinage town. Loe Bar had not yet finally blocked the River Cober, cutting Helston off from the sea, but much of the tin had to be carried from the Penzance district by land, by packhorse along the rough muddy tracks in order to make the date. The coinage process in a busy time might take several days, keeping the tinners from their work and obliging them to stay in and increase the prosperity of the coinage towns that hosted them, so that the right of coinage became a jealously guarded privilege.

Hamilton Jenkin describes the solemnities,

At noon on the first day of the coinage a great company of people assembled in the Coinage Hall, the controller and receiver with the stamping hammer, the weigher and assay master, porters, country chapmen, merchants from London, pewterers, factors and a sprinkling of Italian and Flemish traders.

When the order had been made an open space was roped off in front of the company, the King's beam was brought out, and the weights were solemnly unsealed and handed to the weigher. The assay master then made ready his hammer and chisels and the steward, controller and receiver took their seats facing the beam.

When all was in readiness the porters brought out the blocks one at a time and placed them on the scales. The weight of each was shouted out by the 'peaser' or weigher and was taken down by the three officials. The blocks on leaving the scales were taken in hand by the assay master who chiselled a small piece from the corner of each and rapidly assayed it to ensure the metal was of proper quality. If satisfactory the controller, with a blow of the hammer, struck upon the block the Duchy Arms, a guarantee of both its purity and of its having paid the coinage.

Coinage took place only twice a year, making the tinners' cash flow a fraught business. It was not surprising that a flourishing black market developed where small blocks of portable 'pocket tin' were cast and sold to seamen to be smuggled abroad.

All over Cornwall the prosperity led to a large increase in population, probably three times as many in 1336 as the reckoning in the Domesday Book. Another consequence of prosperity was the number of granite churches being built all over the county. Reliant on wooden scaffolding, hempen ropes, painstaking quarrying and shaping of individual stones, pulleys, levers, capstans, man and horsepower, all marshalled without written plans by the master-builder, they made their slow and elegant way up into Cornwall's skyline. Gothic arches rather than the heavy masonry of the Norman style allowed walls and windows to soar higher and aisles to be added to the sides. Already the focus of each parish, the church became the visible centre of each community.

Edward III made it his crusade to recapture France and reunite the two nations under his kingship. The Vikings had ceased to harry the west Cornish ports, but now the French took their place as occasional raiders and vessels to avoid at sea. Cornish ports as far west as Mousehole were obliged to provide seamen and four ships each to defend the coast, even Bodmin, whose leading burgesses were imprisoned for failing to supply the ships until they managed to convince the government that Bodmin was not a port. Edward's huge fleet descended on France and campaigned so successfully that the whole of France, including last of all Calais, was taken. The country was at high-water mark.

It was now 1346.

10

Plague

By the end of 1346 it was widely known throughout European ports that the Far East was suffering from an unprecedented plague. Such things were far from unfamiliar and caused little panic, but the disease spread rapidly to the Crimea, the Mediterranean, Genoa, Venice, Sicily and Marseilles. In the summer of 1348, a ship came to harbour in Melcombe Regis near Weymouth, and the plague which had been raging all over Europe finally made its landfall in Britain.

The toll of life the plague had taken throughout the world was known in advance of its coming. It is difficult to imagine the terror of its steady and irresistible progress as it spread rapidly in all directions from Dorset. News would be carried from village to village or by royal proclamation and the rumours of its advance would have long preceded its arrival. Tales of mass sickness and death ran before it, along with those trying to escape its grip. They were met with fierce resistance by every community, desperate to keep strangers away, hoping to keep their communities immune. The new churches were packed as a terrified public turned to God as their only salvation. But, one at a time, churches would hear a dreaded spate of coughing or observe the growing absence of members of the congregation. Within a few days, the plague would be felling swathes of the community, killing some in days, some in hours and some overnight.

Social structures crumbled and broke. The priests and friars did their noble best at first to minister to the sick and the dead, but were overwhelmed themselves by plague and the magnitude of their task. Orderly burials carried out at the onset of the plague became impossible. Often the priest was himself afflicted, no bearers could be found, families did not want to gather together and no one wanted to leave their home except for basic necessities. Soon the dead were thrown into pits, unmourned and not even recorded. Eventually, when even that dire process failed, the dead were left to rot in their houses or out on the roads. It was clear to those who survived that the world was ending, and some spent their time in prayer for their mortal souls, while others looked for scapegoats and persecuted strangers, Jews, foreigners, the disabled, anyone different.

How many died in the plague's first thrust will never be known. Parish registers did not exist and only their families knew the identities of the dead. The accepted estimate of the death toll is taken from the only recorded members of the parish population, the priests and their clergy, monks, friars and canons. Of these, a little over a third died. Though they were more in harm's way than most of the populace, they were well housed and well fed unlike many of their parishioners, so even that dreadful proportion may be too low. It was a random process – no one knew who had a resistance to the disease until they survived, and no one knew why, although many supernatural explanations arose.

These were the darkest days in European history, a calamity unprecedented and unmatched by any later attacks of plague, war, famine and death. Unlike other disasters that only affected one community or another, this came home to everyone. History in fact came to a halt while humanity swirled in the hurricane of pestilence, and then tried to piece their lives back together in a devastated landscape, once it had passed on to afflict somewhere else.

When it was over, those remaining were curiously numb, carrying on their lives as closely as possible to what they had known before. Mourning was meaningless as almost everyone was bereaved. Faith in God and the future was shattered and the spectre of death became part of the national consciousness, prominent in contemporary works of art and music. But communities did survive and did their best to rebuild themselves. Least affected were the richest, who were able to close the doors on their self-supporting estates, and the poorest living in the remote countryside. By this, one can suppose that West Cornwall paid a moderate price compared with some, though the towns, especially seaports, would have felt its full force. The main historical effect of the plague was to raise the status of land workers, still serfs – virtually slaves – under the Saxon feudal system. Labour became scarce, and healthy labourers found themselves in greater demand and therefore free to choose where they worked and strike better wages. Starvation due to loss of farm produce was offset, grimly, by the huge loss of life – there were so many fewer mouths to feed.

The tinners had no such essential market to support them or any pool of skilled men to replace those lost, and the production of tin crashed down to a trickle. It was the end of the century before it regained its 1337 level of 650 tons.

But Penzance was firmly rooted by now and like other communities pulled itself back from the brink of ruin and despair, aided by the increase in birth rate that so often follows a catastrophe. Quietly and unrecorded, it spent the rest of the fourteenth century recovering and building on the past, improving its quays and extending its buildings.

11

Growth

Evidence of the town's growth came by royal command on 8 April 1404:

GRANT BY KING HENRY IV TO THOMAS LORD BERKELEY OF A
MARKET AND THREE FAIRS AT PENSANS
The King to the same greeting

Know that there does not exist in the village of Pensans in the County
of Cornwall or in any other village for twenty-four miles around any
market on Wednesday, or for sixty miles around the said village of
Pensans any fair on the Eve and the Day of the Conception of the Blessed
Virgin Mary [8 December] or on the Eve and the Day of St Peter in
Cathedra [22 February] or on the Eve and the day of the Nativity of the
Blessed Virgin Mary [8 September] to the grave detriment of the same
village of Pensans and the whole country round about as our trusty and
beloved Lord de Berkeley has given us to understand.

We considering these circumstances of our special grace have given
and by this our Charter have confirmed to the said Thomas that he and
his heirs may have forever at the said village of Pensans one market every
week on Wednesday and three fairs every year lasting for six days...

His Royal Highness was clearly not aware that Penzance had already had
a Wednesday market since 1332, but the three fairs, with the addition
of the seven-day fair already granted, were a great spur to the town's
prosperity. It also confirmed that, although still mentioned in the charter
as a 'village', Penzance would now have dominance over most of the
trading west of Helston.

One thing still lacking to bring Penzance up to the status of other
Cornish towns was a parish church of its own. The aftermath of the plague
had inspired another widespread wave of church building, in thanks for

the fact that the world had not actually ended. But Penzance's mother church was still at Madron, obliging the townspeople to trudge up and down the long hill on every church occasion. These were numerous. There was no question of not going regularly to church. If possible, children were baptised on the day they were born and were expected to attend all their lives. This included every Sunday, local feast days and the great feasts of the church, marriages, which were celebrated in the church porch, and funerals on the day of death. The calendar, as the charter extracts show, was predicated on the major saints' days, which would have been known to everyone. During Lent, all adults were obliged to go to confession. The most devout would attend all day on Good Friday when Mass was not said, no bells were rung and a silent vigil was held. On Easter Day, adults took their annual Holy Communion, and processions – both large and long – took place on St Mark's Day (25 April), the first three days of Rogation week (the sixth week after Easter), Ascension Day (the following Thursday), and Corpus Christi (the second Thursday after Whit Sunday).

The previous half-century had not been entirely peaceful. War with France ensured that the ever-present threat from the sea continued. Cornwall complained to Parliament that so many of its seafaring men had been conscripted to join the King's Navy that not enough were left to protect their own ports. Cornish ports provided a set levy of ships for Henry V's next invading fleet, including four from Penzance and two from Marazion. In response, a grant was made to keep a garrison on the Mount to look after Mount's Bay. Nothing protected Looe in 1405 when French and Spanish galleons sank nineteen fishing boats and raided and burned the town. Piracy was now being practised not only by the French but by the Cornish too, who proved rather good at it. Shipping in general was burgeoning, and in 1427 the Mount petitioned for funds to create a harbour able to shelter 200 ships.

The peasantry had found a newfound confidence to stand up to injustice. The imposition of a poll tax – never a good move – and the criticism of clerical greed and corruption, in particular by John Wycliffe's Lollards, roused local people to protest. Though there was no local equivalent of the Peasants' Revolt, there were some acts of violence aimed against the clergy, including a shocking episode at St Hilary where the parish priest was attacked and beheaded. Retribution came with the assizes of the merciless Robert Trevanion, originally from St Buryan, who was appointed chief justice and was reputed to have hanged everyone who came before him.

Church tithes were especially resented. The gift of a tithe made sense when communities were tiny, produce was little and the church's needs were humble. But when the population grew both in size and output, the proportion required by the parish church remained the same. Tithes were levied on everything. The great tithes included grain, livestock and other less perishable items which could be stored or turned into cash. The rest were known as small tithes – meat, fish and other crops – and altarage that were offerings brought into the church itself. Tithes applied even to a tenth of the vegetables grown in the congregation's own gardens, their peas, beans, etc.

This was effectively a 10 per cent tax on all goods, which soon made the Church embarrassingly wealthy. For the parish, once the church was built, the only expenses were the upkeep of the inner and holiest part of the church, the chancel (the nave was the responsibility of the local parishioners), and the stipend of the priest or rector. This was covered many times over by the tithes, but the Church increased its revenue even further by employing lower grades of clergy to look after the lesser parishes at very small cost. The rest of the river of wealth went into the bishop's coffers, to build the cathedrals, keep the high clergy in outrageous comfort, and send a small contribution – 'Peter's Pence' – to the mother church in Rome.

Corruption grew with the riches. The excess funds from parishes could be diverted to other parishes or other projects while the local vicars got by on their pittance. Parishes were 'farmed', and therefore the right of the tithes was leased to local landowners and grand families for cash. Even the right to choose a rector for a particular parish, a privilege known as an advowson, had a market value. The gap between the Church's teaching and its practice became cynically wide, and its respect in the community subsequently suffered.

The income from Madron had been gifted by Henry de Pomeroy in 1206, along with that of the otherwise unrecorded chapel of St Clare, to the order of the Knights Hospitaller. It was recovered by the Crown in Queen Elizabeth's reign in 1574. No other trace of the chapel of St Clare remains except in the name of the higher part of Penzance.

Skirmishes between England and France continued during the Hundred Years' War, finally ending in 1453. However, soon afterwards England itself burst into flame with the Wars of the Roses. Cornwall's knack for picking a losing side did not fail and it threw in its lot with the Lancastrians. The very last action of this conflict occurred in 1473 at St Michael's Mount where John de Vere, 13th Earl of Oxford, who had been trying to foment revolution from abroad, made a landing in Mount's Bay. On the pretence of being pilgrims, he and his eighty men seized the Mount. The weary country failed to rise with them and they were soon besieged, though the Sheriff of Cornwall, Sir Henry Bodrugan, failed to press the siege home and insisted on keeping the rebels victualled. A foray was made from the shore by Sir John Arundell of Trerice, but he was cut down in a fierce fight on the causeway. The Earl held out for a whole winter, but eventually most of his men were lured away with bribes and he was forced to surrender.

The Mount had by then been severed from its senior establishment at Mont St Michel by Henry IV in 1408, who decided its revenues would be far better put towards his own private household expenses. Henry V transferred its income to his new foundation of Syon abbey in Twickenham. Henry VI took it back again and made it part of the foundation of his new college, St Nicholas (later King's) College, Cambridge, but Syon abbey fought a long legal battle for its return and succeeded in seizing it back twenty years later. It was worth fighting for, not only for its revenue (£33 6s 8d in 1437), but also its collection of highly prized holy relics, important ecclesiastical currency (including the Milk of St Marie the Virgin, the jawbone of St Mansuetus, stones from the Holy Sepulchre, a portion of the girdle of the blessed Virgin Mary and a fragment of the finger bone of St Agapitt), which was of dubious derivation but priceless for the attraction of pilgrims. However, the French never ceased to regard it as stolen French property. This led to another assault on the Mount by a shipload of marauding French soldiers. The Mount, as before, successfully resisted attack but the French did not leave without a sting in the tail, burning the village of Marazion and around thirty boats as they left.

Cornwall bowed to the Yorkist victory, though never really embracing it. Many of the increasingly influential Cornish families secretly cherished hopes that the choice of the defeated Lancastrians, a young man with a vanishingly small claim to the English throne called Henry Tudor, would invade from his chosen exile in Brittany, and did their best to succour and support his cause. In 1485, Henry landed at Milford Haven, with the same Earl of Oxford (who had in the meantime been exiled in France, imprisoned, and escaped from a castle by jumping into the moat) as one of his lieutenants. Betrayed by treason and his own impetuousness, Richard III lost his life at the height of the battle of Bosworth and the crucial reign of the Tudor dynasty began. For most of England it was the beginning of a golden age, but Cornwall and the Tudors very soon turned out to be the worst of friends.

12

Tudor Days

Henry's particular talent was for economics – he was one of the very few monarchs ever to run Britain at a profit – and Cornwall's enthusiasm for Henry was quickly cooled by large increases in taxation and the increased officiousness displayed in collecting it. Despite his stunning victory, Henry VII's hold on the crown was tenuous. He had many enemies and other claimants to his crown, including the famous 'pretenders' Lambert Simnel and Perkin Warbeck. Insurrections and the ongoing territorial skirmishes with the Scots required more soldiers, more campaigns, and therefore more taxes. Henry angered many Cornishmen when he abolished some of the ancient stannary rights that protected them against outside taxation.

In early 1497, a man of St Keverne, Michael Joseph an Gof (blacksmith), was provoked to distraction by the King's collectors, lost his temper with one of them and struck him down. Instead of waiting for the inevitable reprisals, he raised the countryside in rebellion, aided by a young lawyer named Thomas Flamank. Oppressed sympathisers from all over Cornwall flocked to their banners, including many tinners from the west, and they decided to march on London, led by Lord Audley. Their purpose was not to unseat the King but (in their naivety) to appeal to him to recognise their plight and modify his collectors' greed. It was the first time in its history that Cornwall, so often invaded itself, had instigated an attack on its eastern neighbour.

The sad story of the outcome of the rebellion is well known. The large army Henry had amassed to march on the Scots was still camped close to London, and fell on the lightly armed Cornish with no mercy. Many were cut down on the field of Blackheath, and those who failed to run away were captured and executed. The ubiquitous Earl of Oxford helped lead the king's forces and took full revenge for his undignified exit from St Michael's Mount. Cornwall was defeated, though it remained unappeased, still thirsty for justice and revenge.

In Scotland meanwhile, Perkin Warbeck, who had made an alliance with the Scots and married the Scottish King's cousin, Katherine, heard of the Cornish rebellion. Having had little luck in rousing the northern English counties, he took ship with his wife and a small number of men and set off for Cornwall. Like King Stephen 350 years earlier, Warbeck came ashore at Sennen Cove, to the puzzlement of the Sennen Covers and the equal confusion of Perkin Warbeck who, though he was a noted linguist, had never encountered the Cornish language before. However, by the time he arrived in Penzance the news had spread and the delighted population of the town gathered to greet Henry's enemy. He was acclaimed King Richard IV for the first time in Penzance's marketplace.

Having lodged his wife in St Michael's Mount, he repeated his claim to the throne in Bodmin and led a large Cornish militia, some of whom had only recently escaped from their last disastrous expedition, towards Exeter. Despite a determined siege, they failed to take the city. They carried on towards Taunton instead, harried all the way by Henry's troops. Warbeck lost his nerve outside Taunton and fled in the night, leaving the Cornish furious and disconsolate. After slaying a hated tax collector they had captured, they scattered to straggle their way home once again.

Henry's response was typically cautious and thorough. He travelled to Exeter and stayed there for a month '... to order the parts of Cornwall'. This meant in effect levying an additional fine to punish the Cornish for their rebellious ways on top of the already swingeing taxes. He detailed a representative in each parish to be responsible for exacting it, often the local priest. Henry always preferred money to blood, and while he executed comparatively few he extracted a grand total of £600 from the Cornish as the price of their insurrection, with ruinous consequences for the whole county. The consequent choice for many was either starving or leaving their homeland, a familiar if bitter theme in Cornish history.

The spirit of the Cornish was broken and it would be another fifty years before they raised their hands in revolt again. In the meantime, those remaining made their slow painful steps back to normality and prosperity. They wished for a peaceful life with as little disruption as possible from their rulers. In 1509, Henry VII died and was succeeded by his son Henry VIII; as disruptive a monarch as ever sat on England's throne.

Henry VIII's lifelong ambition, apart from producing an heir, was to regain what he regarded as his heritage, the throne of France. It was an

obsession that, added to his own excessive venality, made him desperate
for money during most of his reign. He lost little time running through his
father's incredible personal fortune of £1.25 million, and then, like his father,
turned to taxation to further his aims. He married Catherine of Aragon,
previously betrothed to his deceased brother, Arthur, and having thus made
an alliance with Spain began his campaign against France in 1513. Once
again, the English Channel became a battlefield, a lawless wilderness where
semi-legal privateers and illegal pirates might appear at any time to rob and
kill under the guise of legitimate warfare. Cornish ports once again supplied
defensive ships and men, and not a few pirates, to join in the fray.

Around this time, West Cornwall and Scilly were graced by one of their
first recorded tourists. Apart from Pytheas, only William of Worcester had
previously set down his brief impressions of Mount's Bay in 1478. John
Leland was far more thorough. He never finished the book of his travels,
but his snatched notes are one of the first non-official texts available as a
view of the county through an outsider's eyes.

Leland goes first from St Ives to Land's End, then works his way around
the southern coast. He accurately assesses the coast between Land's End
and Newlyn as 'without havyn or creeke, saving yn divers places ... shyppes
draw the bootes up to dry land and fisch but yn fayr wether.'

Newlyn is clearly up and running with its stone quay, but Leland is
not impressed, calling it, 'A poore fisschar towne and hath only a key for
shyppes and bootes ... it is an hamlet to Mousehole.'

Mousehole had had its pier since around 1392, and fares better, being,
'A praty fisschar town. Withyn a arrow shot of the sayd key or pere lyith
a lytle low island with a Chapel yn it and this lytle islet bereth gresse.'
Proceeding east, Leland notes: 'Also yn the bey be Est the same towne a
good roode for shyppes cawled Gnaves Lake. Kiwartun [Chiverton] lives
at Newlin by Mousehole and John Godolcan [Godolphin] at Mousehole.'

He then makes reference to a former settlement in which many
archaeological finds had been made but which was possibly 'devourid
of the sea', though Leland places it between Newlyn and 'Pensandes',
possibly a reference to the tiny port of Porthplemynt between Penzance
and Marazion of which no trace and few references remain.

As for Penzance itself, Leland has little good to say, and like many later
travellers cannot wait to get past it in order to rhapsodise on the wonders
of the Mount. He dismisses it thus,

Pensants ... ys the Westest market Towne of al Cornwayle and no socur
for botes and shyppes but a forsed pere or key. Ther is but a chapel yn
the sayd towne, a ys in newlyn, for theyr paroches chyrches be more than
a myle of.

Leland, though part of Mount's Bay's earliest written history, was himself
an antiquarian, fascinated by the past, and he noted: 'In the bay betwixt
the Mont and Pensants be fownd neeree the lowe water marke rootes of
trees yn divers places as a token of the grounde wasted', marvelling on
the remnants of the forest that had once filled the bay and whose petrified
remains still occasionally break the surface of the sand.

Henry, keenly aware that all southern ports needed strengthening
during his foreign adventures, had at least done his best to ensure that
Penzance was 'socur for botes'. In 1512 his attention was drawn to the
port, and he gave an order to devolve the harbour dues, paid at that time
to the Crown after the royal assumption of the manor of Alverton, back to
the townspeople:

To our Styward, Receyvour, Auditor, Reves and Baillyfs of our Towne of
Pensans ... by this our placard we gyve and graunte unto our tenants ...
for and toward the reparacion of our key and bulleworks at Pensance for
saufgard of alle shippes resortying to the same and alle manner of profits
that unto us or our heirs Kyngs of England shold or ought to growe by
reason of the ankerage, kylage [duty paid for the privilege of resting a
ship by its keel in a harbour], busselage [duty paid on transported goods
reckoned by the bushel], of every shippe that shall herafter fortune to
arrive and resorte to our seid towne and key, to have, holde and enioye
the same profits ... from the Feste of Seynt Mighell Tharchaungell last
past as long as they do well and competently repayr and maynteyn the
seid key and bulleworks for the saufgard of alle suche shippes as shall
lond at the same, and for the saufgard and defence of our seid towne.

Henry VIII's bravado made him popular at first. However, in 1527, he
attempted to have his marriage to Catherine annulled for reasons well
enough known. His appeal to the Pope was unsuccessful, and this would
have persuaded most noblemen in Christendom to give up such a quest – or
at least to indulge themselves in private. But Henry's wilfulness and increased

sense of his status as God's personal representative encouraged him to proceed with the unprecedented step of a divorce and re-marriage without papal consent. There would be no way back. Henry was excommunicated and became head of the Church as well as the state. England became isolated from mainland Europe under the new Church of England.

In return, he began the process he had long contemplated, one that gave him personal satisfaction and also provided him with an almost inexhaustible source of wealth and revenue. The monasteries had fallen far from the solemn houses of prayer and good works of their inception. Many had become little more than private clubs for selected clergy. Others were still faithful houses of worship that carried on their traditions as before and provided social services to their local population. It did not matter to Henry and his reliable servant, Thomas Cromwell. The most corrupt were targeted first, including the small monastery of Tywardreath, near St Austell, described in Daphne du Maurier's novel, *The House on the Strand*, as a community of venal self-seeking frauds.

Closer to Penzance was the Benedictine priory of St Michael's Mount, now separated from its French masters and part of the property of the dissolved Syon abbey. Due to its strategic defensive position in a time of such maritime tension, Henry did not sell or give away the Mount. He instead leased it to a local landowning family, on the understanding that they would keep it in repair and support a garrison of five soldiers. The fourteenth-century church was also spared, but the clergy, the last of a faithful line that stretched back 1,000 years, were sent packing down the hill.

The Mount was fortunate in being left intact. All over Cornwall, monasteries were dismantled, all their artefacts valued, the lead sold from their roofs, the bells sold for their metal, even the good stones, archways and lintels ripped out and taken away to other buildings. As for their lands, Carew says, 'A golden shower of the dissolved abbey lands rained well near into every gaper's mouth.'

Not everyone was dismayed by the disappearance of the monasteries. The abbot and the senior clergy were sweetened with adequate pensions, and the prospect of the distribution of their treasures was welcomed by local inhabitants. However, they were destined to see little of the proceeds as the commissioners made a careful inventory of every item of value, which were then taken away by the King's men for purposes from which no local would have felt any benefit. Angered by these brutal changes, a large faction broke out in rebellion in the north of England in 1536. Its subsequent name, the Pilgrimage of Grace, disguises what was England's most serious social unrest until the days of Charles I. Henry invited the rebel leader, Robert Aske, to London and promised him numerous concessions, then sent him north in chains to be hanged at York, a lesson to anyone who dared cross him.

Having succeeded in his first depredations, Henry then turned to the friaries and treated them to the same process of dissolution, including the Franciscans at Bodmin and the Dominicans at Truro. Bishop John Veysey of Exeter proved a flexible supporter of the new order. He insisted to his diocese that the King should be acknowledged as the head of the Church. Popish idolatory was to be outlawed, relics and images were to be forbidden, Latin was largely abolished and there was to be no more observance of superstitious holy days (though, knowing his Cornish flock, he excused the parish feast days from this order).

There were genuine reforms of some of the clergy's excesses. An illuminating passage related to their table habits. As part of a campaign for self-denial, it was decreed that at mealtimes an archbishop should in future never exceed 'six divers kinds of fleshe, or six of fishe on fishe days', while a bishop was restricted to five of the same, a dean to four and so on down. A dish was defined as 'crane, swan, turkey-cocke, hadocke, pyke, tench, or two of capons, pheasants, conies, woodcocks'. But an ordinary clergyman had to satisfy himself with 'Two partridges or three blackbirds or twelve larks or snipe'. Pudding was not forgotten: 'An Archbishop may have of second dishes four, the Bishop three, and all the others but two; as custard, tart, fritter, cheese or apples, peares or two other kinds of fruites.' It was gracefully agreed that the surplus food saved by these new restrictions should be distributed 'for the relieving of the poore'.

However, not all of the money had been wasted in such grossness. The wealth of a church was demonstrated in many ways: in its construction, using the best and most able masons; in its furnishings, from the elaborate rood screens with their affecting wooden images gazing down into the commoners' nave to the carved pulpits and quirky bench-ends; in its artwork, as many church walls were illustrated with huge coloured murals depicting biblical tales; in its windows, the tracery filled with individually coloured pieces of exquisite stained glass; in its rich hangings, altar-cloths, and vestments; in its music, now a considerable feature with organs beginning to appear, local ensembles and choirs sending adventurous church harmonies and simple plainsong echoing from the walls; in its many candles, its incense and its lofty height, where the coloured light played on the pillars. It was no wonder that local parishioners living in their dark, low dwellings regarded their church as a vision of the promised heaven to come, the most uplifting and vital feature of their lives. The Reformation came crashing into this well of comfort and spiritual refreshment.

Henry's own part in it ended in 1546, after another few years of fruitless war with France. He died of his personal excesses, a paranoid megalomaniac best described by a later commentator as 'England's Nero'. Those who hoped his nine-year-old son, Edward VI, would modify the assault on the Church were dismayed to find that his protectors and the boy himself were, if anything, more zealous in their determination to force the country towards a Protestant ideal. Henry had died still equivocal regarding the Catholic faith, but the new order had no such scruples.

For Cornwall, the crunch came in 1547 when William Body came to Penryn – presumably to the centre of Cornish ecclesiastical life, Glasney College – and summoned the clergy and churchwardens from all over Cornwall to hear the new King's injunctions. Body was a man of his time. The properly appointed archdeacon of Cornwall was one of Cardinal Wolsely's sons, Thomas Wynter. However, he had no interest in this remote archdeaconry and leased the office for a fair rent to Body, a corrupt administrator in the King's favour who was not even ordained. Body informed his audience that in future there would be no more processions, no more images or pictures or candles burning before them, no ringing of the Sanctus bell, and commanded them that,

> They shall take away, utterly extinct and destroy all shrines, covering
> of shrines, all tables, candlesticks, rolls of wax, pictures, paintings, and
> all other monuments of feigned miracles, pilgrimages, idolatry and
> superstition, so that there remain no memory of the same in walls, glass
> windows or elsewhere within their churches or houses.

Body returned the following spring to see how well his commands had been carried out. The local clergy had been less than diligent in destroying their most precious artefacts and Body decided to set an example. He and his men went into Helston church and began to set about attacking the proscribed articles and images with hammers and picks. The Cornish rage finally burst and men came from all the surrounding parishes to stop the desecration. In the ensuing struggle they chased Body out of the church and into a stranger's house, where they stabbed him to death.

13

Rebellion

Relations between Cornwall and the Tudors had been poisoned by the two previous rebellions and no mercy was granted following Body's murder. Seven ringleaders were arrested and quickly condemned. They were taken on hurdles through Launceston, where, like Michael Joseph before them, they were hanged and while still alive cut down, their entrails removed and burned before their eyes, their heads cut off and their bodies quartered. The parts were taken away to be displayed in town centres with a suitable notice attached as a warning to others.

The religious assault continued without abate. Glasney College had been exempt from the previous dissolutions. However, despite the heartfelt efforts of the people of Penryn to save its magnificent structure, it was condemned and utterly destroyed and the site left bare. Glasney had been at the heart of the Cornish clerical system, functioning as a regional centre of the Exeter diocese. It had great influence in terms of education, helping to establish what was to become Exeter College, Oxford. It also served as Cornwall's cultural heart where, among other works in the Cornish language, the great sequence of mystery plays, the Cornish *Ordinalia,* was almost certainly written. Its reservoir of Cornish culture was probably the principal reason for its destruction, a punishment to deny the Cornish a focus for their nationalism and whip them to heel. The site, as consecrated ground, was never built upon and remains an open field within Penryn.

The final straw for Cornwall and Devon was the Act of Uniformity in 1549. This abolished the Latin mass altogether and substituted the English Book of Common Prayer. Although most Cornish people were not schooled in Latin – or at all – the Latin Mass was a comforting litany they had become accustomed to all their lives, the rhythms and cadences part of their consciousness. To cut that away was a profound blow to add to all the other destructive changes. This was felt most keenly in West Cornwall. The English language had percolated in a slow way across the county from the English border, and was probably understood in most of it, but west of Truro Cornish was still the everyday language of both high and low society. Translation of their services into English merely changed them into a different foreign language. It was a line they refused to cross.

On Whitsun Day 1549, the Book of Common Prayer was instituted and spontaneously rejected in Cornwall with a furious groundswell of resentment. A rebellious crowd gathered at Bodmin and set off with thousands of followers, determined to march to London yet again to lay their complaints before the King. This time their purpose was not political but strictly religious, and they marched in procession carrying some of the condemned banners and crosses from their churches. Meanwhile, in the small Devon village of Sampford Courtenay, outraged villagers had forced their rector to return to church and repeat the Whitsun service as the traditional Latin Mass. When local law enforcers arrived, there was a serious fight and one of the local squires was lynched on the church steps. With blood spilt, the die was cast.

The Devon rebels rose in force and joined with the Cornish army at Crediton. Together they proceeded to Exeter, which they besieged for five weeks. However, the city remained loyal to the new monarch and remained unconquered.

It was a declaration of war, and the King despatched his most trusted general, Lord John Russell, to stamp out the fire. Russell had distinguished himself in Henry VIII's service and had plenty of brutal experience with rebels in campaigns during the Pilgrimage of Grace. As a reward for this, Henry made him a steward of the Duchy of Cornwall, warden of the Stanneries, and granted him extensive lands in the South West.

The Cornish had in the meantime sent the King a rare message of defiance outlining their sixteen 'Final Demands'. These were uncompromising indeed, including item four:

> We wyll have the Sacramant hange over the high aulter, and there to be worshypped as it was wount to be: and they which will not thereto consent we wyl have them die lyke heretykes against the holy Catholyque faith.

Item seven stated,

> We wyl have holy bread and holy water made every sondaye … images to
> be set up again in every church, and all other auncient olde ceremonyes
> used heretofore by our mother the Holy Church.

Finally, the best-known of all, item eight:

> We will not receyve the newe servyce because it is but lyke a Christmas
> game, but we will have oure olde service of Mattins, Masse, Evensong,
> and Processions in Latten not in English as it was before. And so we the
> Cornyshe men (whereof certen of us understande no Engyish) utterly
> refuse thys newe Englysh.

They also demanded the return of many of the confiscated monastic
lands and manors, which put them at odds with some of the new Cornish
aristocracy who had been pleased to receive them. Some of these panicked
and fled into St Michael's Mount for their safety, but were smoked out
– literally, as the rebels covered their assault on the Mount with burning
hay-bales – and captured. However, the rebels had no thirst for local blood
and sent them back to their homes.

The pitched battles of the Prayer Book Rebellion took place in West
Devon. The first was at Fenny Bridges. After a fierce and bloody fight, Russell
– reinforced with mercenaries from Italy and Germany – forced the rebels to
retreat. After another skirmish the next day at Clyst-St Mary, Russell gained
his shameful and notorious place in Cornish history by responding to an
'alarum' and having all his prisoners put to death. Within ten minutes, the
blood of an estimated 900 unarmed Cornishmen was running into the river.

The following day, his forces won their decisive battle, forcing the Devon
men north and the Cornishmen scattering to the south. Russell celebrated
his victory in the relieved city of Exeter, but heard that the Cornish had
reformed where it had all begun at Sampford Courtenay. There, further
reinforced by a contingent of Welshmen, Russell, after a terrible fight,
finally put Humphrey Arundell and the Cornish rebels to flight with many
casualties. The Prayer Book Rebellion was over.

The King's retribution was put into the willing hands of Sir Anthony
Kingston, another lord who had perfected the art of suppression following

the Pilgrimage of Grace. He made his leisurely way through Devon and Cornwall, hosted by the defeated and often terrified worthies of the towns while he dealt out execution after execution in judgement, including many of the clergy. On one infamous occasion he dined companionably with the Mayor of Bodmin. After dinner, the mayor inquired for whom the new gallows had been erected outside his door. Kingston replied that they were for the mayor's own benefit and had him immediately hanged, much to Kingston's grim humour.

As a rebellious force, the Cornish were finally cowed and went back to their homes to make the best of it. How they adapted to the Reformation – the removal of stone altars, the marriage of priests, the looting of virtually all valuable church property (except for what they had taken the precaution of hiding) – will never be known. Dissent of any form was too dangerous to be written down and they kept their grief between themselves, but it was a hurt that went deep. The ruling factor of their everyday lives had been betrayed and despoiled, their traditions forbidden, their customs outlawed and their beloved churches turned into bare comfortless halls shorn of all their former magic. The Reformation was in its way as profound a disturbance of the normal lives of ordinary people as the Black Death had been. Both can often be silently traced in the lists of vicars and priests on the walls of Cornish churches: a sudden change of incumbent in 1346, and another around 1549.

The number of rebels who came from Penzance and district will never be known. Those who survived would have been particularly careful to conceal any part they played in those dangerous years. It is certain that Penzance was at the heart of the Cornish-speaking area, and there is something in the uncompromising and unprecedented confrontation of the King's wishes that smacks of the tough western communities of Penzance, Mousehole, St Ives and St Just.

Madron church would have been put through the same destructive rigour as all the others, but at least Penzance did not suffer, as many towns did, with the humiliation of having a church in the centre of their community sacked. Indeed, the town came close to having one of its dearest wishes granted. The King's commissioners in their pernickety zeal did not fail to notice the chantry chapel of St Mary, which had been endowed by the Le Tyes family. Their main object was to strip any such institution of its valuables and close it down, but they were empowered to recommend the continuation of any that seemed to be of benefit to the wider population.

In 1548, the commissioners reported that the chantry was a private one with a seventy-year-old priest who had no other income. However, they were good enough to note that Penzance was a town 'inhabited by fishers and others to the number of 340', and that their parish church was 2 miles away. Their concern was not for the drudgery of the walk up to Madron, but something more suitable to their paranoid times:

> This ministration in the said chapel may ... conveniently be spared, for
> if the people of the said town should go daily to the Parish Church the
> town would be in peril of burning with the Frenchmen and other enemies
> in time of war.

Sadly, their advice went unheeded and the parsimonious King opted to grab the £4 per annum endowment for himself, though the chapel managed to survive through local charity.

The melodrama of the Tudor dynasty continued. Edward VI presided at the opening of Parliament in March 1553, a pale boy of fifteen who was as determined and inflexible in his opinions, especially concerning religion, as his father had been. However, as soon as Parliament had been officially opened, it was suspended 'because the King was sickly'. While on his sickbed he drew up plans to ensure that his sister, Mary, should not succeed him and undo all his good Protestant work. Instead, he nominated his cousin Jane as queen and arranged a swift marriage in hopes that a male heir should be born to Jane that would ensure the succession before he died. Lady Jane Grey married Guildford Dudley on 21 May, but Edward's condition was deteriorating and he died on 6 July, praying with his last breath that England be defended from papistry.

It was not to be. Mary's reign began, and with it an attempt to turn back the religious clock. However, even after so short a time, the return to Catholicism was not greeted with the delighted relief that could have been expected. In many parishes the money could not be found to restore the church's treasures. Some priests had married, and were now left with the choice of losing their living or their wives. Even the congregations had become accustomed to 'this new English'. Most of the recently enriched owners of the confiscated Catholic lands were quick to readopt the

Catholic faith, but not so easily persuaded to give back the land. The times remained uneasy and dangerous, where an overheard word of dissent could cost a man's living or, in extreme circumstances, his life.

The full horror of heresy and public burnings of Mary's reign mostly passed the West Country by, with the exception of a spirited old woman of Exeter called Agnes Prest who would not cease to insult and rail against the Pope until she was silenced by the flames outside the city walls.

Mary was never popular, especially in her marriage to Philip II of Spain. Many feared that England would become no more than a Spanish colony. It was a depressed time, with a succession of cruel winters, poor harvests, high food prices that led to poverty and beggary and, worst of all, a return of the plague. Dismayed and disgusted by the savagery of the religious persecutions, the populace was glad to see the back of Mary and turned to her sister in hope of better days.

Elizabeth was crowned in 1558 and quickly reinstalled the Protestant regime of her half-brother. She was worldlier than Mary, with all the charm her sister had lacked. She took steps to temper the second sudden change of faith with greater tolerance of Catholicism. Gradually, the awful tension of the last thirty years began to diminish. Although there was still division between one community and another, within communities and even within families that would never completely disappear, the terror of spies and betrayal, denouncement and ruin slowly faded away.

What local people longed for was a period of stability. There is a beautiful and famous coloured map of Mount's Bay painted around the middle of the sixteenth century. It artistically exaggerates the basin of the bay as a complete semi-circle, its arms embracing a delightful variety of shipping. Dominating the foreground is the Mount, its castle and church similar in profile to today. Opposite, Marazion is as long and straggly as ever, a sizeable town for its times, and a solid spit of land still attaches Chapel Rock to the mainland with the small pilgrims' chapel of St Catherine perched on top. Penzance is shown as a dense settlement, unified around the harbour with its single pier, the chapel of St Mary with its substantial tower and spire directly above the Battery Rocks, and the harbour, which held only a couple of humble merchant and fishing boats. Newlyn sits under its protective hill. Mousehole also had its pier and fishing boats, and the island of St Clement is topped with a good deal of grass just as Leland described it, with St Clement's chapel still in place. Above, the church of St Paul looks down from its cleft in the hills.

It is a picture of peace, harmony and industry, an idyllic scene, the first detailed scheme of early medieval Mount's Bay, and sadly the last. No one can be sure exactly how much the previous wars and outbreaks of internal strife affected the town of Penzance, but there is no doubt how totally and profoundly the next period of international tension came home to the shores of Mount's Bay.

14

Spanish Fire

Elizabeth liked to keep her enemies on the wrong foot. Would she marry this one or that? Would she make alliances with one nation or another? Or would she follow the family tradition of territorial ambition? She kept them guessing and remained on terms with all rival nations, which included – by the friendship of her brother-in-law – Spain. However, in 1568 there was a revolt in the Spanish colony in the Netherlands. This was put down with great cruelty and caused a large Spanish garrison to be posted just across the English Channel. She deftly encouraged her supporters to make the Channel as inhospitable as possible for the Spanish, privateers and pirates alike. This was to the taste of most Cornish ports: Saltash; Fowey; the nascent Falmouth from which the notorious Killigrew family plied their trade; and Mount's Bay. The Spanish responded in kind, and a vicious unofficial contest was joined in the Channel, to the terror of those with more peaceful purposes. A Spanish fleet attacked a British expedition in San Juan in Mexico. The Queen then seized the treasure from Spanish ships that had been driven to shelter in Cornish ports. The Duke of Alva detained all English ships in port in the Netherlands and Elizabeth seized all the Spanish ships in English ports.

The pretence of peace was maintained against all credibility. Elizabeth, with her tongue firmly in her cheek, even appointed Sir John Killigrew to chair a commission of enquiry into piracy in the west.

The conflict was wide in scope and fought on the other side of the Atlantic by Drake in particular, but neither side was yet ready for all-out war and the skirmishes continued. Despite the Queen's attempt to avoid the religious aspect of the undeclared war, the zealously Catholic Spanish agitated to make it a critical issue, a holy crusade against the infidel English to go with the cruel persecutions they were carrying out elsewhere in Europe. In 1570 the Pope declared Elizabeth an illegitimate heretic and excommunicated her. Though English Catholics were mainly loyal to the Queen they all came under suspicion of betrayal and treason, poisoning the formerly tolerant atmosphere. Catholics were persecuted and rounded up, some were tried and imprisoned, a few executed for their refusal to recant.

The terror and paranoia of Henry's and Mary's respective reigns was returning, and matters were not helped when Parliament passed an Act making it treason to join the Catholic faith or to persuade others to do so. Tension rose, and every major seaport was garrisoned with soldiers. In 1578, the plague returned with horrifying suddenness into this ugly scene. While it was not as devastating as its fourteenth century equivalent, it still took a crippling toll on the population, especially in the seaports. Penzance suffered heavily, with some accounts reckoning that up to 10 per cent of the population died.

By 1584, all pretence of peace was at an end. The Spanish were all around, in possession of the Netherlands to the east and established in Ireland to the west. Cornwall was on the front line. Tinners and farm labourers were conscripted into a rough militia, given the most basic agricultural weapons and a few days training. Earthworks were thrown up on the most vulnerable beaches and beacons were manned on the hills and headlands. In 1587, England waited breathlessly for the blow to fall, until Drake slipped out of Plymouth and accounted for the loss of almost 100 of the enemy's ships in several bold engagements, which put off the expected invasion for another year.

In July 1588, the watchers on the Cornish coastline gazed at the apocalyptic sight of the reassembled Armada, nearly 150 ships laden with fighting men, as it passed slowly by up the Channel. With fair weather they would have been almost impossible to resist but, harried by Drake and Howard and scattered by contrary winds, they were unable to make a concerted landfall. Sailing around Scotland and the west of Ireland, they were stricken by a series of storms that led to the loss of almost half the Spanish fleet, while the rest limped home without ever having given fight.

The Spanish were not finished and helped fuel the flames of a French civil war. In 1590 they took sides with Catholic Brittany, thus acquiring yet another base from which to harass the coast of England, including the conveniently near coast of Cornwall. Raleigh and Drake saw to the fortification of Plymouth and Sir Francis Godolphin was sent to the vulnerable Scilly Isles to add new defences to Henry VIII's Star Castle. The great estuaries of Falmouth and Fowey were defended with chains and booms, difficult to assault between their well-defended headlands. But one western bay was not defended at all, a tempting target for an admonitory raid, and a message to a heretic Queen that stated her realm was not as secure as she imagined.

Fear of invasion spread throughout Cornwall. Watchers had sighted a large fleet of Spaniards off Falmouth, while smaller detachments were sighted off Padstow to the north and St Keverne to the east of the Lizard; their intentions were clear enough.

The morning of 23 July 1595 dawned fine, though the Mount's Bay was obscured by an early mist. As this cleared, the people of Mousehole were horrified to find four Spanish galleys emerging from the fading mist, right next to their village.

The galleys had sailed from the Breton port of Port Louis, near Lorient, under the leadership of Don Carlos de Amesquita, stuffed with around 400 arquebusiers (riflemen). They had sunk a French barque captured by an English crew on the way, and ghosted into Mount's Bay under cover of darkness. They quickly launched around half their soldiers in pinnaces, who landed in Mousehole just a few minutes later. If they had been expecting a fight with a prepared garrison, all they found was a terrified civilian population from which many of the abler men had already been pressed into service in Ireland or in the Queen's privateers. Of the villagers, only Jenkin Keigwin appears to have shown any resistance, or perhaps he was the only one armed, and he was immediately shot dead. To their credit, the Spanish forces restrained themselves from massacring the families who were fleeing up the hill towards Paul. They divided their forces. Half remained in the village, some to set fires while others stood guard over the firing party against any returning villagers. But there were none. The other half went eagerly up to Paul. Among the raiders was an English spy, Richard Burley, a staunch Catholic from Weymouth, who 'sat next to the captain'. Burley clearly knew the terrain well and had helped in planning the raid.

Paul church was an important target for the Spanish leaders, who regarded the raid as a holy crusade. They found it full of refugee women and children, but once again refused to emulate savage atrocities elsewhere and removed them from the church before setting it alight. The body of the church was destroyed, though the fifteenth-century tower survived. Other raiders foraged a little wider around the countryside to terrify the peasants and burn nearby farms and crops. After around five hours, their work was done and no opposition had presented itself; they returned to their galleys in triumph. The rest of the bay watched in horror as the plume of smoke stained the sky, hoping they would see the galleys put back to sea and disappear.

The Spanish indeed weighed anchor, but instead of turning seaward they drew further into the bay. Sir Francis Godolphin happened to be in Penzance reviewing the local defences. He had not been idle during the sack of Mousehole, and with Thomas Chiverton of Kerris he had summoned their ragged militia, mostly armed with little more than pikes and pitchforks. They formed up on Newlyn Green while Godolphin wrote a hasty note to Drake and Hawkins in Plymouth:

> Four galleys are at anchor before Mousehole, their men landed and the town and other houses in the country thereabouts are fired. No more of the fleet are in sight; fifty or sixty were seen Monday evening and yesterday athwart of Falmouth. Pray consider what is to be done for safety and defence.
>
> PS About two hundred men have assembled; we attend the coming of more, so as to make head towards the enemy.

Despite the icy calm of the message, Godolphin's position was hopeless. Among his company there were, according to Carew's account, 'About thirty or forty shot, though scarce one third of them were serviceable'. The Spanish galleys moved nearer and anchored again, close to the Western Green. They then landed their whole force of 400 armed and armoured soldiers and quickly put the smaller community of Newlyn to the torch without opposition. Scouts mounted Chywoone Hill to check whether other defending forces were marching against them or if ships were attempting to cut them off. Hearing that no defensive action had occurred, the Spaniards turned their attention towards Penzance.

Godolphin saw the futility of trying to defend the open green and called his forces to retreat towards Penzance town. The galleys, being close enough to open up with their firing-pieces, rained Godolphin's men with shot, turning their retreat into a rout:

Though none were hurt but only a constable unhorsed, without any harm saving the show on his doublet of the bullets sliding by his back, yet many in a fearful manner fell flat to the ground and others ran away.

The Spanish soldiers convened on the vacated green and marched in formation to the western outskirts of Penzance, with the firing parties busily setting alight every house they passed. Godolphin did not lack courage and tried to marshal the forces he had to form up in the marketplace by the ancient crossroads. However, if he expected the unarmed townspeople to stand with him in the face of a disciplined and heavily armed enemy, he was gravely disappointed. The population fled to the hills as their fellows in Newlyn and Mousehole had done, and when Godolphin assessed his force it consisted of a small number of local men, plus, 'but two resolute shot who stood at his command and some ten or twelve others who followed him, most of them his own servants.' As the Spanish forces came within earshot, even this small number began to diminish further and though Godolphin stood firm, the rest 'neither with his persuasions nor threatening with rapier drawn could he recall'.

The enemy entered the town in three detachments, one up Chapel Street, one along Alverton and one encircled North Street (Causewayhead) to meet at the marketplace. By the time they had assembled there, their bright banners and pikes catching the sun amid the smoke, even the furious Godolphin had seen the pointlessness of making a stand and retreated in frustration.

The firing parties continued in their task of destroying the buildings, most of which were thatched and of wooden construction, while another party went down to the harbour to fire the ships in the port. One of these was carrying three newly cast bells, which were destined for the smouldering Paul church. Having completed a satisfactory day's work, they decided that Penzance was too dangerous to defend in case of any forceful reaction and marched back to Newlyn, leaving utter ruin behind them. Most of the troops returned to the galleys for the night, but a small group of their leaders, including Don Carlos, ascended Chywoone Hill once more. There, as the sun went down, they had the pleasurable view of the smoke from the three communities they had attacked. They held a spontaneous Mass of celebration and thanksgiving, vowing to consecrate that very place as a Catholic friary once their countrymen had succeeded in making England their own.

By the next morning, they were still calmly anchored off Newlyn Green, ostentatiously in charge of the situation. However, defenders had been gathered in from other parts of the west. The invaders made to land once again in Newlyn. But, on seeing a number of organised and armed men ashore, they changed their minds. The defenders turned their fire on the galleys. They were too far off to be greatly harmed, 'but finding themselves annoyed by the shooting of bullets and arrows where they rode at anchor they were forced to remove them further off.'

A greater Cornish force had convened to the west of Marazion, determined to defend the town and in particular the Mount. By a twist of fate, Marazion had received Mount's Bay's first Charter of Incorporation as a borough from the Queen on 13 June, just six weeks earlier. By 24 July it was the only town in the bay left standing. However, the Spaniards were better equipped to sack and burn than to lay siege, and their spy would have told them the Mount was garrisoned by professional soldiers. Besides, they realised their time was running out.

Wednesday July 23

St Mawes Fort

Hanibal Vyvyan to Sir Francis Drake and Sir John Hawkins

Generals of the fleet at Plymouth: I think you are informed of the Spaniards landing this day in the western parts; they have burned Penzance, Newlyn, Mousehole, Poole Church and Churchtown, and other villages adjoining without resistance; I speak it to the disgrace of those people.

There is great want of leaders; the Spaniards' conquest without resistance may give them greater encouragement to land along the coast as well to the east as north. I beg you if your ships are not fit to fight to send into these parts some of their leaders who have commanded in war, as they are greatly needed now and will be even more so if the Spaniards should land. If you lack mariners I think a hundred could be procured in ten hours in Falmouth harbour.

Hannibal Vyvyan's letter reached Plymouth the next day and Drake and Hawkins, without any need to beat the inns of Falmouth, detached part of their fleet to sail to Mount's Bay with due speed. The Spaniards made no further raids the following day. They had with them a number of English prisoners, whose later testimony helped to explain their thinking. Barnaby

Loe of Ipswich explained that the original goal of the Spanish had been the Isles of Scilly, which they proposed to seize and hold, but the winds proved adverse for that venture. Among other things, their galleys contained 'a good store of treasure, which was to be used for pay, and for the corrupting of some'. In keeping with the overall civility of the raid, they proposed to pay their men enough to save them from helping themselves to spoil.

The wind prevented a quick getaway from Mount's Bay, blowing strongly from the south-east and keeping the galleys embayed. Though they would have liked to land once more, they did not need the treacherous Burley to inform them that English ships would soon be bearing down on them. One of their own ships had sprung a leak and they were all running short of fresh water, so it seemed, as the English boats sailed hungrily for their revenge, that the raid would be a costly failure. Their only venture to the shore was to send in a boat containing all their English prisoners.

However, the fortune of the weather, which had deserted the Spanish so thoroughly during the Armada, turned in their favour. On the morning of Friday 25 July, as the English ships were making the difficult passage of the Lizard, the wind turned round to the opposite side of the compass, north-westerly, hampering the English fleet and ushering the galleys safely out to sea, 'as if God had a purpose to preserve these his rods for a longer time.' The raid was over, and only the post-mortem remained.

The verdict of nearly all those who put pen to paper was that the townspeople of Mount's Bay had disgraced themselves with their failure to stand and give battle to the enemy. Vyvyan's harsh words – albeit despatched from the safety of the well-garrisoned St Mawes Castle – were echoed by others. Sir Nicholas Clifford, one of the reinforcement captains who had arrived in Penzance shortly after the Spaniards left, was equally scathing: 'Had the people stood with Sir Francis Godolphin, who engaged himself very worthily, it had been saved, but the common sort utterly forsook him saving four or five gentlemen.'

Most cutting of all was the opinion of Sir Thomas Baskerville, a diligent general and admiral who had fought (and quarrelled) with Drake:

If any captain of judgement had been there to conduct the people, with only 200 men, and had accosted the enemy in flank, the country would have been saved from spoil and fire, and without any loss; had they attempted it whilst the enemy followed the spoil in the sacking of the towns, their disorder would undoubtedly have overthrown them.

This was all very well from those who had not been there. Carew's verdict on the incident – his report came straight from the mouth of his friend, Sir Francis Godolphin – was more measured:

> There you have a summary report of the Spaniards' glorious enterprise and the Cornishmen's' infamous cowardice, which (were there any cause) I could qualify by many reasons: as, the suddenness of the attempt, the narrowness of the country, the openness of the town, the advantage of the galleys' ordinance on a people unprepared against such accidents through our long continued peace, and at that very time for the most part either in their tin-works or at sea, who 'ere the next day made resistance even with a handful, and entered a vowed resolution to revenge their loss at the next encounter if the enemy had landed again. So might I likewise say that all these circumstances meeting in any other quarter of the realm would hardly have produced much better effects.

However, the ultimate judgement of the wisest course of action for unarmed civilians faced with a phalanx of trained and well-armed invaders was that of the townspeople themselves. They instantly decided that while buildings could be rebuilt, the people of Penzance would be an irreplaceable loss and pragmatically ran for it, uncaring of their future reputation among the military classes. And their decision proved the best.

15

Taking Stock

The story of Penzance is one of many sudden setbacks followed by slow regrouping and growth. It was and is a durable town, used to the blows of fate, sufficiently rooted to start again and again.

At the end of July 1595, it appeared to have little future and seemed destined, along with Mousehole, to spend the rest of its days as a minor fishing port while Marazion turned into the major and only conurbation of Mount's Bay. It was at least summertime, and the people cleared away the ashes of their homes, turned the few stone buildings into rough shelters, sought the assistance of their friends and relations in the surrounding farms, and took stock.

It was probably then that the western part of the town began to rise in prominence. The main thrust of Penzance until then had been more or less the straight line from Causewayhead to the sea (marked even now by the location of the older inns that still follow this line). This would seem to have been the logical stretch for a main street as the highway between the two original settlements. But it was not to be. In the devastation following the raid, a makeshift market was set up as close as possible to the burnt marketplace, and the side road pointing towards Market Jew (Marazion) came into its own.

By 1598, a lively but illegal market held in Penzance on Saturdays was proving such a successful attraction that the recently incorporated Corporation of Marazion sent a strongly worded complaint to the Attorney General, demanding that Penzance either show by what warrant they held the market or desist. It turned into the classic mixture of obstinate Cornishmen and legal delays that would emerge again and again in subsequent years. Penzance did not cease its trade and boldly continued, despite threats of action. It was not until 1602 that an injunction was finally issued by the Court of Exchequer that prohibited three named offenders – Richard Fenney, Robert Hamett, and Richard Bennett – and other inhabitants of Penzance from their illegitimate carryings on. The Penzance contingent insisted that they were not holding a market but merely a meeting, a pleasant social occasion. Marazion countered this nonsense by trying to have the ringleaders imprisoned for contempt of court. Penzance's flimsy excuses could not stand examination for long and the court did finally enforce its ruling in 1604, though allowing a limited meat market to be held in recognition of the losses Penzance had suffered by the Spanish raid.

Though the inhabitants of Penzance had suffered comprehensive losses, there were those outside the town who saw an opportunity in the disaster. The ruined town plots could be obtained for a small fee, and landowners and well-off tenant farmers began to take an interest. Foremost among these were the Tremenheeres, a farming family from Ludgvan whose dynasty rang down the ages of Penzance's development and whose name is still not hard to find in Penzance today. Along with others, they invested in obtaining and rebuilding parts of the old town.

On the world stage, the battle with Spain went on and England was to be saved from invasion twice more by the intervention of the weather. The Spanish were also being rivalled by retaliation from the Netherlands and the complex seaborne power struggles went on without cease. The Cornish coast continued to form one of the most vulnerable borders but, shocked by the raid on Mount's Bay, the Queen sent serious reinforcements of well-trained professional soldiers to ensure that no more such events took place. By the end of the Elizabethan era, the country was sick of war but seemingly unable to end the international stalemate.

Just before the death of the Queen, a major work of literature concerning Cornwall was written – Richard Carew's *Survey of Cornwall*. He has little to say about Penzance itself, except the report of the raid quoted above, but his observations in 1602 paint the first comprehensive picture of the county's wildlife, agriculture, fishing, mining, governance and the Cornish way of life.

Carew is always more comfortable with the ruling classes and local Cornish aristocracy, though he archly observed of their isolation: 'The angle that shutteth them in hath wrought many interchangeable matches with each other's stock, and given beginning to the proverb that all Cornish gentlemen are cousins.' He casts a wry glance on the lower orders, in what became a tradition for outside travellers, pointing derisory fingers at the primitive Cornish. 'Their chiefest trade,' he says, 'consisteth in offering their petty merchandises and artificers' labours at the weekly markets'. He criticises the coastal dwellers for their lack of ambition in failing to create industries such as shipbuilding or large-scale trade in goods, though he acknowledges their expertise in 'free trading'. The state of their hospitality comes in for its share of abuse:

> Strangers occasioned to travel through the shire were wont to inveigh against the bad drink, coarse lodging, and slack attendance which they found in those houses that went for inns, neither did their horses' better entertainment prove them any more welcome guests than their masters.

He notes some improvements in the fortunes of farmers from recent times. In the past, he says,

> Their grounds lay all in common, their drink water, or at best whey, for the richest farmer in a parish brewed not above twice a year, and then God wotte what liquor; their apparel coarse in matter, ill-shapen in manner; their legs and feet naked and bare, to which sundry old folk had so accustomed their youth that they could hardly abide to wear any shoes, complaining that it kept them over hot ... The meaner country wenches of the western parts do yet ride astride ... their household walls of earth, low thatched roofs, few partitions, no planchings [floorboards] or glass windows, scarcely any chimneys other than a hole in the wall to let out the smoke, their bed straw and a blanket.

Happily, he finds the Cornish husbandman can now

> maintain himself and his family in a competent decency to their calling and findeth money to bestow weekly at the market for his provisions of necessity and pleasure, for his quarterly rent serveth rather as a token of subjection to his landlord than any grievous exaction on his tenement.

The Cornish husbandman may have had his own opinions about this assessment, but he might recognise Carew's observation of his suspicion if not actual dislike of the English foreigner and still more the sad fact, noted down the centuries: 'It might be wished that divers amongst them had less spleen to attempt law-suits for petty wrongs, or not so much stiffness to prosecute them; so should their purses be heavier and their consciences lighter.' In resolving these, the local JPs also failed to earn Carew's respect. Trials were often 'posted on with more haste than good speed'. A magistrate 'takes on him peremptory judgement in debts and controversies great and doubtful'. As for the mayor, Carew's view is even more cynical: 'Exercising his office but during one year, for the first half is commonly to learn what he ought to do, and in the other half, feeling his authority to wane, maketh friends of Mammon and serveth others' turns to be requited with the like.'

Despite his superior stance, Carew writes with great insight and enthusiasm on local customs like parish feasts and hurling. The feasts were hosted by the wealthiest of the parish and could last up to a week, with good food and relaxation from the usual hard labour. In addition to hurling, he notes: 'Gwary miracles and three-mans' songs, hunting, hawking, shooting, wrestling and other such games.' 'Gwary miracles' refer to the miracle plays which took place in a 'Plen an Gwary', a circular playing place such as still exists in St Just, where cycles of religious plays like the Cornish *Ordinalia* were performed. 'Three-mans' songs' were ever-popular catches or rounds. 'Shooting' was archery, at which they excelled. Wrestling was of the Cornish variety, exactly as practised today using coarse canvas jackets with which to make a hold or throw, within a ring – in fact a square – of four 'sticklers' to see fair play. Hurling was described as far more than a rough battle to carry a silver ball to a goal. Its complex regulations covered tackling, offside, releasing the ball from a scrum and seems to have much in common with present-day rugby, still the favourite game among Cornishmen everywhere.

Some of the most illuminating parts of the survey relate to the three Cornish trades of fishing, farming and tin-mining. Fishing was as varied as it is now, but Carew gives us the first description of the huge shoals of pilchards that used to come into Mount's Bay every year, enough to form a specialised trade of its own. He describes the open seine nets, the technique of surrounding and catching the shoal directed from high above by a 'Huer', 'crying with a loud voice, whistling through his fingers and wheazing certain diversified and significant signs with a bush'. The fish are then 'first salted and piled up row on row in square heaps on the ground for some ten days until the superfluous moisture of the blood and salt be soaked from them'.

Salted fish proved to be one of the cornerstones of West Cornwall's economy for the next 300 years. Catholic Europe was restricted to eating no meat on Fridays or during the whole of Lent and this created a hungry market for salted fish, which Cornish pilchards filled to perfection. The three villages of Mousehole, Newlyn and Penzance had partly evolved to serve this trade, with courtyards full of 'fish cellars', which were open-fronted buildings over which an upper floor, often reserved as the family's dwelling, was propped on granite columns. It was there that the fish were processed as Carew describes. The oil was collected and used for various local purposes, including lamp-oil. The resulting stench of fish, oil and blood can be imagined and would have made the port areas of the villages something the gentler classes would have done their best to avoid. Pilchards destined for France were packed at once in hogshead barrels and sent off. Those sold to Spain and Italy had already been smoked and were sent as *fumados*, but at this time were packed into barrels and pressed with great stone weights until most of the oil had been extracted.

Farming is briefly described, noting that the Cornish sheep and cattle are smaller and tougher than their English cousins. Local wildlife is portrayed with genuine insight and fondness, except for the rats, which 'dance their gallop galliards in the roofs at night'.

Carew waxes poetical over tin:

In working so pliant; for sight so fair; in use so necessary ... and with such plenty thereof hath God stuffed the bowels of this little angle it overfloweth England, watereth Christendom, and is derived to a great part of the world besides.

Mining was by Carew's time far more advanced than streaming or digging alluvial soil. All the techniques of later works are already in use:

If the load lie slopewise the tinners dig a convenient depth and then pass forward underground so far as the air will yield them breathing, which as it beginneth to fail they sink a shaft down thither from the top to admit a renewing vent. Notwithstanding most of their work is by candle-light. In these passages they meet sometimes with very loose earth, sometimes with exceeding hard rocks, and sometimes with great streams of water.

The loose earth is propped by frames of timber-work as they go, and yet now and then falling down either presseth the poor workmen to death or stoppeth them from returning. To part the rocks they have axes and wedges with which mostly they make speedy way, and yet not seldom a good workman shall hardly be able to hew three feet in the space of so many weeks. While they thus play the moldwarps [moles] unsavoury damps do here and there distemper their heads.

For conveying away the water they pray in aid of sundry devices as adits, pumps and wheels driven by a stream inerchangeably filling and emptying two buckets. Notwithstanding the springs so encroach as to keep men, and sometimes horses also, to work both day and night without ceasing.

Once being brought above ground in the stone, it is first broken with hammers and then carried to a stamping-mill where great logs of timber, bound at the ends with iron and lifted up and down by a wheel driven by water do break it smaller. From the stamping mill it passeth to the crazing-mill, which between two stones turned also with a water-wheel, bruiseth the same to a fine sand. The stream, after it hath forsaken the mill, is made to fall by certain degrees, upon each of which at every descent lieth a green turf three or four foot square and a foot thick. On this the tinner layeth a certain portion of the sandy tin and with his shovel softly tosseth the same to and fro, that through the stirring of the water it may wash away the light earth from the tin, which of a heavier substance lieth fast on the turf. The best of these turfs (for all sorts serve not) are fetched about two miles to the eastward of St Michael's Mount.

Carew then details the hazardous smelting process and concludes,

I know not whether you would more marvel whence a sufficient gain should arise to countervail so manifold expenses; or that any gain could train men to undertake such pains and peril.

A tinner called Beare, of Blackmore, writing shortly before Carew expands on this:

The most part of the workers of the black tyn are very poore men, as no doubt that occupation can never make them rich. And chiefly such tyn workers as trust only to their wages, although they have never so rich a tynworke, have no profit of their tyn as their masters have their tyn. The wages of a tynner working his dole ... is but £3 a year. This poor man happily hath a wife and four or five small children to care for, which all depend upon his getting. O God, how can this poore man prosper?

As for the class among whom Carew was most comfortable, Beare's 'masters', things were a little less onerous.

They converse familiarly together, and often visit one another. A gentleman and his wife will ride to make merry with his next neighbour, and after a day or twain those two couples go to a third, in which progress they increase like snowballs til through their burdensome weight they break again.

Beneath them as they rode were men gasping in the semi-darkness 'working their dole'.

16

Incorporation

The class of people Carew found least interesting were the burgesses, the increasing cohort of bourgeoisie, yet it was they who kept communities together, attended to day-to-day matters and pushed for progress. They can take the greatest credit for the remarkable fact that less than twenty years after being burned to the ground, Penzance was granted its own Royal Charter of Incorporation on 9 May 1614 and became a borough.

James I had been on the throne since the death of Elizabeth in 1603, and had finally negotiated a peace with Spain. Even so, it was the strategic military importance of Penzance that was among the foremost justifications accepted by the King for the Incorporation. He wrote,

Whereas our village of Penzance in the County of Cornwall bordering the sea there is an ancient village and port both populous and of great force and strength to resist the enemies that shall there invade and to defend the country there adjoining and our subjects there residing and is also a village that exercised merchandise from time immemorial with much commerce upon the sea whereby many mariners are brought up in the art of navigation there constantly instructed and practiced who for naval service and the defence of our kingdom are fit.

And whereas also the inhabitants of the same village divers laudable services to our predecessors and to us have rendered.

And whereas also the inhabitants have been burdened with the expense in the fortification and defence of the village and the port and in the maintenance and repair of a pier or quay and other necessary charges and especially in the taking of pirates and lately in the rebuilding of the village which was by the invasion of the Spaniards insidiously and in a hostile manner demolished and burned to the injury of the inhabitants.

And whereas the inhabitants by their very great pains costs and expenses have rebuilt and repaired the village and the port and quay and have humbly supplicated that We by our royal grace and munificence the said inhabitants of the village would make into one body corporate and politic by the name of the Mayor Aldermen and Commonality of Penzance with the grant of certain liberties as to us might seem expedient.

It is notable that the Charter still mentions the village and the port as separate entities, and it is by the Charter that this distinction – at least in legal terms – was finally ended. There is also no doubt of the ongoing significance of the Spanish raid. England's defences had been breached, albeit for only three days, and the shock and shame of that event still haunted her rulers. Many aspiring Penzance residents had wished to 'put Penzance on the map', but its destruction achieved that, however painfully, and was in many ways a spur to its future progress.

Penzance is also praised for training mariners to be fit for naval service, however unwillingly they provided them, and given credit for defence against pirates, many of which they did willingly provide. Such facts are smoothed over if they were ever acknowledged. The Charter continues,

We therefore being willing that henceforth forever one certain and undoubted manner order and form in the same village should be observed for the custody of our peace and the good government of the village and of our people there inhabiting, and that the village in perpetual future times may be and remain a village of peace and quietness to the dread and terror of the bad and to the reward of the good and that our peace there may the better be kept.

The aspirations of the Charter, 'to the dread and terror of the bad and to the reward of the good', in the original Latin became the borough motto, which later appeared on its coat of arms, '*Quod improbum terret pobo prodest*'.

There was also something of a 'quid pro quo': 'Hoping that if the inhabitants shall by our grant enjoy more ample liberties and privileges they may feel themselves more especially bound to render services to us and our successors'.

Then came the words the burgesses were longing to hear:

By the present letters declare that the aforesaid village of Pensance be and remain henceforth forever a free village of itself and that all inhabitants thereof and their successors shall be in perpetual future times one body corporate and politic of itself called and known by the name of the Mayor Aldermen and Commonality of Pensance in the County of Cornwall ... and may be in law capable to have and possess lands and other hereditaments and goods and chattels and other things whatsoever ... and that they may have forever a Common Seal for all their public causes and affairs.

It was an achievement which laid the foundations of a new era for the town.

There was one curious feature of the Charter which led to administrative problems from then until the next redrawing of the borough boundaries in 1835. Instead of defining the boundaries as was common in terms of roads and streams – the streams of Lariggan and Ponsandane were highly suitable choices – the borough of Penzance was instead defined by a circle half a mile in radius, with its centre at the market cross. This eccentric choice excluded some of the existing fringes and included a considerable area of the sea. The latter was never a problem, but as the town expanded in a non-circular way it formed an awkward artificial line between the town and some of its suburbs. Boundary stones were duly set up at Chyandour, St Clare, Alverton and Wherrytown.

The Charter drew up the future administrative hierarchy in some detail. The corporation was to consist of a mayor as leader of a body of eight aldermen and twelve councillors, known as assistants. To keep order, two sergeants-at-mace were also appointed with an assistant known as 'le yeoman', together with the power to appoint such constables as might be necessary. Also appointed was a recorder 'to give the counsel direction and advice in the execution of the laws and decrees to be made', and a town clerk. The mayor was to be chosen from among the aldermen to serve an annual term, beginning on the Friday after Michaelmas (29 September). The retiring mayor served for a further year as a JP before resuming his office as an alderman.

There was no question as to democratic representation. The aldermen and assistants were appointed to hold their offices for life, with aldermen being replaced on their death from among the assistants, and assistants being appointed when necessary by the aldermen's choice among 'the more sufficient, discreet upright and honest inhabitants of the village'. This was a workable if self-perpetuating system liable to the formation of a ruling elite, entirely in tune with its times.

The mayor and corporation administered the law within the borough boundaries, excepting 'determination of any treason murder felony or other criminal or capital offence touching loss of life or limb', or personal actions in excess of £50 that were reserved for the assizes. Courts were to be held every fortnight under the mayor or the recorder, who was also responsible for establishing and looking after a town prison. Penzance was permitted to keep any local fines or forfeitures for itself. It was also granted, in recognition of the considerable sums it had expended on the town and the quay (of which it was presciently said 'it will be forever burthensome'), half the value of the forfeitures of properties belonging to 'felons, fugitives, outlaws and persons adjudged attainted or convicted of felonies murders or petty treason ... and suicides, deodands and other forfeitures within the village'. Deodands were an ancient practice by which any article that had caused an accidental death, which could be as little as a falling slate or as large as a horse, a cart or even a boat, were forfeited, originally to the victim's family in compensation, subsequently to God, which meant to the Church, and later became yet another right of the Crown.

The greatest of all of the King's favours were the confirmations of the trading rights by which the town's future prosperity would be measured. Penzance was granted two weekly markets on Tuesdays and Thursdays, and a generous allowance of seven fairs: the Eve and the Day of Corpus Christi (the Thursday after Trinity Sunday, a date between 17 May and 20 June); the Thursday before St Andrew's Day (30 November); the eve, day and morrow of St Peter ad Vincula (1 August); the eve, day and morrow of St Bartholomew (24 August); the eve and day of the Nativity of St Mary the Virgin (8 September); the eve and day of the Conception of St Mary the Virgin (8 December; and the eve and day of St Peter in Cathedra (22 February).

The second of these had already been granted, and the fair celebrating St Bartholomew was stated to have, 'Heretofore been kept in a certain place near Penzance and is there obsolete.' The 'certain place' was in fact Mousehole, and is one of several indications that Mousehole, although continuing as a thriving fishing port, never fully recovered its status as a community following its destruction in 1595.

In return for all these privileges the King set an annual rent for himself of £3 6s 8d, happily not index-linked, which continued to be paid until 1832.

The inaugural corporation consisted of: John Madern, mayor; Thomas Seyntawbin (St Aubyn), recorder; Thomas Rosewarne, town clerk; John Clyes, John Game, Robert Dunkyn, Roger Polkinhorne, Joseph Lympayne, William Yonge, William Madern Jnr and Robert Luke, aldermen; and William Luer, Richard Sampson, Morice Roche, William Tonkyn, John Davye, Richard Bennett, Richard Finney, David Penlease, Nicholas Game, Richard Trott, Richard Penquite and Simon Hooper, who were assistants.

Local people will recognise many family names that are still common in Penzance. Being nominated among the assistants must have been a particular pleasure to Richard Finney (Fenney) and Richard Bennett, as they had been among those who were prohibited by the Court of Exchequer from holding their illegal markets in Penzance in 1602. Their incorporation must have been a sweet revenge on the borough of Marazion for the dispute following the Spanish raid.

Among its privileges the corporation was able to choose for itself a heraldic seal (similar to a coat of arms). Guided by the institution known as the Heraldic Visitation of Cornwall, local men who were not well versed in such matters sought for a suitable emblem for the seal. They decided that it should refer to the origins of the town's name, 'Pen sans' – the Holy Head(land). They sought the Bible for an appropriate 'head' and decided upon the detached head of St John the Baptist on a charger (dish). With an appropriately grim illustration, this became Penzance's emblem. Representations of the head are still to be found on several buildings in Penzance, including the current market house.

While King James was conducting his long quarrel with Parliament, the corporation of Penzance was choosing robes and ornate maces embossed with the royal arms, and settling down for the first time to take charge of their town's affairs.

17

Consolidation

One of the corporation's first tasks was to redefine its relationship with the still extant manor of Alverton (by now known as 'Alverton and Penzance'). It had reverted to James I, who had sold it to two London businessmen, one of whom died shortly after. The survivor sold it to his stepfather-in-law, Richard Daniell, a wealthy merchant of Truro. The corporation opened negotiations with Mr Daniell, with the result that they agreed to purchase several of its important rights. These included the harbour dues that Henry VIII had granted to the manor, and also the rights and profits of the now considerable markets and fairs. Mr Daniell reserved for himself the right of 'boatleave', presumably an exemption of the harbour dues for himself, and an annual payment of £1, which continued to be faithfully paid to his heirs until the final dissolution of the manor in 1936.

Importantly, he also agreed the sale of

One three-cornered plot of waste lande lying in the saide town ... towards the west side of the Towne ... and bounded on every part thereof with the king's high waye ... and one tymber howse lately erected upon the same plott. To have and to holde the saide tymber howse markettes liberties free customes of tolle stallage, peckage [leftover food], coverage, fayres ... unto the saide Maior Aldermen and Communalty of Pensance forever.

For the sum of £34, the town had not only acquired the markets and fairs, but also a site and building in the centre of the town in which to hold them, an excellent piece of business and the source of income on which to build the town's future prosperity.

Rivalry with Marazion continued as Penzance's wealth and influence grew. With the port now in their hands, the corporation made great improvements to the quay's facilities which, coupled with the tidal inconvenience of St Michael's Mount, began to draw the lion's share of commercial shipping into its sphere. Within a few years Marazion was forced to write a resentful petition, copied to the corporation of Penzance and presumably intended for Parliament:

> The Mayor, Magistrates and inhabitants of the town of Penzance out of self ends to themselves do endeavour as much as they can to deprive us of our ancient privileges and to constrain us and all others concerned with us to land all goods and merchandises on the stone quay of Penzance, pretending there to be the fittest place but intending their own interest; and to make us pay for cellarage what they please (we not having any cellars here); and also to make us pay for quay duty, boatage, porterage, and several other charges ... which will not be only to us an exceeding great prejudice but also to many others of His Majesty's subjects, *viz* merchants, owners of ships and seamen which are and may be concerned with us, the said stone quay at Penzance being about three miles distant from our town.

Their fears were well founded. The main imports, vital for local trade, were the bulk raw materials that West Cornwall significantly lacked: salt, iron, coal and timber – the last two usually provided from other English ports. In return, Penzance exported hogsheads of pilchards, the numbers fluctuating (according to customs) from 148 in a bad year to over 2,000 in a normal year. Although customs' records then classed the whole of Mount's Bay and the stretch from the Lizard to Cape Cornwall as 'the Port of Penzance', it was the town itself that claimed the major part of the business. It benefitted from much more than the harbour dues. All the above imports were labour-intensive to handle, requiring dockers, labourers and waggoners, the storage facilities that Marazion lacked, and the market house where buyers and traders could gather to bid for the products.

The most significant absentee from this industrial scene was the shipment of tin. To the town's increasing frustration, the wardens of the Stanneries refused to grant any further coinage rights in Cornwall, a decision vigorously defended by those towns like Helston which held the lucrative privilege. The long and dreary twice-yearly trek of wagonloads of tin to Helston continued.

The port fees were graded according to the origin of the customer. Local Penzance inhabitants naturally enjoyed the most favourable rates. Those from elsewhere in England, known as strangers or denizens, paid an intermediate rate, while all foreign traders, or aliens, were charged the most – a significant difference as the borough records show:

> Every ship that shall come within the pier having a top shall pay twelve pence, every smaller bark without a top belonging to a denizen shall pay eight pence, and every ship or bark belonging to an alien of what burden soever they be shall pay two shillings.

Small wonder that Marazion bewailed its disadvantages.

Shipping continued to be a most hazardous occupation. Merchant ships suffered the usual seasonal dangers of the western coastline, of storms, reefs, fog and the risk of being trapped within the wide arms of Mount's Bay in a contrary wind. A regular toll of ships and men was a sad strand of the far west's maritime heritage.

An attempt by one of the Killigrew family in 1619 to erect a lighthouse on the Lizard was met by a furious if cynical reaction from nearby coastal communities. Killigrew recorded their objection, 'that I take away God's Grace from them'. By this he understood correctly that every wreck that came ashore was regarded as divine good fortune, for the locals if not the unhappy crew. Wrecking – as in the art of recovering cargo and other valuables from a wreck – was part of Cornish life and culture, so much so that it was regarded as a right that the courts on many occasions were petitioned to uphold. The protests by the locals together with the reluctance of ship-owners to pay his considerable costs caused Killigrew to give up the enterprise, and the coast and headlands became dark and frequently deadly once more.

Added to the natural hazards was the risk of running into one of the Dutch privateers, who had replaced the Spaniards as the English Channel's regular scavengers. Most fearsome of all was a new menace from the north coast of Africa. The Dutch had made an alliance with the Moorish pirates from Algiers, Sallee, Tripoli and Tunis. In return for the use of the Dutch ports it encouraged the Moors to fare further north from their former sphere of influence.

Pillaging adventurers from the British-named Barbary Coast (from the native Berber population) had already caused some Mediterranean states to abandon their coastal communities altogether. The pirates first explored the west coasts of mainland Europe and then fell upon the lucrative traffic in the western approaches. Their oar-powered galleys were augmented by light sailing xebecs, too fast to be pursued by heavy warships. Unlike the privateers whose main goal was merchandise, the Moorish Corsairs – known along the Cornish coast simply as the 'Turks' – were still more terrifying due to their trade in humans. In the Ottoman Empire slaves were a crucial part of the economy, amounting to perhaps a fifth of the population. Many were captured in central Africa, but Caucasians were far more valuable in the slave markets. Adding religious zeal to this mercenary trade, Christian slaves who were forced to convert to Islam were the most prized of all. Captives from prosperous families supplied a regular stream of ransom money, while those with no particular background faced a miserable choice of hard labour on the land or worse, being chained to an oar as galley-slaves. The prospects for captured women were equally dire. White concubines were a status symbol for prominent Berber families and the most favoured were reserved for the sultans' own harems. Between the sixteenth and nineteenth centuries it is estimated that well over a million souls were taken as slaves to North Africa, the last one as late as 1908.

These raiders could strike anywhere at any time. They were not restricted to encounters at sea but landed ashore at will, rounding up as many terrified civilians as possible, and quickly fleeing before help could arrive. Their depredations increased throughout the first half of the seventeenth century. By 1625, Penzance's alderman Roger Polkinghorne petitioned the government for shore batteries and a grant of £600 for fortifications, presumably without much success as the next year it was reported that even the fishermen dared not put to sea. In 1640 it was reported to the Privy Council that a fleet of four 'Turkish' ships had captured no fewer than nine ships in the bay in a single day, including five fishing boats, and had continued to take a further three off Mousehole in the evening, which left over sixty people condemned to a life of slavery. In the same year, the Corsairs landed at night and are said to have carried off most of the inhabitants of an unnamed village on Mount's Bay – whole families including women and children who had sought sanctuary in the church.

In spite of such atrocities, the life of the borough went on. It followed the tradition of the Church in 'farming' its rights and dues to private individuals. This meant that its income from the port, markets, and fairs was less than what was actually paid, but this was more than compensated by the fact that it was paid in advance by the middlemen and spared the town officials from the burdensome task of chasing the ship-owners and market traders for the money.

Far less orderly was the question of the right to grind corn. This had not been included in the manorial rights the town had purchased from Mr Daniell. Instead, on one of the occasions when the manor had reverted to the Crown, the right had been sold or granted as a favour to a branch of the Godolphin family who lived at Trewarveneth, Newlyn. The manorial mill was just across the river at Tolcarne, and to this mill all harvests of corn from Penzance and within the bounds of the old manor of Alverton had to be brought, to the great profit of its owners. Having been freed from the other restrictions of the manor, the local farmers and millers in outlying villages looked forward to the lifting of the obligation to patronise Tolcarne, but found it was not forthcoming. Offended by this setback to their entrepreneurial spirit, various bodies tried to bypass this tiresome monopoly, principal among them those tasked with the upholding of the law, the mayor and corporation. The Godolphin family first went to law to defend its rights in 1623, naming the mayor, Pascoe Ellis, for encouraging rather than punishing farmers and local bakers for using other mills.

A few years later, Ellis, along with Roger Polkinhorne, William Maddern (the mayor), and other magistrates, took it upon themselves to authorise 'various horse-mills, hand-mills and querns' to grind on a less than industrial scale within the manorial bounds. This was challenged at law in its turn and Godolphin's rights were upheld. In response to this the obstinate defendants set up a rival mill at Gulval just outside the old manor bounds, which proved very popular with local bakers. Litigation recommenced and in 1639 the redoubtable Polkinghorne was ordered to close his Gulval mill and 'to cease making unlawful orders and constitutions within Penzance'. Polkinghorne complied and Penzance bowed, at least officially, to the law, though further lawsuits regarding Tolcarne's monopoly carried on well into the eighteenth century.

It was not the only manorial lawsuit to involve Mr Polkinghorne. Along with the same William Maddern, Robert Luke and John Game – all appointed by the King in the original 1614 Charter as aldermen – Polkinghorne had made use for himself along the length of the shoreline and meadows stretching from St Mary's chapel to Lariggan stream. This was variously known as The Greens, Adgeaporth, and Le Logges, the extent of the current promenade. These had been used or rented out for such uses as the drying of nets, the building of fish cellars and cattle grazing. Polkinghorne claimed rights from an ancient and dubious lease granted by Elizabeth I. Alexander Daniell, son of Richard Daniell, who had inherited the rights of the manor not assigned to the town by his father, claimed the land as his own and demanded its return and £40 in unpaid rent.

The case was undertaken in 1635 and typically trailed on for another two years before being heard. The judgement went Daniell's way and Polkinghorne was ordered to pay damages of £70, which he unsurprisingly refused to do until committed to Fleet Prison for contempt. Even then he managed to satisfy the court with a payment of just £17. The farcical aspects of this typically Cornish piece of litigation were further illustrated when it was revealed that a crucial document on which the buccaneering Polkinghorne and his fellow Aldermen depended was – allegedly – destroyed when,

> It pleased God that a dog catched the said deed from the table where it lay [written no doubt on vellum] and tore it into pieces and ate it while they caroused and rejoiced in their mischievous purpose.

It will also come as no surprise to those familiar with the history of corporate bodies that one of Daniell's complaints was that the defendants

> do pretend and give out that they can make friends to jurors in these parts and will by one means or another detain these same premises from your subject, notwithstanding that he has good right and title thereto.

Some 300 miles and a whole world away from these parochial matters, Charles I had ascended to the throne, recommenced hostilities with Spain, and made himself vastly unpopular with coastal communities by imposing payments of 'ship money'. This had replaced the Tudor obligation on ports to provide ships and men for the defence of the realm with suitable payments in cash (so much more amenable for royal purposes) but had never before been imposed in peacetime. Charles was not afraid to make enemies and continued to antagonise far more powerful lobbies than coastal towns – Parliament, the Church, the Scots – his confidence being such he was sure he could overcome all three.

Parliament was simply bypassed and its members were sent home. This had less impact in Penzance than other parts of Cornwall since it had never been favoured with a parliamentary seat. St Ives had returned two members since 1558 and Marazion had reputedly been granted the same privilege around the same time, but could or would not raise sufficient funds to support them. A few years later, Marazion changed its mind and dutifully sent up two members, who found on entering the Commons that they were no longer on the lists and were sent back to Cornwall in ignominy. Penzance appears to have taken the electoral slight well and a later anonymous commentator by the name of 'Penzantiensis' writing in the *London Magazine* in 1749 concluded,

> The most sensible and rational part of the inhabitants think it an happiness not to be a parliamentary borough, for they observe that elections poison the morals and are productive of discord, idleness, drunkenness, perjury, poverty and ruin.

The Church was riven by extreme factions, especially the reaction to the perceived toleration of Catholics, exemplified by Charles who had taken a Catholic wife. This led to the increasing grip of rigid Puritan values, allied to the Scottish Presbyterians, on the wider Church. These included an extraordinarily zealous observance of the Sabbath, on which, according to Exeter's Municipal Records, it was forbidden to do almost anything – entertaining guests, walking in the fields, even knitting could lead to a session in the stocks. Uttering of oaths had a graduated scale of fines depending on the offender's social station. Even speaking – or not even speaking – with the opposite sex was hazardous: 'Jane Dicker was seen in her own house suspiciously near Francis Hamlin by a person who was passing near the door', which saw both imprisoned. Fortunately, the Puritan zeal affected the East far more than the conservative West.

As for the Scots, their patience eventually ran out and they crossed the border to occupy the northern counties of England. The King's need to mobilise an army made further demands on Cornwall, which saw money badly needed for the coastal defences withheld and pressed many able-bodied men into military service. These were mostly tinners and farm labourers, with consequent damage to mining and the harvest. He also revived the execrated fourteenth-century poll tax. While angry with the government, the Cornish retained a traditional fondness and loyalty for the King. But when hostilities looked inevitable, the great Cornish families were as profoundly split as the rest of the country. On the Royalist side were Sir Bevill Grenville, Sir John Arundell, Sir Richard Vyvyan, Lord Mohun, Sir Henry Killigrew, Sir Francis Godolphin, Sir Nicholas Slanning, and Sir Francis Basset, Lord of St Michael's Mount. Ranked against them were Lord Robartes, Alexander Carew, Sir Richard Buller, Richard Erisey, John St Aubyn, Edmund Prideaux and many others. It went even deeper in some families, including the Arundells and the Godolphins, who were divided among themselves in their loyalties.

The division into camps and the beating of war drums must have seemed until the last moment a high-stakes confrontation, a national trial of strength from which one side would inevitably draw back. Following the final parliamentary challenge entitled the Grand Remonstrance, Parliament granted itself permission to call up troops with its Militia Bill. The King declared it illegal and responded by issuing the Commissions of Array to summon his own supporters to arms. On 18 August 1642, Parliament proposed a fifteen-day truce 'to quiet the country'. But it was too late. By then the King had committed himself too far. Three days later, facing the prospects of defeat by Parliament or a full-scale invasion by the Scots, he set up his banner at Nottingham and the bitterest war in England's history began.

18

Civil War

In Cornwall, the first forlorn response was to turn to Cornwall's favourite resort, the courts. Local representatives of both factions met at Launceston Assizes and argued the legality of each other's cases. This ended in a reading of the King's Proclamation of the Commission of Array, which ended all discussion. The parliamentary lobby sent a letter to London, after which Parliament demanded the presence of Sir Bevill Grenville, Mohun, Arundell, Slanning and others to answer for their 'iniquity'. Unsurprisingly, they declined to attend.

The Royalist forces were established in three principal areas: the central south of England under the King himself; the North under Lord Newcastle; and the South West, nominally under the supervision of the Marquess of Hertford but in practice under the able command of Ralph Hopton. Hopton had been successively an Oxford scholar, a soldier and an MP in his native Somerset, and in the unavoidable choice he opted firmly for the King's side. Much of the West Country was inclined towards the parliamentary cause, partly due to Puritan influences, and Somerset and most of Dorset and Devon declared themselves against the King. Support was never simply divided; the City of Exeter was for Parliament while the dean and chapter of the diocesan authorities remained loyal to the King. However, Parliament's grip on the western counties made the only remaining Royalist stronghold, Cornwall, a major strategic objective for both sides.

The first attempts to recruit a royal Cornish militia were a failure. Harvest time had taken away many able-bodied men, despite the urging of Sir Bevill Grenville who had called a muster at Bodmin. Only 180 men, most of them Grenville's tenants, attended. Hopton arrived with troops in late September and in such farcically confused times was promptly arrested for bringing armed forces into the county. Following 'a leisureable and legall debate of the business' at the Assizes, he was unsurprisingly acquitted and thanked for coming to Cornwall's aid. Brightly using the law as his friend, Hopton issued a *Posse Comitatus*, an ancient legal instrument that permitted him to indict the opposition before a Cornish Grand Jury as 'disturbers of the peace' and gave him license to gather a militia in order to expel them. The *Posse Comitatus* gathered a very respectable muster of 3,000 men in October (after the harvest was in), volunteers from all over Cornwall, though who were poorly armed and mostly untrained. Hopton was obliged to use what he had and proceeded to use all of his skill to organise them as well as he could. However, when he marched them on their first engagement at Launceston they were so excited at finding it undefended they immediately began to burn and plunder the town. Hopton was a fair man but a stern disciplinarian. 'Pay well, command well, hang well' was his motto, and he began to turn his ramshackle force into an effective army.

All of Cornwall's western ports, especially Penzance, were playing a vital role in the King's cause. Queen Henrietta Maria was in France and organised a steady supply of arms, ammunition and other essentials to be landed in the far west and distributed from there. In return she had been given a pre-exemption by Charles over the tin trade that she used to fund these supplies, all output of tin to be sold abroad by her at 20s per hundredweight, almost a third of its pre-war market value. Those tinners who were left after the military call up suffered accordingly, but the port and town of Penzance were never busier. Offshore Parliamentarian men-of-war attempted to harass this trade and together with the African Corsairs who were still active made the voyage to France a highly fraught passage.

Skirmishes continued along the Cornwall–Devon border. Plymouth was resolute for Parliament. Hopton took his forces to Exeter but found it too well defended and retreated back into Cornwall. This suited the Cornish contingent who were generally unwilling to fight outside their county bounds. Another *Posse Comitatus* was held in Modbury, which was well attended, though the volunteers still seemed to take the war lightly. According to Hopton, 'they were so transported with the jollity of the thing that noe man was capable of the labour, care, and discipline'. A rare piece of good luck occurred when three Parliamentary men-of-war full of arms and money were forced by bad weather into Falmouth and captured. Hopton, now able to 'pay well', fought and won the first local pitched battle at Braddock Down near Liskeard. This was followed later in January 1643 by a further victory that relieved Saltash.

After a period of truce due to both sides refreshing their forces, further battles were fought at Launceston and Stratton – both were triumphs for Hopton. On 18 May, following the gallant victory at Stamford Hill in Stratton, Sir Francis Bassett wrote to his wife at St Michael's Mount in an exuberant mood:

> Oh Deare Soule prayes God everlastingly, ring out yo bells, rayse bonfires, publish these joyfull tidings, believe these truths ... Your duteous prayers God has heard and blest us accordingly...

Though he is aware enough to add a coda, 'Send word to ye ports south and north to search narrowly for all strangers travelling for passage, and sease them and keep them close and safe.' These were dangerous times ashore as well as at sea.

Cornwall was secured, a Royalist island in a hostile region, entirely dependent on replenishment from the sea. The victorious Royalist armies struck eastwards with further stunning successes at Bath and Devizes, and in July joined forces with the army of Prince Rupert for an assault on Bristol. The city was taken after a short but immensely bloody fight. The formerly disorderly Cornish contingent, which had by then gained a reputation as a fighting force, took the full brunt of the defence and lost around half its number. By then it had also lost several of its personal heroes: Sidney, son of Francis Godolphin, had been hit by a sniper's bullet at Chagford; John Trevannion and the dashing Nicholas Slanning were killed at Bristol; but worst of all had been the loss at Lansdown Hill, Bath, of Sir Bevill Grenville.

Grenville was loved by Cornishmen everywhere. Grandson of Sir Richard Grenville of the *Revenge*, he was a landowner, scholar, poet, MP and only latterly a soldier. His memorial at Kilkhampton church, near his now-demolished country seat of Stowe, reads,

> He was an excellent person whose activity, interest and reputation was ye foundation of what had been done in Cornwall ... a brighter courage

and gentler disposition were nevar marry'd together to make ye most chearfull and innocent conversation.

He had lost his life to a battleaxe at the climax of the battle, to the great distress of the Cornish troops who found in him more of an inspiration than any other cause for which they fought. The day after his death, Hopton himself was seriously injured when an ammunition cart in which several prisoners had been confined (possibly passing the time by innocently lighting their pipes) exploded. Hopton was found 'miserably burnt, his horse singed like parched leather', but recovered enough to lead his troops on to Bristol.

After the awful slaughter at Bristol, the Cornish army lost heart. Joseph Jayne, MP for Liskeard, wrote that there was 'a general damp upon the people, so that though they reteyned their loyaltie, they lost much of that life which appeared in their first actions'. Some were absorbed into Prince Rupert's army, but many, finding themselves so far from home and dispirited by the loss of so many of their fellows and their iconic leaders, took the long road back home to Cornwall and their home towns and villages.

Despite their absence, the terrifying reputation of the Cornish army went before Hopton's troops and many West Country towns surrendered without a fight, including Dorchester, Weymouth, Portland, Bideford, Barnstaple, and eventually Exeter and Dartmouth. Plymouth remained in Parliamentary hands, though besieged, along with Poole and Lyme Regis. The vastly satisfied King sat down at his camp at Sudely Castle near Winchcombe in the Cotswolds and wrote a proclamation to his loyal subjects in the county of Cornwall, thanking them for their heroic efforts on his behalf and promising that, 'As long as the history of these times and this nation shall continue, the memory of how much the County hath merited from Us and our Crown may be derived with it to posterity.' He ordered that the proclamation should be displayed in every church in Cornwall, and copies of it lettered on to wooden boards may still be seen in some of them today.

The Earl of Essex led the Parliamentary troops in a major counterattack and actually reached as far as Bodmin, but his army was harassed on all sides by the Cornish population and was eventually all but destroyed at Fowey. Over 6,000 Parliamentary prisoners were taken captive to

Lostwithiel, from where they were ordered to march under guard to Launceston and thence back to their own headquarters at Poole. However, such was the hatred of them among the Cornish who had suffered as their battleground that they were attacked, robbed, and stripped of most of their clothes, even their boots, and marched half-naked, starved of food, exhausted, half wounded and were assailed by old men, women and children every step of the way. By the time they reached Launceston half had died, and only around 1,000 ever lived to see Poole.

However, this tainted victory was the high-water mark of the Royalist cause in the west. Delay and indecision as well as dissension and jealousy between Royalist generals prevented any further advances. Leadership was completely lacking, each general acting on his own initiative, as if with his own private army. Cornwall's hopes rested on the uncertain shoulders of the irascible and self-seeking Lord Goring and the brutal but more effective younger brother of Sir Bevill, Richard Grenville. Meanwhile in Yorkshire, Sir Thomas Fairfax was gaining a reputation for the Parliamentarians as head of his new model army.

The King appointed his son Charles, Prince of Wales and Duke of Cornwall, to command the western armies though he was only fifteen years old, assisted by his advisers Lord Hyde and the ennobled Lord Hopton. However, this made little improvement to the internal strife and indiscipline of those on the ground.

Fairfax gained a critical victory at Naseby in Northampton in June 1645 and the Parliamentary armies, secure at the rear, began to take back the territories they had lost. Sherborne, Yeovil and Bridgewater fell. Bristol, gained with so much Cornish blood, surrendered, cutting off the west from Wales. Exeter capitulated. Dartmouth was recaptured and Fairfax gained considerable prestige by sending home every Cornish prisoner with two silver shillings in his pocket, a mighty contrast to the brutal treatment meted out by Grenville and Goring. These two meanwhile continued to fight among themselves and Goring gained few friends over the Tamar by claiming that each one of his Irish soldiers was worth ten of Grenville's 'Cornish cowards'.

The Cornish were not so much cowards as sick of war. Although, while they remained loyal to Richard Grenville due to the memory of his brother, they refused to fight anywhere but on their own soil. Fairfax won a signal victory at Torrington, crossed the border and took Launceston. By now he was seeking terms of surrender from Cornwall. But it was not until his troops reached Truro that a ceasefire was ordered and the indefatigable Hopton negotiated terms of surrender, to include all Cornish territories except Pendennis Castle and St Michael's Mount, which remained garrisoned and defended.

And of course the Isles of Scilly. The young Prince Charles had already fled there from the Mount and Hopton joined him to form a final redoubt of Loyalist supporters. Penzance was not – so far – involved in direct fighting, but was at the very heart of the fading Loyalist cause, with Parliamentary troops all around, the besieged Mount on one side and intrigues coming from Scilly on the other. It was a tense and nervous time for all its inhabitants and their fears were fully justified when Parliamentary troops finally entered the town in the spring of 1646 and spent two days contentedly robbing and plundering all they could carry away. The Mount remained garrisoned and besieged for a while, but its owner Sir Arthur Basset had already virtually bankrupted himself in funding its defences, and after a skirmish and many desertions the Mount too laid down its arms.

It had been the ugliest conflict in the history of England, with counties, towns, villages and even families divided between warring factions, fighting not only on the battlefield but in their own hills and fields where no one could be sure from one day to another by whom their neighbourhood was held. It was described by Cornish author Sir Arthur Quiller-Couch in his novel *The Splendid Spur*, in which his two protagonists travel across the war-torn country from Oxford to Cornwall:

There sounded a crackling and snapping of twigs ahead and two figures came rushing towards us, a man and a woman. The man carried an infant in his arms and though I called on them to stop the pair ran by us with no more notice than if we had been stones. Only the woman cried 'Dear Lord save us!' and wrung her hands as she passed out of sight ... Up amid the pines I clambered and lo! In a minute I looked down as if into the infernal pit. There was a whole town burning below ... in the streets the shouts and the rattle and blaze of musketry, the flames of burning thatches, and quick jets of fire-arms like lightning in a thunder-cloud ... Now and then you might hear a human shriek distinct amid the din which spoke terribly to the heart.

The peaceful and beautiful West Country countryside and villages through which tourists now pass on their way to West Cornwall had all seen similar times of threat, betrayal, conflict, destruction and bloodshed. Even the far west was not united. Penzance, though it contained a small Parliamentary faction, was stoutly for the King, but much of St Ives had a different allegiance and had risen in sympathetic rebellion in advance of the Parliamentary victory.

Peace, such as it was, did not last long. The Parliamentary victory carried with it a new host of strictures regarding churches and Christian worship. With the inspiration of the Puritans, many of the churches that had escaped being stripped of their goods and architectural treasures 100 years before were literally attacked with saws and sledgehammers to produce the modesty and plainness required. The prayer book service, against which the Cornish had once risen, was condemned, to the grief of its former opponents. Added to this was the imposition of heavy new taxes on a county that had already suffered so many losses, in which the old trades of farming, fishing and mining had been devastated by the disruptions of war and the lack of men. The harvests remained poor, and, to add another of the apocalyptic curses, the plague returned in 1647 to claim many of the weakened populace.

Loyalist outbreaks occurred in many parts of England and Wales. Knowing its inner sympathies, however concealed, the Commonwealth regarded Cornwall as particularly unstable. In the spring of 1648, Sir Hardress Waller was sent with troops to arrest known Royalists and keep the countryside quiet. However, his influence did not extend to the end of the peninsula. One of the few Parliamentary supporters in Penzance was ex-mayor Anthony Gubbes, who, with his son, had narrowly escaped execution for high treason. He warned the occupying forces that Penzance was ripe for insurrection but no one took any notice until 16 May 1648. Led by Maj. Thomas Grosse of St Buryan, William Keigwin of Mousehole, Capt. Maddern of Penzance and Capt. Tresillian of St Levan, and secretly backed by other Cornish Loyalist families, they seized Penzance for the King and arrested Gubbes. Despite considerable support from the Helston and Lizard area, the neighbouring communities failed to flock to the Royal Standard and six days later a Parliamentarian army was marching on the outskirts of the town. Refusing its terms of surrender, the Penzance rebels resolved to meet the heavily armed Parliamentary troops on the eastern Borough boundary near Gulval.

There could only be one outcome between seasoned troops and the local militia, and the rebels were quickly driven back into the town. Penzance's hopes rested partly on a detachment of fellow rebels from St Keverne who were to attack the Parliamentary forces from the rear, but some of the parliamentary cavalry were detached to meet them and successfully fought them off. The battle of Penzance, according to the report by John Moyle, one of the Parliamentary committee for Cornwall, was short and bloody:

> After two hours dispute with the loss of only two of ours and four or five wounded, the enemies were totally scattered and about 60 or 70 slain, some drowned, 60 taken [prisoner], the rest, amongst which the chiefest, fled partly by the advantage of the hedges.

The men of St Keverne met a similar fate: 'the horse fell on them, slew seven or eight, took very few, but all desisted and the business is now quietened.' However, even Moyle admitted, 'if they had not been so seasonably scattered, we fear our country had been by this time universally inflamed.' However, his claim that the 'business is now quietened' was, to say the least, premature. A Capt. Pike escaped from the slaughter at Penzance by sea and made for Mullion. That village rose and joined with other supporters from around The Lizard to group together for a march on Helston. The Parliamentary troops, fresh from their efforts in Penzance, met them at Mawgan-in-Meneage and a battle ensued on a nearby earthwork called The Gear. Once again the fighting forces overcame the local rebels with little difficulty and put them to rout. Some rebels hid in the woods around Trelowarren, some hid in quarries and caves, and some avoiding hot pursuit even jumped into the Helford.

It was the last engagement. Apart from the Isles of Scilly, the whole county bowed down and accepted Parliamentary rule with the best grace they could muster, settling resentfully down under Cromwell to try to restore and make the best of their ruined and divided communities.

Penzance, however, remained in the eye of potential insurrection. The Isles of Scilly had been taken by Royalist forces under Hopton together with yet another Grenville, Sir John, Richard Grenville's son. They were joined by Maj. Grosse, who fled there after his defeat in the streets of Penzance, and Scilly became a base for Royalist privateers, adding another hazard to merchantmen around the western approaches. Penzance was the nearest significant port, and many spies would have been posted there to observe the sea traffic and keep watch on the temper of its inhabitants. Like all Royalist strongholds, it suffered profound disturbance and grief as the trial of Charles I proceeded, and disbelieving horror at his execution on 30 January 1649. However, like all Royalists, they held in their hearts what they dared not express openly, that across the Channel King Charles II was now their monarch. The King was dead: long live the King!

19

Recovery

The years of the Commonwealth were full of tension and unease. The Parliamentarians set about seizing the private estates of their opponents and distributing them among their own, as well as dismantling the Duchy of Cornwall and disposing of its lands. The Bassets were not deprived of St Michael's Mount but were forced to sell it ten years later, after suffering swingeing fines for their support of the King, to a local Parliamentary supporter, Sir John St Aubyn of Clowance. All over Cornwall other great families had to make careful calculations. They wished to accept the shower of rewards they were offered, but many of them opted to accept the properties as tenants rather than freeholders. The shadow of the King, now based in Jersey, made them cautious to rely on gifts that could as easily be snatched away should he return.

Conspiracies continued to haunt the Parliamentary peace, and in May 1650 Hopton wrote from the Isles of Scilly to 'all the King's loving subjects in Cornwall, Devon, Somerset, Wilts, Bristol, Bath and Wells', in a message which was music to many disaffected ears:

Countrymen, I hope you retain still the hearts and courage of true-born English that had rather bow to the Head than worship the Heel ... If there yet remains any spark of loyalty, any sense of duty to God, obedience to your King, affection to your country, love to your friends, pity to your wives, children or houses or to your own souls, shake off this servile yoke of base tyranny and see what a happy exchange it will be when instead of the sword, oppression, and violence of every rebel or rakeshame, you are governed by a hopeful, just and prudent prince.

In the meantime, his ships, sometimes up to twenty at a time, continued to harass merchant shipping and Parliamentary men-of-war. In April 1651,

Cromwell's patience was exhausted and he sent the extraordinary total of 2,500 soldiers supported by an English and Dutch fleet to capture the islands. After a well-defended siege, the Royalists finally accepted terms of surrender. Grenville joined Charles in France while Hopton, exhausted by his long campaigns and many wounds, retired to Bruges where he died the following year.

The last Royalist refuge was extinguished but Parliament made itself no friends by its heavy punishment of 'rebel' lands. Cornwall not only suffered the sequestration and redistribution of family lands but was also afflicted, as ever, with punitive taxation. It failed to rise in support of an abortive rebellion in 1655 due to the vigilance of spies and guards, and was spared the mass executions that followed, but it remained sullen and riven by internal conflict right up to the time when fate took a hand in the Commonwealth's prospects.

In September 1658 Cromwell died, naming his son Richard as his successor. Virtually no one favoured this course and eighteen months of chaos and intrigue followed. Eventually, a Free Parliament was elected in April 1660 and agreed that for want of a better alternative, England's government would be best served by the return of the King.

Charles II landed at Dover in May and was received in triumph and to the considerable relief of those moderate factions who looked for a period of stability above all else. Prominent Cornish Loyalists were jubilant. Parliamentary supporters faced the expected reclaiming of the lands they had been granted but, apart from vengeance on the body of Cromwell and the zealous pursuit and execution of the regicides, the Restoration was not marked by mass arrests, punishments or executions. Loyal Cornish families received the full gratitude of the King, especially the faithful Arundells, Godolphins, Killigrews, and Trelawnys who had survived such dangerous times. Moderate Parliamentarians, many of whom had eventually voted for the King's return, were treated moderately, including Sir John St Aubyn who was permitted to retain St Michael's Mount, where his family remains until today.

Cornwall's days as a separate armed force were over. Sick of its losses and the vicious poverty war left in its wake, it was never again to rise as an independent body. Instead, it left national politics to others and concentrated on trying to restore its own fortunes.

The first objective was to revive the tin trade. This had suffered terribly from the pressing and slaughter of so many experienced men, and the royal pre-emption that fixed the price of tin against the purchase of arms for the Royalist cause. The Commonwealth had unfrozen the tin market to considerable effect, the price of raw tin rising from 65s a hundredweight in 1650 to 125s in 1660. Best of all for the tinners of the far west was one of King Charles II's personal expressions of gratitude to his loyal supporters in Penzance, written on 18 August 1663:

> Whereas wee have byn informed that the greatest part of the tynne now and for some years past gained within our said Stannery of Penwith and Kerrier, and hath byn soe gained in places within the said Stannery very farr distant and remote from Helston, and by reason of ... the straitness and deepness of the wayes by which the same must bee conveyed to Helston, it will be of great inconvenience and noe lesse charge to most of our Stannators and tynners if they shall bee compelled to carry all their tynn by them gained to Helston ... and more especially in the winter season, and that it would bee a very great ease and encouragement to all our said tynners ... if they might have a coynage hall provided and appointed for them in some other place within our said Stannery nearer to the tynnworkes.
>
> Wee takinge these premisses into our princely consideration ... do nominate and appointe our Towne of Pensance ... to bee from henceforth forever one of the Coynage Towns of us for coyning and weighing of tynn gayned and to be gayned within the said Stannery.

It was the answer to prayers and representations repeated for more than 100 years. With a single flourish of his pen, the King transformed the prospects of the western tin fields. There was more, as the King empowered the mayor and corporation to enact what they longed to achieve:

> Wee graunt free liberty, full power, licence and authority unto William Godolphin of Trewarveneth, esquire, Martin Maddern, Thomas Grosse, Nicholas Sherme, John Keygwin of Pensnace, gentleman, John Tremenheer, gentleman, Walter Finney, Thomas Benver, Richard Veale, Edmund Davy of Lusvan, gent, John Lanyon of Sancrett, John Usticke, John Burlace, Charles Usticke, and Richard Edwards of St Just in the Hundred of Penwith, gent, ... to make and erecte a Coynage Hall in such convenient place as they shall thinke fit att our said Towne of Pensance aforesaid...

The corporation lost no time in identifying a site on 'wastrel of the street below the Market House', which still belonged to Richard Daniell as part of the manor of Alverton. The cost exceeded the town's resources and the shortfall was made up by advances from mine owners and the corporation's first ever capital loan, of £200. The coinage hall was erected on its site in the marketplace, where it remained until replaced by one nearer the quay in 1816.

The response from the other four stannery towns was not in the spirit of the King's generosity, and they made themselves as uncooperative and obstructive as possible to their new fellows, requiring Penzance to defend its new status in law. The good effect of the local stannery was not immediately felt in the Penwith mines, but it encouraged fresh capital to look again at the area. The increased profitability and savings gained by avoiding the expensive haul of every ounce to Helston and back was a powerful incentive. The return of the coinage system following the Restoration had dampened down the free market that had developed with the Commonwealth's laissez-faire attitude, and put a stop to the soaring increases in price, but local landed families quietly increased their holdings where they could. The Godolphins, Pendarveses, St Aubyns, Boscawens, Tonkins, Borlases and others looked forward to better times.

Penzance absorbed the extra business, the twice-yearly bustle and trade, the year-round visits and meetings and negotiations now that the tin industry was firmly based there. The coinage joined the markets and fairs as part of the annual calendar. Freed of the tension and suspicion of the Civil War, the town's entrepreneurial ability to face down adversity and regenerate itself came to the fore.

As for the tinners themselves, their lives continued to appear to outside observers as barely worth living. A commentator named Westcote, wrote in 1630 that,

It seems to me that no labourer whatsoever undergoes greater hazard of peril and danger, nor in hard coarse fare and diet doth equal him, bread the brownest, cheese the hardest, drink the thinnest, yea commonly the dew of heaven...

The unnamed author of a pamphlet entitled 'The Tinners' Grievances' was one of many who described the poverty of their diet. He recorded how

tinners would even search the fields for sheep or cattle that had died of
accident or disease:

> I am persuaded that a great many families do not make use of any other
> flesh at their own tables twice in the year, their ordinary food being
> potatoes and barley-bread as coarse as horse-bread, with gruel thickened
> oftener with barley-meal than oat-meal. In summer they have the same
> sort of bread with milk only. I have further observed in twenty or thirty
> years past, by reason of the cold and hunger their youth suffer, having
> not rags enough to cover them, men are so reduced from well-grown
> persons to be now comparatively mere pygmies in stature and strength,
> lamentable to behold.

Apart from the sheer tenacity required to burrow through solid rock, the
most constant output of labour was that required to drain the workings.
Most Cornish mines tunnel through underground watercourses and flood
easily unless regularly pumped out. In 1695, the admirable traveller Celia
Fiennes decided to adventure all the way to Land's End on horseback and
her eye for detail illuminated current mining practices as well as many
other aspects of local life. Her first experience of tin mines was near St
Austell, where,

> There were at least 20 mines in sight which employ a great many people
> at work almost night and day, but constantly all and every day including
> the Lord's Day, which they are forced to prevent their mines being
> overflowed with water. More than a thousand men are taken up about
> them, either down in the mines digging and carrying the ore to the little
> bucket which conveys it up, or else others are draining the water and
> looking to the engines that are draining it. Those above are attending to
> the drawing up the ore in a sort of windlass, as it were a well. Two men
> keep turning, bringing up one and letting down another. They are much
> like the leather buckets they use in London to put out fire...

She came upon copper mines near Redruth, noting that the ore was not
smelted in Cornwall but taken to Bristol by sea. The ports on the north
coast, St Ives, Hayle, Portreath, had come into their own, partly due to
the age-old danger of the Land's End passage but also because of the

activities of pirates and privateers. The sea was still a lawless wilderness. Nearing Penzance she found the people fascinated by her presence but not necessarily helpful. Their attitude to visitors will be familiar even today:

> The people here are very ill guides and know very little from home, only to some market town they frequent, but will be very solicitous to know where you go, and how far, and from whence you came and where is your abode...

Celia Fiennes' first impression of Penzance is charming:

> Pensands lies just as a shore on the main South Ocean, and being on the side of a hill, with a high hill all around the side to the landward, it looks so snug and warm, and truly it needs shelter having the sea on the other side.

She notes the shortage of coal and wood, all the cooking being done on furze fires, but on enquiry she is told that, 'it must all be brought round the Land's End, and since the war they could not have it'. She also notes St Mary's chapel and a 'good meeting place', and draws an accurate picture of the town's geography:

> There is a good quay and a good harbour for the ships to ride, by means of a point of land which runs into the sea in a neck or compass which shelters it from the main, and answers The Lizard Point, which you see very plain...

Like many travellers she is not willing to stop until she reaches Land's End, stepping out on the headland as far as she dares and making out the Isles of Scilly on the horizon. Cornish people will recognise an early reference to their native sense of humour, even if Fiennes did not:

> I saw the island of Sily which is seven leagues off the Land's End. They tell me that in a clear day those in the island can discern the people in the main as they go up the hill to church, and they can describe their clothes...

As Celia trotted off back to more civilised parts she left large areas of Cornwall buzzing with mines, still in a primitive state of technology. What innovations there were brought their own legacy of extra hazards. Six years before Celia Fiennes' account, the parish register at Breage records the first casualty from 'Shooting the rocks' – explosives. Gunpowder had been introduced from Germany and was presumably viewed, like all innovations in a traditional industry, with great suspicion at first. However, the sight of rocks broken in a moment that would otherwise have taken days of weary drilling must soon have changed the miners' minds. The method was simple – to drill a hole into which they would previously have forced their wedges and metal 'feathers', stuff it with gunpowder, lay a primitive fuse, back away and hope for the best. It is easy to imagine the toll of death and injury, the roof falls and water incursions produced by such a crude method, but there was no going back and blasting became a craft of its own. Despite the invention of safety fuses and increasing awareness of the specific effects of explosives, they became a constant danger to add to all the other hazards miners faced.

What was incomprehensible to most observers was the positive spirit of those who followed a miner's calling. Their most horrific working conditions were still to come, but even around 1700 their daily routine consisted of walking to the mine through all Cornish weathers; descending by rickety ladders to their level; dragging their tools to the face through tunnels sometimes so narrow that their sides were as polished as glass; examining their 'pitch' by the dim light of tallow candles stuck into their hats; hammering, drilling and shovelling for hours in the heat of the mine, beset by the bad air, the smoke from explosives and their own candles; climbing back up and walking home to a damp cottage and a poor meal.

Several things sustained them: the care and camaraderie of their companions; the rich sense of humour and constant satire of their supposed betters; the constant gambler's compulsion of the possibility of wealth and treasure behind the next rock; and above all the pride in their status as tinners, independent and free men. Westcote wrote, 'Miserable men, may some say in regard to their labour and poverty, yet having a kind of content within, and these people, though the most inferior, are notwithstanding free-men of state and condition, no slaves.' Carew was even more cynical, not surprisingly since he was of the class that owned mines rather than worked in them, and yet he too remarked on the self-esteem that the freemasonry of such professions granted:

Between their numerous holidays, holiday eves, feasts, account days, one way or another they do not work half the month for their owners or employers. It is further observable that once a fellow has taken to work tin he shall hardly be persuaded to do anything else, though it were to keep his family from starving. In which respect the tinners are followed by the fishermen, of whom I have seen twenty or thirty together basking themselves in the sun when there has been no fish upon the coast, rather than they would go to earn a penny at husbandry work to buy bread for their wives and children...

The wives and children were often part of the profession themselves. Women and girls were not allowed to go below but were the mainstay of the equally arduous surface work, attending the stamps that broke the rock into smaller pieces and reducing these to gravel with hammers for hours, unprotected in all weathers, while the children carried out whatever menial tasks they were able to perform. Every penny counted.

By contrast, Penzance's middle class was flourishing. These were men of commerce rather than land, living within the town rather than in grand houses around the outskirts. Prominent among these was the Tremenheere family who had seized the opportunity of acquiring cheap building land after the destruction of the Spanish raid.

John Tremenheere, known in his family as John the first, was elected mayor at the age of twenty-seven. He had been a prominent Royalist and taken part in the Penzance rising in 1648, but had kept out of serious trouble. In 1662, he helped the corporation to entertain Catherine of Braganza, Charles II's queen, as she made landfall in Penzance and was given the town's hospitality (to the recorded expense of £7 2s 11d). Anticipating Penzance's stannery, he had added to his many business interests by setting up Penwith's only smelting works, just outside the borough boundary at Chyandour. This was a speculation only available to the wealthy due to the high price of coal and the difficulty and danger in importing it, but it was most successful and became one of the most important smelting houses in Cornwall.

Tremenheere's will following his death in 1686, gives an idea of the spread of interests a wealthy commercial family might own. As well as his own two dwelling houses he left:

Eight houses in New Street
Property in St Just, Trewellard, Lelant, Paul, Sancreed, Tregadgwith, St

Buryan and Mousehole

The lease of the Chyandour blowing house and a house

Shares in tin works

Ships and boats, with seine nets and tackle

Two milk cows and his second-best horse to his wife (the Lord of Alverton Manor still had the right to the best horse), plus all his furniture and effects

£10 to the poor of Penzance and £2 to the poor of Madron.

His main dwelling house was in the centre of town, just above the old alley then known as Beare's Passage, now Harvey's Ope, facing down Market Jew Street. However, he had a retreat that his wife preferred further down Chapel Street away from the bustle and business of the market, which was a 'new brick house in the French fashion' with a courtyard and garden going down to a little cliff to the west side of the Battery Rocks. This was next to St Mary's chapel. In 1680, he donated money and endowed 'land adjoining the highway at Leskinnick' on the Eastern Cliff, then worth £5 per annum, to support its running costs.

The chapel had never been formally consecrated, only licensed from time to time by bishops of Exeter. In 1672, the corporation undertook to rebuild it completely. The date was inscribed in a granite block over the south porch of the chapel, and can now be seen above the little door facing what is still known as Under Chapel Yard on the seaward side of the current church. The new chapel was a substantial building, low in profile, hugging the crest of the hill, but with a tall and delicate spire which must have been as iconic for approaching sailors as for the townspeople. It occupied a similar space as the current church, and stood until 1832. It was still subordinated to Madron, officially designated as 'A Chapel of Ease subject to the Parish Church of Maddern as Mother Church'. All burial and other fees would still be paid to the vicar of Madron, the inhabitants of Penzance would still be liable for the repair and maintenance of Madron church, and the faithful were required to take the sacrament (Holy Communion) there at least once a year at Easter or Pentecost.

The corporation undertook to pay the curate of the chapel a salary in addition to John Tremenheere's endowment. The new building was consecrated in 1680 by Bishop Lamplugh, and though it was accepted that it was not their parish church, the townspeople began to attend its new and comfortable interior on a regular basis, the pews nominated for prominent families and the corporation, with the gentlemen seated around the sides and the ladies in the centre.

The nominations of the corporation in the chapel registers of 1693 give an interesting insight into their occupations. They were Thomas Eastlake (mayor); George Richards (justice); seven other aldermen, including three gentlemen, two merchants, a fellmonger (dealer in hides and skins), and a mercer (dealer in textiles); eleven assistants, including two merchants, another fellmonger, a yeoman, a cooper, a shoemaker, a haberdasher, a butcher, a shipwright, a shopkeeper and a blacksmith; James Praed (recorder); Frances Paynter of Boskenna (town clerk); the vicar of Madron and Penzance, Revd Reginald Trenhayle; Revd Thomas Billot (the curate of Penzance chapel); four constables; two chapel wardens; two overseers of the poor; and the two official sergeants at Mace.

The History of the Town and Borough of Penzance by P. A. S. Pool includes a long account of a mayoral dispute that began when an attorney, John Carveth, married the widow of John Tremenheere's son, Henry. Henry Tremenheere had inherited his father's status in the town and was mayor himself in 1674 and 1682, but died on falling from his horse in Camborne in 1686. Once Carveth had married this extremely well connected widow, he quickly began to fall out with several members of her family. However, his divisive and litigious style did not end there. He was elected mayor in 1703 and re-elected the following year. By then he had amassed many bitter enemies, led by prominent local landowner alderman William Tonkin, and rather than surrender the mayoralty to Tonkin when his second term expired he simply sidestepped the whole process.

On the day of the election, according to an affidavit,

In the Town Hall of Penzance (the defendant) Carveth and the major part of the Aldermen and Assistants had assembled to elect a Mayor. The Defendant declared he would have the Town Court first called before the election of a Mayor should be. After the calling of the said court it was proposed by the Town Clerk and some of the magistrates there present that they might elect a Mayor, to which the defendant replied that he would adjourn the court until four of the clock in the afternoon of the same day and then would come to the said hall and proceed with the election as usual. The Defendant absented himself from the said hall for the remaining part of that day without any election, yet he did afterwards act as Mayor from the said Friday.

William Tonkin also claimed the mayoralty from that day, leaving two opposed factions supporting two different mayors, both of whom claimed the considerable powers of that office in terms of justice, finance and administration. When after a year no solution had been found, each one proposed his own successor, Carveth naming John Grosse and Tonkin nominating Daniel Hawkey. Considerable legal fees were incurred and both 'mayors' tried to use the town revenues to meet them, adding to the confusion. Even a writ issued by Queen Anne demanding that a proper election be held failed to solve the dispute, and it was not until 1708 that William Tonkin assumed his second term free of opposition.

In the meantime, Carveth had also fallen out with the vicar of Madron. When the curate of St Mary's chapel left for another post, Carveth, without justification in law or precedent, assumed the power of appointing his successor. He accused Madron's vicar, Revd Thomas Rowe, of refusing to take services there, and further, 'although the yearly income he has out of the town amounts to generally sixty pounds or upwards ... he does nothing for it.'

Revd Rowe applied in hurt terms to the Bishop of Exeter:

How Mr Carveth's face should be so much altered towards me is difficult to guess and can arise from one cause, which is that he supposes that I have favoured the interests of those honest gentlemen in an honest cause about a late unhappy election of a Mayor, which has been the bottom of his hotspurred temper and occasioned his angry words.

The bishop in question was Sir Jonathan Trelawny (the same Bishop Trelawny, in whose cause 20,000 Cornishmen were reputed to have asked James II the reason why), and he was not prepared to take any nonsense. He wrote in lofty terms,

I had not heard that the Mayor of Penzance was Vicar General ... till he can produce such a power over me I shall approve and establish Mr Rowe's curate as soon as I know his name unless I have any objection to his manners or his learning, as I believe I shan't...

The matter descended into farce. Revd Rowe explained to the diocesan registrar,

> Some time after morning service (Carveth) sent his apprentice, one Francis Simons, to demand the key from Mary Cock who had locked the door and took it out. Mary Cock refusing to deliver it Francis Simons wrestled it out of her hands by force, so that when I came to chapel in the afternoon I found the doors shut against me and could not perform the duty of that part of the day. Inquiring of Mary Cock she said she demanded the key of Mr John Carveth but he would not nor did not deliver it.

Carveth had gone too far, and facing imminent prosecution by the bishop he gave way and largely disappears from the scene, one of Penzance's more colourful and eccentric figures.

A further court case involved the ancient grudges surrounding Tolcarne Mill. The ownership of this monopoly had passed from William Godolphin of Trewarveneth to his nephew, William Nicholls of Trereife, thence to Nicholls' son, John. Unlike his predecessors, John was not prepared to wink at the obvious abuses of his ancient right to be the sole grinder of corn in the manor of Alverton. When the Penzance Corporation failed to enforce these he sued the whole corporation in 1711, sixty-eight individual defendants headed by the finally installed mayor, Daniel Hawkey. Despite the enterprise of other rival grinders and bakers, judgement was entered for Nicholls to the considerable profit of himself and his successors, the Le Grice family of Trereife. The mill wheel has gone but the building survives near Newlyn Bridge, with the grooves cut by the wheel's edge still visible, a sentinel to a century of dispute.

One notable piece of business that concerned the value attached to the right of deciding the incumbent and administering the income of a parish church, the advowson. In 1731, the corporation, under James Tremenheere, obtained the advowson of Madron church from Robert Coster for £481 10s. The wisdom of this was fully justified fourteen years later when it was sold to John Borlase for £800.

The manor of Alverton itself was sold by Richard Daniell (whose brother George bequeathed an endowment for the parish school near Madron church still known as the Daniel School). It passed to the Keigwin family, then to Uriah, the son of the disputed mayor, William Tonkin. It had come a long way from the mysterious Alward, through many trials and troubles to deliver the established and successful town of Penzance which retains his name in so many locations.

20

Sinners

In 1724, the author and traveller Daniel Defoe made his recorded tour of the West Country, in particular its ports. Unlike most travellers, he failed to be seduced by the charms of St Michael's Mount, dismissing Marazion for having 'no harbour or safe road for shipping' and the Mount itself as no more than 'a high hill standing in the water'. The Mount was indeed in a poor state, the lowest in its history. Its garrison had gone and its importance as a stronghold and prison had disappeared. The St Aubyns still lived at Clowance and the castle was not fit for habitation. As for the village on the Mount it was recorded by William Borlase in 1702 that only one inhabitant remained, a widow by the name of Orchard. By Defoe's time a new attempt had been made to revive the village, but the Mount was certainly no longer the jewel of the bay. However, Defoe approves of Mount's Bay itself as 'a very good road for shipping which makes the town of Penzance be a place of good resort'.

His account reads less as a travelogue and more as a kind of strategic survey, possibly in accordance with his lesser-known career as a government agent and spy. His fascination with the sea led him to write a vivid account of the Great Storm on the night of 26/27 November 1703 that swept over Cornwall and severely damaged Bristol and London, uprooting thousands of trees and killing around 8,000 people on land and sea. He recalled an incident during the storm when a ship laden with tin was blown out to sea from Helford and arrived at the Isle of Wight seven terrifying hours later, manned by just one man and two boys.

Of Penzance itself he writes,

Penzance is the farthest town of any note west, being 254 miles from London and within about ten miles from the promontory called the Land's End. This town of Penzance is a place of good business, well built and populous, has a good trade and a great many ships belonging to it, notwithstanding it is so remote. Here are also a great many good families of gentlemen, though in this utmost angle of the nation. And, which is yet more strange, the veins of lead, tin and copper ore are to be seen even to the utmost extent of land at low-water mark and even in the very sea. So rich, so valuable a treasure is contained in these parts of Great Britain though they are supposed to be so poor because so very remote from London.

Copper was becoming a significant factor in Cornish mines. There had always been some trade in it though the bulk had come from Ireland, but as tin mines delved deeper they sometimes found rich lodes of copper below the tin. There was an attempt to extend the stannery laws to include copper. It would have been a mixed blessing since it would have been subjected to the same taxation, but it was too expensive to smelt and prepare it in Cornwall. Instead, it was taken out of the county in its raw state. Once again the price of coal was a deciding factor.

Another was the price of corn, which was in short supply after many bad winters but also by the manipulation of the market by the corn factors (merchants). The shortage hit everyone equally but the tinners lived closest to the margins of life and in 1727, shortly after Defoe's visit, they rioted in many parts of Cornwall. Sir John St Aubyn responded in a reasonable fashion. He built a new quay at the Mount to further its trade and advanced miners in his area a 'sufficient sum of money to prevent them from starving and the necessity of plundering their neighbours'.

The miners received harsher treatment a couple of years later when they again rioted in several places, including Penzance, and broke open storehouses to carry off the corn. This time magistrates petitioned the Secretary of State to demand that,

As tinners and others have ravaged up and down the country in a very insolent manner and great numbers, presuming so far as to break open and enter dwelling-houses and outhouses out of which they have forcibly carried corn and other things...

They suggested that a royal proclamation be issued naming certain ringleaders, offering a reward for apprehending them and a pardon for those already held providing they impeached their fellows. This had the desired result and several miners were executed, one of them 'hanging in chains on St Austell downs'. Despite this dreadful warning, further riots ensued in Penryn and St Agnes. As a contemporary saying had it, 'The belly hath no ears'.

Tinners in revolt would have been a frightening prospect. They were desperate beyond all reason, and by the hardship of their labours they were as tough and persistent as any men alive. They were skilled enough to break and dismantle any gates or walls put up to guard against them. They were also often drunk, as violent in their pleasures as in their work, and the increasing imports of raw liquor from the continent gave them some release from the burdens of the world.

The age of smuggling is still often seen in romantic terms, and the Cornish took an undeniable pleasure in outwitting the revenue men to keep the illicit trade alive. But in reality smuggling of liquor to miners was no more romantic than the present-day smuggling of hard drugs to helpless addicts. Vast fortunes were made by a few, but the quality of the liquor could be lethal. Like the gin trade in London famously advertised as 'Penny drunk, tuppence blind', there might be minerals in the raw spirits that would in fact cause blindness or other disabilities. Drunkenness also led to injuries due to accidents and fierce and bloody fighting.

Tinners were also notoriously skilled in the art of wrecking. The legend of deliberate wrecking probably arose from the not uncommon sight of a ship in distress struggling along a coastline in search of a haven. For the local people it was essential to be first at the wreck, partly to salvage it before it broke up but also because the news of it would spread like wildfire and huge crowds would descend on it to pick it clean. Therefore, at night a procession of people, men women and children carrying lanterns might follow a stricken vessel along the cliff-paths as it drove parallel to the shore, to be certain of identifying its final resting place and taking away what they could of 'God's grace' before everyone else arrived. Any stranger seeing this macabre sight might imagine that the lights were a deliberate lure, but in such circumstances the unfortunate vessel was usually beyond control and running for its life.

Once a vessel had struck however wrecking began in earnest. The law declared that a wreck was the property of the landowner on whose shore the ship had foundered, so for the wreckers time was of the essence before the landowners' men arrived to secure it. They were well drilled and fearless on the scene, forming human chains and venturing out into the surf to collect whatever was coming ashore. Their attitude to the surviving crew was ambivalent. The law stated that a ship did not officially become a wreck unless no person (or animal) survived, and no doubt some hellish deeds were inflicted on exhausted crewmen as they struggled ashore. On the other hand, most Penwith residents had friends or family members at sea, some unwillingly pressed long ago, and this inspired them to acts of great heroism, rescuing seamen in the most desperate conditions – presumably on the understanding that they would deny they had been crewmen if later questioned.

Having disposed of the crew by either means and taken ashore all the floating cargo, one party would obtain horses and carts to carry it away to a local smugglers' hide while the others waited for the tide to fall so they could set about the wreck itself. Armed with suitable tools, they unloaded what cargo was left and then cut away all useful timber, blocks, pulleys, ropes and anything else of value. These were carted away in turn. If they had done their job properly nothing would remain for the landowner by morning but the main spars and a great deal of rubbish.

The Land's End peninsula had always been a terror to sailors. The turbulent conditions where two tides meet, the sprinkling of unmarked rocks, the lack of lights ashore to give any warning in a storm until the ship was already in danger and the fogs and mists had persuaded early traders to choose an overland passage to avoid it. In bad weather Mount's Bay was a haven but it was also known as a 'maritime trap'. If ships took shelter there and the wind direction changed there was no chance of escape via Land's End or the Lizard, and their only chance was to anchor fast and pray. Other vessels blundered into the bay in fog, and some made the error at night of mistaking the Land's End peninsula for the Lizard and turning into the bay, believing they were entering Falmouth Roads. If they were lucky they might drive on to a sandy beach, but otherwise a granite reef would soon tear the ship to pieces. The shores of Mount's Bay witnessed the destruction of thousands of ships, and disposing of the wrecks was in the local inhabitants' blood (and it must be said that even in these civilised times a large crowd materialises from seemingly nowhere whenever a wreck occurs).

Wrecks were therefore an intrinsic part of the local economy. Killigrew's abortive Lizard lighthouse had shown that any serious attempt to warn ships of potential danger was considered an affront to the local population.

As parson Troutbeck, vicar of St Mary's in Scilly had famously preached, 'We pray Lord, not that wrecks should happen, but if they do Thou wilt guide them to the Isles of Scilly for the benefit of Thy poor inhabitants there.'

Landowners were naturally infuriated to find these beneficial acts of God anticipated by others. George Borlase complained in 1753,

> The people who make it their business to attend these wrecks are generally tynners, and as soon as they observe a ship on the coast they first arm themselves with sharp axes and hatchets and leave their tynn works to follow these ships.

He cites the example of a wreck near Helston of a large merchantman laden with claret: 'In twenty-four hours the tynners had cleared all.' As a mine-owner Borlase had other reasons to complain:

> Sometimes the ship is not wrecked, but whether 'tis or not the mines suffer greatly, not only by the loss of their labour, which may be about £100 per diem if they are two thousand in quest of the ship, but where the water is quick the mine is entirely drowned (in their absence).

It is not difficult to sympathise with the miners. A wreck was a welcome diversion from their usual toil and an opportunity to gain some valuables, or at least to be let loose on a ship laden with claret. Also, as Halliday points out in his *History of Cornwall*, if the loss of a day's work by 2,000 miners cost the owners only £100, the tinners stood to lose just a shilling a day each, and it would be a poor wreck that would not reward them with something better than a shilling. No doubt when they had recovered from their nocturnal efforts they quickly set to work to drain their workplace and carried on as usual.

However anti-social the effects of smuggled spirits, the insatiable demand and the huge sums of money to be made pervaded society at all levels around the Cornish coast. It became a hidden industry in which whole communities might be implicated. There was little sympathy for the task of the revenue officers. Though the local gentry might offer them apparent support, the officers could never be sure that they themselves were not part of some illicit organisation. They were sometimes paid to keep the revenue men amused, distracted, or to give them false information. Lower down the social scale they would find communities united in a conspiracy of lies and silence.

All kinds of trades were involved: the fishing boats with their coastal expertise; the farmers with their horses and carts; barns, secret caves, holes in the ground and countless other places of concealment; and the tinners with their labouring men and ready money. The revenue men rarely took on the tinners on their own ground. Even if they succeeded in catching smugglers red-handed they could see their success turned upside down by a sympathetic Cornish jury, immune to evidence or reason.

Smuggling goods into Penzance where the revenue men were often quartered was unwise and usually unnecessary (though excavations in the lower part of Chapel Street have turned up more than one hidden tunnel, including one from the Abbey Basin to the rear of the Turk's Head Inn). The coast of Mount's Bay offered plenty of opportunities for night-time landings by small boats while the larger supply vessel stood off in the darkness. Every cove around Penzance was suspect, and that could include Porthgwarra, Porthcurno, Penberth, St Loy, Lamorna, Mousehole, Newlyn, and to the east Marazion, Boat Cove, Perranuthnoe, the much-favoured Prussia and Pixie's Coves, Praa Sands, Rinsey, Porthleven and Loe Bar. The north coast had the passage of Land's End and fewer convenient coves which discouraged the trade, but carried out its share on a smaller scale.

Detachments of armed soldiers acted as something of a deterrent but their placement was often a mere token. They would be billeted in the town for a short period following complaints to make a show of force and then withdrawn again.

The smugglers grew bolder. Officers complained to their superiors that 'The smuggling trade is carried out to such a height that they carry goods at noon in defiance of the officers.' Another complaint named the mayor of Penzance himself, John Pender, who despite his office and status as a magistrate was already bound over for a large sum in 1773 not to involve himself again in smuggling. In 1778 Edward Giddy, curate and JP of St Erth, wrote to a friendly peer,

Smuggling since the soldiers have been drawn off has been carried on almost without control. Irish wherries carrying 14, 16 or more guns and well-manned frequently land many large quantities of goods in defiance of the officers of Customs and Excise, and their crews armed with swords and pistols escort the smugglers a considerable distance from the sea.

The smugglers themselves, armed with offensive weapons and bidding defiance to all the opposition the officers can make, carry their goods from one part of the country to another almost every night.

About a fortnight since a large wherry landed 1,500 to 2,000 ankers (9½ gallons) of spirit, about twenty tons of tea and other kinds of smuggled goods on a sandy beach in Mount's Bay between the towns of Penzance and Marazion near a public road, which while the goods were discharging was filled with armed men in order to stop every traveller in whom they could not confide for a few hours until the goods were safely lodged in the country.

A few days after two officers got information that a very considerable quantity of these goods were concealed in the house and premises of a well-known smuggler, obtained from me a search warrant and were forcibly hindered from executing it by four men, one armed with a pistol and a large whip, the others with sticks or bludgeons, and were told that if they persisted they would have their brains blown out.

It would be mere pedantry to attempt to describe the shocking effects, the moral and political consequences of smuggling carried out to such a daring height, but I cannot help saying that perjury, drunkenness, idleness, poverty, contempt for the law, and a universal corruption of manners are in this neighbourhood too plainly seen to accompany it.

If this was not bad enough the Penzance officers were still smarting from a prior humiliation when an Irish wherry came into Penzance quay itself, stole a revenue boat that had just seized a quantity of contraband, relieved it of its stolen goods and set it adrift. On another occasion the famous John Carter, the 'King of Prussia', had some of his goods seized and locked away in the customs' warehouse in Penzance. Carter never broke a promise to his customers, so when the customs' men arrived the following morning they found their store broken into. Carter's confiscated goods had been carefully removed and all the other contraband left untouched.

There seemed no way of stopping a trade that so appealed to Cornish hearts. The officers' task, short of turning Cornwall into an armed camp, was impossible. The eventual solution was to come from the least likely source, and was already in process by Edward Giddy's time. One extraordinary man, John Wesley, did what troops of soldiers could not, and began to stem the demand at its source.

21

'... Even in this Place'

Wesley and his brother, Charles, were born near Lincoln in the early eighteenth century, into a large religious family. John went to Charterhouse School and Oxford University and took holy orders as a conventional Anglican, but it was not until he returned from an unsuccessful mission to America that he found his true vocation. Attending a meeting of the evangelical Protestant Moravian church, he 'felt his heart strangely warmed'. After being inspired by his friend George Whitefield on the merits of outdoor preaching, he began his extraordinary mission. This took him on a continuous circuit of England, Scotland, Ireland, Wales, and Cornwall. He travelled around 5,000 miles every year on horseback, preaching on average three times a day.

Although he was an accredited member of it, the Anglican Church and its traditional congregations took exception to his fiery style of preaching. Established Christian communities distanced themselves from him and their reaction ranged from apathy to hostility to incitements of actual violence.

His phenomenal success cannot easily be explained. It was partly the quality of the man, his sincerity and courage, partly his unshakeable faith, and above all his ability to speak to all classes of people in ways they could understand. He had a talent to communicate and inspire that only those who heard him would have experienced.

Wesley visited Cornwall on no fewer than thirty-two occasions between 1743 and 1789. On his first tour he was greeted as a curiosity, except in St Ives where the people responded with immediate extremes of love and hate. Realising they had to take his mission seriously, his opponents were ready for his next appearance. A rumour was spread that he was a sympathiser with the Jacobite rebels in France and this gave licence for angry mobs all over Cornwall to threaten him personally.

One of his chief opponents was Dr Walter Borlase, vicar of Madron and local magistrate, and he may have been responsible for spreading these rumours.

Wesley preached at Morvah in 1744,

About eleven John Nance and I set out [from St Ives] for Morvah. Having both the wind and the rain full in our faces we were thoroughly wet before we came to Rosemergy where some of our brethren met us. I found there had been a shaking among them, occasioned by the confident assertions of some that they had seen Mr Wesley a week or two ago with the Pretender in France, and from others that he was in prison in London. The wind and rain beat hard upon us as we walked from Morvah to St Just, which also frighted many from coming. However some hundreds were there. It is remarkable that those of St Just were the chief of the whole country for hurling, fighting, drinking and all manner of wickedness; but many of the lions are become lambs, are continually praising God and calling their old companions in sin to come and magnify the Lord together.

He was soon regarded as a definite threat to the established churches of the area. Since preferment in the church had become largely a matter of a reward for birth and influence, much of the ground-level parish work was carried out by lowly paid curates, or neglected altogether. The parishes worked well enough as administrative institutions, but as beacons of faith and belief they had become ineffective and uninspiring.

Wesley's words were a breath of fresh air to the poor working classes. He alternated terrifying threats of purgatory and eternal hellfire with rosy promises of an afterlife in which the poorest and meekest would be exalted to his beautifully described visions of heaven, while the rich would be laid low. This was exactly what his listeners wanted to hear. Even those who were not persuaded by his oratory were impressed with the personal bravery of a man who often endured abuse and physical ill-treatment, yet still continued to visit in the hope of saving their souls. All over Cornwall it was the roughest, poorest and most oppressed who responded most quickly to the balm of his sermons, while more prosperous places rejected him. Working-class Newlyn and middle-class Penzance were prime examples:

I rode to Newlyn to rising ground near the seashore where there was smooth white sand to stand on. An immense multitude of people gathered together. Before I had ended my prayer some poor wretches of Penzance began cursing and swearing and thrusting people off the bank. I was thrown into the middle of them, when one of Newlyn, a bitter opposer until then, turned about and swore 'None shall meddle with this man, I will lose my life first'. Many others were of his mind so I finished my sermon without interruption.

As his journals showed, even Penzance eventually succumbed to his persistence:

17 September 1760 'I preached on the cliff near Penzance, where no-one now gives an uncivil word'.
6 September 1766 'I preached in a meadow adjoining Penzance. The whole congregation behaved well. The old bitterness is gone...'
5 September 1768 'I preached at Penzance. Surely God will have a people even in this place where we have so long seemed only to beat the air.'
21 August 1776 'I preached at Penzance in a gentleman's balcony which commanded the market-place to a huge congregation. Such an opportunity I never had at Penzance before.'
23 August 1780 'I went on to Penzance. It is now a pleasure to be here, the little flock being united together in love...'

As Edward Giddy's account of smuggling shows, there was no miraculous transformation from smuggling and drunkenness to piety and moderation in Wesley's time. Some smugglers were fervently religious too, as described in the imaginary encounter between a local youth and the legendary smuggler 'King Nick' (a disguised portrait of John Carter) in Crosbie Garstin's novel *The Owls' House*:

By the fire sat a tall old man dressed in unrelieved black from neck to toe. A wreath of snowy hair circled his bald pate like a halo...
    King Nick rose to his feet. 'Now let Jacob rejoice and Israel be glad ... so shall the poor tinner be comforted at a reasonable price and the Lord be praised with cymbals, yea with trumpets also and shawms. Gather in the young men and maidens that we may ask a blessing on our labours. I can feel the word of the Lord descending upon me!'

... Dawn saw the entire Kiddlywink family packed shoulder to shoulder singing lustily while before them on a chair stood a benevolent old gentleman in black, beating time with one of John Wesley's hymnals...

It was not until the next century that one of Penzance's biographers, Dr Paris, was able to write,

The Methodists in West Cornwall are very numerous, and the change they have effected in the morals of the miners is really incredible, the habits of sobriety and order which they have happily introduced have tended as much to the mining interests as to the quiet and comfort of the neighbourhood.

22

Steam

Mining requires considerable nerve from its backers. There was no question in the eighteenth century of insufficient demand for tin, copper and other minerals, but every mine seeking to supply it had to take an immense capital gamble. The easy lodes and streams had long been worked out and adventurers had the choice of taking over an existing mine and digging further, or taking a chance on sinking a completely new shaft. In either case the money had to be outlaid first, with no certainty of return.

Investors grouped together in partnership to pledge sufficient sums to get the work under way. They then met for regular monthly meetings where either demands for more development money had to be honoured or, preferably, profits would be distributed. These could sometimes be of legendary proportions – in 1757 one mine in Gwennap was reputed to have produced £5,700 worth of copper in its first fortnight of operation. Such overnight fortunes led investors with a gambler's spirit to pour money into prospecting and exploratory works. Some of these were local families but many more were appearing from the emerging cities, drawn by the lure of instant riches. They knew that a single fall of rock might reveal nothing at all, or a broad seam of minerals that would keep them wealthy for years. In the history of mining there is little sympathy for the investors, but mining is essentially a capitalist industry and the speculators were the engine room that made the whole enterprise possible, risking and sometimes losing everything. William Pryce wrote in his *Mineralogia Cornubiensis,*

If a mine when she is first discovered throws up a large profit to the adventurers and fails soon after that to their loss and detriment, they nevertheless pursue their object under the most unpromising circumstances with unremitting ardour, patience, industry and resolution scarcely parallel in any other unfortunate undertaking under the sun.

Every little stone of ore brings with it new hopes and fresh vigour. It fans the glimmering flame of adventure which seems to animate the natives of Cornwall and to deserve that success that they cannot always command.

However, in such a labour-intensive venture their consistent desire was to obtain the maximum amount of labour for the least possible cost.

They achieved this by making the workers compete with each other for the work. The labourers were divided into two main classes, those who did most of the heavy work ('tutworkers') and those more skilled in the extraction of the ore itself ('tributers').

Tutworkers formed teams known as 'pares' and would bid for specific jobs, driving a tunnel so many feet, removing so many tons of waste, etc., for a fixed price. Other pares would bid against them, and driven by the pressure of their hungry families would sometimes bid down to desperately low sums in order to secure the work. Once contracted they had to fulfil their contracts or no mine captain would ever look at them again.

Tributers shared in the gamble and worked for no wages at all. They received just a small proportion of the value of the minerals they extracted. The individual pitches on which they worked were put up for auction on a monthly basis, so they too had to bid against each other as well as sharing the risk that their labours might produce nothing. It was a cruel system that virtually ensured the poverty of the workers, but it chimed with the miners' ancient love of independence, their status as tinners, 'no slaves', and their pride in their profession.

Their main challenge was the vast amounts of water that gush through Cornwall's terrain and constantly threatened to flood the workings. By the eighteenth century some mines had dug down below sea-level, making their old hard-won adits redundant except as drains when water had been drawn up to their level. New adits were driven in others, sometimes with the happy result of finding an unexpected lode on the way. Water was drawn up in leather buckets or barrels on a belt powered either by men or horses, unless the mine was sufficiently advanced to own a waterwheel. Not all had vertical shafts and the wear and tear on the equipment was considerable.

Newcomen's 'Atmospheric (steam) Engine' was patented as early as 1712, but it was not efficient and needed large quantities of expensive coal to make very limited amounts of steam. Cornwall did not generally take to it and continued to use larger and larger waterwheels. In 1777, James Watt and Matthew Boulton's more efficient steam engine transformed the scene and cut the consumption of coal by a third. This was timely as the copper mines, which were producing around 28,000 tons of copper a year, were suddenly undone by the discovery of the Parys Mine in Anglesey. This was less a mine than a hill full of easily worked copper, which undercut and closed down many Cornish enterprises for a decade.

Penzance could only claim one tin mine within its borough limits, though its unique features were a famous example of the enterprise and imagination of mine adventurers. Thomas Curtis, a miner from Breage, was examining the foreshore to the west of Penzance when he found rock formations favourable to potential tin deposits. The problem was that the site was only accessible at low water and about 250 yards out from the beach.

Nevertheless, in the brief time available between tides he persuaded his co-workers to dig a shallow shaft around 15–20 feet deep. He was encouraged enough by this to take more ambitious steps and in 1778 he constructed a cofferdam to keep out the sea, a roughly circular wooden structure anchored to the levelled rock with metal rods, covered inside with pitch and outside with rough mortar. The Wherry Mine started operations in earnest, and thoroughly rewarded Curtis' diligence. At first the crude ore was carried into Penzance by boat, but as the mine grew busier and more successful he was able to finance a long wooden platform leading to the head-works. In such a position the mine was more prone to flooding than most, as the walls never ceased to leak and storms sometimes broke over the structure, but it prospered enough to justify a steam engine of its own, based on the shore.

A travel writer, W. G. Maton, visited the mine in 1794 and explored its seventeen fathoms by the same basic means the miners endured:

> The descent is by means of a rope tied around the thighs, and you are let down in a manner exactly the same as a bucket is into a well: a well indeed it is for the water is more than knee-deep in many parts of the mine.

He was impressed with the courage of the men, 'momentarily menaced with an inundation of the sea, which roars loudly enough to be distinctly heard in it.'

Fortunately, no one was below on a stormy night in 1798 when an American merchantman sheltering in Gwavas Lake was driven off its anchorage straight into the mine's protective barricade, destroying it completely and flooding the mine beyond repair. The ore of the Wherry Mine was known to be extremely rich and two serious attempts were made to re-establish it in the nineteenth century, one actually going to the length of creating a new company and restoring the head-works and platform. However, it gave up after four unproductive years. Exploratory works were carried out from a drilling rig as late as the 1970s, but the results were again – so far – not sufficiently encouraging to justify recommencement of operations. A metal plate still marks the entrance to the old workings and can be seen off Wherrytown at low water.

23

Local Difficulties

Apart from mining, Penzance's preoccupations were much as before, including the usual quarrels and disputes. One of these led to a stand-off almost as ridiculous as that of the celebrated Mr Carveth. Not for the first (or last) time, the dispute centred on the state of the quay and the need to extend and rebuild it. In 1765 the mayor was Dr Walter Borlase, who had committed the town's revenues to a new extension, but this was not popular with all the aldermen and as his term of office ended he was afraid that the post would fall to one of the scheme's powerful opponents. To ensure his plans could not be reversed, he managed to divert the town revenues by serpentine legal means to the control of nominated trustees, so that until the loans secured against them were honoured subsequent mayors could not touch them. When the new mayor, William John, was elected he arranged to let the harbour to George Ley and the markets and fairs to John Read. On the same day, acting on Borlase's instructions, the trustees of the loans let the harbour to Thomas Tonkin and the markets and fairs to William Rawles and William Richards.

Chaos ensued, with both sides claiming the essential rights and income, leading to ridiculously undignified behaviour among the gentry. According to Borlase's account, the new mayor appointed eight constables instead of the usual four:

> With these he has paraded every market day since, and by force prevented the Trustees' farmers [agents] from receiving the dues and profits of the markets and quay. The Mayor did himself in the open market seize Mr Rawles by the collar and drag him to the market house and there imprisoned him for more than an hour and refused to let him out though sufficient bail was tendered him, and this for no other offence than Rawles civilly asking a butcher that stood in the market for his stallage [fee].

Two of Penzance's oldest religious artefacts: the damaged statue from the old St Anthony's chapel, and the 1,000-year-old granite cross, which stood in various locations at the crossroads in the marketplace.

Elizabethan Mount's Bay pictured before the Spanish Raid – note the chapels on St Clement's Island next to Mousehole, and Chapel Rock, Marazion.

Early nineteenth-century view of Penzance from the east.

Rare early watercolour of Penzance from above Newlyn, dated 1813, with terraces beginning to emerge.

The extraordinary Egyptian House in Chapel Street.

The old St Mary's chapel from the Western Green, now the promenade.

In this atmospheric scene of the quiet early eighteenth-century harbour, the artist is sitting outside what is now the Dock Inn, looking towards the original stone lighthouse.

The Greenmarket 1829. Note the market cross to which pigs used to be tethered, and the women collecting water from the shoot at the bottom of Causewayhead on the right.

The old market house at about the same date. Humphry Davy's statue now stands close to where the wagon is parked.

These two photographs were taken around the time of the Newlyn Riots in 1896. Above are the Lowestoft boats (registration letters 'TT') enjoying port facilities in Penzance. The image below is a rare photograph of the Royal Berkshire soldiers showing off on Newlyn Pier to some unimpressed locals.

RIOTS.

The peaceful scene of the late Victorian promenade at low tide, showing the full length of the Battery Rocks.

Penzance harbour mouth dominated by the distant St Michael's Mount with RMV *Scillonian III* by the South Quay.

Army cadets, schoolboys and local people try to clear wreckage from what remains of the road following the Ash Wednesday storm in March 1962.

Market Jew Street on a quiet winter's day.

Penzance from Lescudjack Hill Fort.

Penzance viewed from Newlyn.

Market Jew Street on Mazey Day during the Golowan Festival.

High summer and the Jubilee Pool at its best.

The gala opening day of the Jubilee Pool in 1935. Note the partly demolished cottages in the right foreground.

Around the turn of the twentieth century, a schooner leaves Penzance Harbour assisted by two pilot boats, while a steam road-roller looks on.

Compare with the historic photograph of the Ross Bridge above – here with RMV *Scillonian III* by the quay.

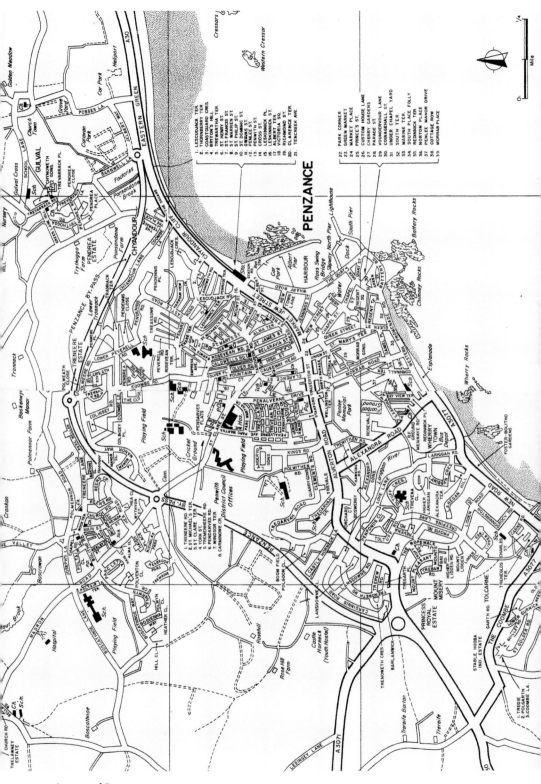

A map of Penzance.

One of Penzance's most famous sons, Humphry Davy was renowned for his scientific explorations and inventions, the most notable being the Davy Lamp.

Thomas John, the Mayor's brother and one of his new constables also one market day seized Mr Rawles by the collar, drew him up and down and used him very ill, and threatened to imprison him and everybody in the markets that will not pay (John) Read. The Mayor distrained and has taken off beef, greens and other things. From one butcher he took a piece of beef worth seven shillings for fourpence or sixpence stallage, and sold it. They have done the same as to the quay dues, taken them by force.

The Trustees put up notices signed by them in all the public places of the town directing the revenues to be paid to their farmers; the Mayor went round with his constables and pulled them down. Messrs Rawles and Richards had some toll-corn of last year in their toll-chest under their lock; one of the pretended constables broke open one of these chests in the Mayor's presence and by his direction and assistance took out the corn and threw it loose into Rawles' shop. In short the Mayor and his constables by force collect the tolls and do everything in this arbitrary way.

Borlase was censured for setting up the unprecedented trust in the first place and for his pettiness in 'refusing to administer the Oath of Office to the new Mayor, or to hand over the Regalia'.

This of course led to a long and complex lawsuit, which took a leisurely sixteen years to extinguish the rights of the trustees, cover its own extensive legal fees, and restore full rights to the corporation.

The unfortunate Rawles was right to object to his stay in the town's prison. When prison reformer James Neil came to Penzance in 1773 he reported that,

Penzance Borough Gaol (or as it generally and more properly called, 'The Black Hole') is a dark room with a double door at the end of the Corn Market in the Market House, a great part of which is not of sufficient height for the prisoner to stand upright in. Straw on the floor. The only light or ventilation it receives is from an aperture 12 foot by 5 ½ foot which opens to the staircase and, being a borrowed light, serves just to make darkness visible. The annoyance of the rats in this place is terrible, so that the wretched prisoner, ever on watch, may perhaps doze in feverish anxiety but never knows the balm of peaceful sleep.

As well as a prison and the town stocks other trappings of civilisation were appearing. The corporation bought a fire engine and then a second.

The first purpose-built reservoir was installed at Causewayhead, supplied by a leat all the way from Madron well, and ran from there to a 'shoot', a place for the public to collect their fresh water at the market cross.

Rumours of war often disturbed the century of peace. Tension rose and fell between England and France, and French privateers and warships joined the ever threatening African corsairs to harass local shipping. In 1739 the situation was so grave that the corporation petitioned the government for serious fortifications and weaponry to protect the town. The government agreed to supply the necessary guns if the corporation undertook to construct a suitable belvedere for them to stand on, a battery. The corporation agreed and erected a substantial battery at the water's edge to the west of the quay, taking full advantage of the rocks that now bear its name. This structure was thought to have been pulled down but a recent survey revealed its outer walls beneath where the war memorial and the Jubilee Pool now stand.

During the Jacobite rising of 1745, a local militia had been formed by George Borlase. A heartily enthusiastic description of them appeared in the area's first newspaper, the *Sherborne Mercury*:

> One hundred tradesmen of this town, animated by a noble zeal for their religion and liberties, have formed themselves into an Independent Company, made themselves masters of the military exercise, and chose some worthy gentlemen of the town for their officers. They are a company of stout men ... and are worthy descendants of Old Britains. The fine appearance which they make and the dexterity with which they perform their exercise have been justly admired by all ... they show great ardour and cheerfulness on every occasion that requires them.

They were disbanded again three years later and the great guns were either removed or put into storage. Penzance was to feel their loss in a near calamity in 1756 when, 'A French privateer of 250 men and 22 nine-pounders endeavoured for three days together to land two hundred men, but the wind being against them they could not get in.'

The privateer was later captured by Capt. John Lockhart of the frigate *Tartar*, and the French captain was interrogated. His purpose was to capture the undefended town, plunder it and if possible burn it down before leaving. It would have been equivalent to a second Spanish raid, prevented only by an unfavourable wind. There were at the time a large number of blocks of tin awaiting coinage lying in the streets, and the French privateer missed not only plunder and fame but an enormous fortune.

Fear of invasion was heightened when on an autumn night in 1760 guns suddenly rang out from the direction of Newlyn Green. The town turned out to discover an Algerian corsair, believing itself to be in mid-Atlantic, had driven into the beach at full speed. A makeshift militia formed up to defend the town against attack by the Turks, but the crew were disoriented by their sudden arrival and shipwreck, in which eight of them had been drowned. The militia disarmed them and took all 172 of them prisoner in the Barbican building:

> A fear seized the town and neighbourhood scarcely less formidable than that of massacre and plunder; namely of the Plague. The volunteers however kept guard and ward to prevent all intercourse.

Finding that the prisoners were not afflicted with plague, the townspeople's curiosity overcame their fear and they crowded to look at the exotic captives. African corsairs had been a constant terror, a story to frighten children, but few landsmen had seen their crews in the flesh. 'Their Asiatic dress, long beards and mustachios, turbans, the absence of all coverings for their feet and legs, the dark complexion and harsh features of the pirate band made them objects of terror and surprise.'

The prisoners were treated kindly, and the novelty of their presence caused a brief sensation in Penzance before a man-of-war picked them up and took them back to Algiers, probably in exchange for other prisoners.

The threat of French invasion increased as the century wore on, and as any other period of international tension the far west felt itself again on the front line. Pleas to the government for more defences led to reassuring replies but very little in terms of weaponry or manpower. In 1779, a combined French and Spanish fleet was seen cruising off the Cornish coast and the Penzance Corporation allocated an emergency sum of £100, 'In support of our defence against the common enemy at this time of common danger when we are actually threatened with invasion.'

However, it was the apparently distant events of 14 July 1789 that set the course of the next twenty-five years. A revolutionary Parisian mob stormed the Bastille, the French monarchy and government fell, and France became a revolutionary republic.

24

Isolation

The immediate reaction to this in Britain was mixed. The British ruling classes were naturally apprehensive that the revolutionary spirit would spread across the Channel and rouse their own peasant classes. However, many enlightened thinkers and intellectuals were inspired by the high ideals of the early revolution. They formed societies with noble titles and distributed pamphlets urging a more equitable social structure, better treatment of the working classes, democracy, and other inflammatory ideas.

Such notions did not wash among the gentry of the Penzance Corporation. The ten times Mayor of Penzance, Thomas Giddy, caused the corporation to send a loyal address to the King condemning,

> ... divers wicked and seditious writings which have been printed and industriously dispersed throughout several parts of this Kingdom, tending to raise discontent in the minds of your Majesty's faithful subjects...

Having received confirmation that the address had been 'graciously received', Giddy went a step further in his determination to claim the hearts and minds of his peers. He set up his own pro-government society, with the typically prolix name of 'The Association for the Preservation of Liberty and Property against Republicans and Levellers'. On his death, Giddy was described in an obituary in the *Gentlemen's Magazine* as 'One who, though not a bigot, disliked innovation in any form', an epitaph that could have applied to so many Cornishmen in the county's long history.

The execution of Louis XVI, like that of Charles I, was greeted with profound and visceral horror, and together with reports of the revolutionary Reign of Terror snuffed out any ideological sympathy with the Parisian regime. In February 1793, France declared war on England. The long tension had broken out at last into open conflict.

Around the Cornish coast the prospect of invasion was at last taken seriously. Four guns were put in readiness on the battery, two more on the Western Green and later another two on the hill in Newlyn. The old guns were carefully inspected. No one wanted a repetition of an event twenty years earlier when a notorious Irish pirate chased a brig into Mount's Bay. It was repelled by the long-disused cannons of St Michael's Mount, one of which exploded in the face of a young Mount resident, Martin Matthews, and killed him.

The corporation began organising its own forces, and set aside sums for such items as gunpowder, flags and drums. A new body of Penzance volunteers was formed, grimmer and better organised than the somewhat comical 1745 equivalent, though there was some inner rivalry between the volunteers of Penzance and those of neighbouring villages, '... competing for recruits from the same towns and villages, riddled with local, family and even personal jealousies'. These were eventually ironed out and the forces combined into the 'Mount's Bay First Battalion'.

The Penzance Corps was led by another John Tremenheere and was widely praised for its efficiency and industry. Less renowned were the Artillery Volunteers, a separate group responsible for the batteries. When Lt-Col Enys inspected them in 1805, he reported in scathing terms,

This is a very indifferent corps, attend their parades very ill, and are very irregular when assembled. The officers appear to have no sort of command among the men. Indeed I have sometimes suspected that many of them were only hired and dressed up for the day, as they did not always know their names when called over until reminded of them by the Commandant. None of these officers have ever been in the service and appear to be of the same class as the men. The Commandant is an American and I could never account for his being suffered to raise a corps, unless from his having married better than he deserved...

However, in action they were a different body:

Their arms were tolerably kept and their accoutrements very good. They were most of them seamen and accustomed to great guns, so that with all their faults – which were very numerous – they could work the guns tolerably and give ball with more accuracy than anyone from their appearance would expect.

Lt-Col Enys returned the following year to review the grandly named but lesser-known Mount's Bay Yeomanry Cavalry:

This troop was originally raised as Guides, for which they are very well qualified, among them many butchers accustomed to search every part of the country for cattle ... I cannot say much in favour of their discipline or looks but they certainly stuck well upon their little cat-like horses. Wishing to show off before General Wilford they proposed to charge in line across so very bad a line of ground that both the General and I tried to prevent them, but they did do it without a man falling off ... Wilford turned to me and said 'Thank God it is done and no-one killed...

Dressed in their coveted red costumes and armed with 'their sabres and a few old Spanish pistols', these were mostly old men. The young and fit were forcibly conscripted by the government, mainly for naval service. 194 men were officially required in 1795 and 252 in 1796, and these reluctant volunteers were of course supplemented by the increasing activity of the press gangs. These dreaded ruffians might arrive at any time in the dark of night and trawl the local inns for any men fit enough to stand on a deck and stop a bullet or worse, the original cannon fodder.

War brought hardship all round. Soon, continental markets were all but closed and trade fell to a trickle, devastating the mining industry, and crippling the fishing trade. This suffered not only by the prevention of supplies of fish to hungry continental Catholics but by creating a shortage of salt, made worse by heavy customs duties levied on it. Salt was absolutely essential for the fishing ports' survival and soon joined the list of desirable smuggled goods.

25

Down the Mine

After the first shock of war Penzance's fortunes recovered. With little opportunity for imports, England was thrown back on its own resources and the demand for minerals, mainly for weaponry, partly reinstated the miners' fortunes. Mine profits had been reduced by the royalties payable for the use of Boulton & Watt's patented steam engines, but the patents ran out in 1800 and others were able to improve the design and efficiency of the pumps. The copper hoard at Anglesey was also worked out, and the deeper lodes of copper were a great temptation, supposing that the pumping technology could bring them within practical use.

Some advances had been made by Jonathan Hornblower of Chacewater, who, aside from fathering thirteen children whose names all began with a 'J', invented a compound steam engine with a separate condenser. However, an inventor even closer at hand was Richard Trevithick, whose extraordinary imagination transformed many of the accepted ideas of what was possible with steam. He was working on the novel concept, of 'strong steam'. Existing steam engines worked at a pressure of no more than 2 or 3 lbs to the square inch, but Trevithick designed an enclosed system that would raise pressure to around 65 lbs per square inch, and later to around 100. The technology for this was made possible by the expertise of his wife Jane's family, the Harveys of Hayle, who had created their historic foundry and could meet his mechanical specifications. The energy produced by these pressures and the saving of wasted power achieved by enclosing the system enabled engines to work at a hugely increased capacity and efficiency, and for far less cost of imported coal.

Trevithick's genius was matched by his mercurial temper. He was too impatient to be concerned with administration or money but quickly took offence if anyone quarrelled with his methods. Once an invention was working successfully, he took little further interest in it and quickly moved on to something else. His steam pumps were draining water from mines with acceptable efficiency, so he began applying the same principles to problems such as the transport of materials. His engines were compact and light enough to be mounted on wheels and it was a short imaginative leap from there to the concept of a self-powered locomotive.

His first 'fire carriage' was trialled on Christmas Eve 1801, and with typical bravado was set not only to travel but to climb a fairly steep hill from Camborne towards Tehidy, to impress the Basset family of mine owners. The event was witnessed by a young Davies Gilbert who later described the occasion. The engine performed splendidly, to the amazement of the large crowd that had come to watch it, and travelled 300–400 yards up 'an ascent'. It then became the victim of the world's first motor traffic accident when, due to fallible steering gear, it swerved into a ditch. However, it was almost Christmas, so in the exuberance of their partial success, '... the parties adjourned to the Hotel and comforted their hearts with roast goose and proper drinks, when, forgetful of the engine, its water boiled away, the iron became red hot'. The great invention shortly afterwards blew itself to pieces. The astonishing event was, and still is, commemorated in song, when,

> The horses stood still
> The wheels went around
> Going up Camborne Hill coming down

Trevithick took another new self-propelled vehicle to the streets of London, but the first 'car' was so far outside anyone's experience that it was regarded as a mere novelty. It ran for 4 or 4 miles at a top speed of 9 mph. 'Captain Dick came alongside of me and said "She is going alright?" "Yes," I said, "I think we had better go on to Cornwall."' Their only incident occurred when they swerved '... tearing down six or seven yards of a garden fence. A person put his head from a window and called out "What the Devil are you doing there! What the Devil is that thing!"'

Having made both the steam locomotive and the motor car possible, both so crucial in the opening up of Cornwall, Trevithick moved on once more. He devised a workable means of refloating a ship sunk in the Thames by pumping air into inflatable bags. Typically, he fell out with the contractor halfway through the operation when the man had the temerity to quarrel with his methods, flying into a temper and cutting the ropes to let it sink again. He then began pioneering work on designs for a screw propeller to replace ships' cumbersome paddle wheels, before sailing away to open up gold and silver mines in Peru.

In the meantime, his pumping engines had transformed the potential of deep mining. The efficiency of engines was judged by a standard known as the 'duty', a calculated measurement based on the number of pounds of water that could be raised 1 foot by a hundredweight of coal, and the cost thereof. Trevithick's engines had raised this to 17 million lbs and it rose during the early years of the century to 125 million, an incredible refinement of effort and expense, so that, as Halliday says, 'one pound of coal in a perfected Cornish engine could lift a ton of water four hundred and fifty feet, at a cost of about half a farthing.' No wonder that Cornish mine engines were exported to mining areas all around the world, where many of them still stand.

The statistics of Dolcoath in Camborne, Cornwall's deepest and richest mine, showed how and why Cornwall became the Klondike of England and the forerunner of the Industrial Revolution that later spread to the Midlands and the north. It was already 600 feet deep by the turn of the nineteenth century and had produced tin and copper worth £1,250,000 when it was closed by the competition from Anglesey. From its reopening in 1799 to its final closure in the 1920s, it was reckoned to have produced a further £9 million of tin, copper, arsenic, silver and other minerals. By 1882, it reached a depth of 2,160 feet and had 12 miles of tunnels. Eventually, it reached a staggering 3,300 feet in depth. Its pumping engine, supplied by Harveys, had a main cylinder of over 7 feet in diameter.

Such increased capacity may have been music to adventurers and mine owners, but the additional burden on the miners themselves became almost unendurable. Before the invention of the 'man machine' to raise miners up and down, a large part of their working day was spent climbing down endless slippery ladders to their pitch and back up again at the end of the shift, sometimes falling off with exhaustion. In between their physical labour they had to contend with the heat, which increased as the mines descended until temperatures of 100 degrees were not uncommon. The air that was pumped down from the surface with variable efficiency was mixed with a fog of grit, gunpowder smoke, and the smoke from the tallow candles and the miners' own clay pipes.

The wider the levels were excavated the more suffocating the air became, together with the constant threat of falls, explosions, lung diseases and even unexpected diseases, such as hookworm from human faeces. At the Geevor-Levant complex, one can still see the spirals of granite steps cut by the miners in the sides of a cleft on the cliffside. Sick of the foul air, they preferred to exit via an old adit at sea level and climb the last 200 feet in the teeth of the wind, rain and spray rather than face the last section of ladders. On the surface in its heyday, this mine had a range of over ninety 'stamps' that operated twenty-four hours a day, which made the ground shake, their thundering heartbeat audible all over the peninsula and far out to sea.

Halliday describes the general scene:

After eight hours work with a pick the miner climbed to the surface where, dripping with sweat, he might find a freezing January evening. Then in an open shed with no facilities for washing he changed his clothes, cold and wet if he had been caught by rain on his way to the mine, and walked home, sometimes five miles away or more.

There was little material comfort to be found there. The typical miner's cottage was a thatched hovel of cob. One room with a damp earthen floor had to serve for all purposes, unless a shelf rigged up under the rafters could be called a bedroom. The usual food of the family was fish, mainly pilchards, potatoes, barley bread and an oatmeal gruel. Meat was a very rare luxury. Conditions in the home varied with the housewife but even a capable woman was helpless against poverty, overcrowding, lack of sanitation and disease... In 1850 the average age of those buried in the mining parish of St Just, male and female, was twenty-seven.

Adventurous travellers took the risk of seeing for themselves, such as James Forbes who wrote a vivid account of his experiences:

It requires a strong stomach to go through all this. The clothes they give you are greasy and filthy to a degree and are often stocked with a republic of creepers. The descent resembles a large well with an immense machine for the purpose of draining the water in motion all the way down. The Captain told us that if we made a false step to one side or the other we would be ground to atoms in the steam-engine or dashed to pieces in the shaft. I only wonder that accidents are not more frequent among the miners, who run up and down these slippery places like lamp-lighters, singing and whistling all the way.

Forbes describes the copper mining he finds at the 80 fathom level, and then descends further:

We stood 130 fathoms below the surface of the earth. We crawled forward on our hands and knees and afterwards had to cross through a rapid stream whose waters rushed abundantly over us. We came at last to the shaft of the tin mine. Here we saw two figures that hardly wore the appearance of human beings, singing at their work! We found it difficult to pay them a visit as we had to descend by a single rope... The heat of a mine combined with the fumes of sulphur is excessive – the miners are quite naked when engaged at their work. It is impossible to describe the luxury one feels in breathing again the fresh air and washing with cold water after these subterranean exercises.

The nineteenth century was the golden age of unfettered capitalism, with all its glorious achievements but also its careless inequity, poverty, and squalor. Haunted by the fear of unemployment, miners continued to bid each other down for the right to work, until the wages barely covered their expenses and they had to borrow from the mine company accounts at suitable rates of interest. They were also encouraged, sometimes forced, to spend their meagre wages in the mine's own stores, or even paid in a mine's own unique currency. Enormous riches rubbed shoulders with conditions that were little different from the overseas slavery that had underwritten the growth of Britain's wealth.

26

The Montpellier of England

In Penzance, a short ride away from the scenes of squalor that sustained it, a different world of increasing prosperity and sophistication existed. The adventurous Mr Maton, who had explored the Wherry mine, described Penzance in glowing terms:

> Penzance is a large and populous town, surrounded by a well cultivated and beautiful tract of country. Notwithstanding its exposure to the sea the corn, and particularly wheat, seemed to be in a remarkably thriving state. There is a fine pier, along the eastern side of which vessels are very commodiously and safely anchored. The mildness of the air, the agreeableness of the situation, and the respectability of its inhabitants render Penzance particularly inviting to residence, and with regard to invalids it may justly be considered as the Montpellier of England.

With the gradual improvement of the roads and turnpikes, visitors of leisure were becoming less of a novelty. The passage from London to Truro by stage wagon drawn by eight horses had been a matter of weeks rather than days, but with the new roads stagecoaches provided much less arduous travel. Fast post-chaises could, at a push, traverse the whole of Cornwall in a day.

In a family recollection, Henry Boase contrasted the Penzance of the late eighteenth century with the early nineteenth century:

> At that time Penzance afforded very little help towards the acquisition of knowledge; no book clubs, no reading rooms, no scientific institutions of any kind. Except for a little stir by the novel introduction of Methodism there was nothing to disturb the long-established smoking, drinking and gaming clubs, of which there were some for all ranks and for almost all

ages. These were distinguished by many ridiculous names, but all agreeing in drunkenness, profanity and card-playing. Hard drinking, gaming and swearing were then considered gentlemanly accomplishments and destroyed the health and fortune of very many.

When I again saw it in 1806 I was astonished at the change. Much of the moral change we have seen may be traced to Methodism which, while it operated powerfully on the labouring classes, reflected a benign influence on the higher orders of society.

Mr Boase did Penzance an injustice. The social life of Penzance had acquired aspirations of culture and sophistication long before the end of the eighteenth century. Notable was the Ladies' Book Club, established as early as 1770 and believed to be only the second institution of its kind in England and the only one outside London. In the town's most central and popular inn, the Ship & Castle (later the Union Hotel), fortnightly assemblies including elegant balls were held, so popular that a new assembly room had to be built to the rear of the inn, along with a small but equally popular theatre above the stables, and, to cater to all tastes, a cockpit.

The Gentlemen's Book Club followed in 1799. The Penzance Royal Geological Society was founded in 1814 and Penzance Library in 1818, sharing premises in North Parade.

It was an age of elegant buildings. Among country houses already in existence were Roscadghill, a possibly seventeenth-century house once owned by the Tremenheeres; Rosehill, built in 1814 by banker Richard Oxnam; Trengwainton, bought in 1814 by Sir Rose Price on the proceeds of his West Indian sugar plantations; Nacealverne, once home of the rebellious mayor John Carveth; Trereife, who owned Tolcarne Mill; Trewidden, home of Thomas Bolitho; Castle Horneck, home of the Borlase family; and Treneere Manor, built by the Robyns family. York House came a little later, built by a Mr Pope of Camelford who had made his fortune in America. It was christened by local poet and wit Valentine Le Grice, presumably in honour of the owner's surname, 'The Vatican'.

Within the town, Chapel Street, the main thoroughfare from the marketplace to the harbour, was filling with large and prestigious dwellings, some of which still survive. A group of houses near St Mary's chapel were made of bricks, reputedly brought to Penzance as part of the ballast of a Dutch merchantman, the *Rotterdam*, which had been captured as a prize by a Penzance privateer. They are still known as the Rotterdam buildings, one of which became the home of Maria Branwell, mother of the Brontë sisters. In Penzance, unlike other English towns, bricks were a comparative rarity and were considered an attractive and unusual feature. The granite pavements stand relatively high in Chapel Street as the roadway itself was often impassably dirty. This was due to more than the usual detritus of town life. Every few days, long trains of mules and packhorses, eighty or ninety strong, would process down it to the docks carrying their leather saddlebags of tin and copper, the latter leaving a trail of red slime on the road behind, later ascending again with a return load of dusty coal.

In Alverton Street, the fine Alverne House (currently known once more as 'Alverne's') was built by the Pascoe family, who purchased the plot opposite in order to obtain a sea view, later obscured by the building of North and South Parade. This was filled in much later and is now a solicitors' office, but its street number, No. 3a, still denotes its late arrival. No. 8 Parade Street, home to Penzance's earliest known firm of solicitors, Cornish & Birtill, until a devastating fire in the 1990s, is another beautifully proportioned eighteenth-century house, built once again in brick. Revd John Swete, who visited in 1780, described the town's geography as a simple crossroads: 'well built, consisting of one very long street leading from west to east and another dividing itself from this at the market place in the middle of the town which conducts itself to the quay.' On the darker side was New Street, probably in fact Penzance's oldest street, leading straight down to the docks, which was known from earliest times until living memory as a haunt of drunken lowlife, criminals and prostitutes.

The eastern part of the town, Market Jew Street, straggled down from the market house and marketplace, always the more commercial side of town with few aspirations to architectural gentility.

Summing up the somewhat 'Jane Austen' atmosphere of the time was a poem by the dashing Valentine Le Grice of Trereife, a paean of praise to his hometown, though not without a hint of irony and even astonishment at the very idea of its social aspirations:

> But now from Back to Betty's Lane
> From Morrop Stile to Ponsondane

From north to south, from east to west
Where 'jennies' spin or hides are dressed
Elliot's Square or Will Toll's bakehouse
Humphry's shop and Phillpotts cakehouse
Woolcock's back-let, Market Jew Street
Everywhere 'tis like a new street.

The poem continues to laud the state of the streets, once muddy and rough but now, with much poetic licence, 'smooth as cheek of lady fair', and the communal water shoot at the crossroads, 'a crystal stream, that sparkles in the solar beam'.

Le Grice proceeds to his peroration:

The Market House that looked so grim
Is now a beau, quite spruce and trim...
Our ball-room too has few compeers
See, see, those blazing chandeliers!
What music! Ravishing the spheres!
And ah! What pretty little houris
Whose charms are more than ample dowries
Lightly thread the mazy dance.
Say, say, ye Gods, is this Penzance!

The assembly room in the Union Hotel has one more claim to fame, being the place where the naval victory at Trafalgar and the death of Adm. Lord Nelson were reputedly first announced. The news was carried home by the schooner *Pickle* under the command of Lt John Lapenotiere. Legend has it that a local fishing boat spoke to the *Pickle* off Mount's Bay and learnt the news from her. The crew then made haste for shore and passed the story to the mayor, Thomas Giddy, who announced it during a ball, and arranged a memorial service at Madron.

There is however no contemporary account of these events. In fact, according to Tony Pawlyn (in his paper for Falmouth Maritime Museum 'Trafalgar – the Race for Glory' in 2005), the likelihood of such an occurrence was increasingly small. The honour of reporting such momentous tidings to the admiralty was a privilege conferring honour and reward on the messenger. This led to a somewhat undignified race between

Lt Lapenotiere and Cdr John Sykes of the sloop *Nautilus* who had heard the news via a chance meeting with the *Pickle* off Cape St Vincent.

While the *Pickle* was making for Falmouth, the *Nautilus* made straight for Plymouth. Lapenotiere landed first but had to cross Cornwall, whereas Sykes landed later in Plymouth but with the advantage of territory. Both hired post-chaises and it is rumoured that they passed through Okehampton within three quarters of an hour of each other, both driving furiously. In the end, Lapenotiere won the race reputedly by minutes after racing neck and neck through fog over Hounslow Heath, and received the reward of honour and fame and a magnificent prize of £500, as well as instant promotion. With such rewards at stake, the idea of such valuable information being shouted out to a passing Penzance fishing boat strains belief, though the topic is still highly contentious and the 'event' is still celebrated in Penzance.

After Trafalgar, the threat of a French invasion reduced and little occurred on the home front until Napoleon's final stand at Waterloo. The news of this did not arrive for eleven days, when the Penzance Artillery Corps carried out one of their rare operations in firing their guns for victory. Valentine Le Grice was among those who went to look at the defeated French leader in Plymouth Sound as he stood at the rail of the *Billy Ruffian* as sailors had nicknamed it, better known as the *Bellerephon*, awaiting transportation to his final exile in St Helena.

Around the time that Bonaparte sailed away, Sir Humphry Davy was occupying an idle fortnight by trying to devise a lamp that could be safely used in coal mines without the risk of an explosion.

27

Humphry Davy

Humphry Davy can fairly claim the title of Penzance's best-known son, his reputation enshrined in every history of the advancement of science, and in particular chemistry. According to Edmund 'Clerihew' Bentley, he 'lived in the odium, of having discovered sodium', but if that sounds boring, this, according to his cousin Edmund, is how it felt:

> When he saw the minute globules burst through the crust and take fire as they entered the atmosphere, he could not contain his joy – he actually danced about the room in ecstatic delight; some little time was required for him to compose himself to continue the experiment.

Davy was one of the children of a relatively well-off family of yeomen farmers from Ludgvan, though he was born at No. 4 The Terrace, Penzance. When his parents left Penzance to take over the family farm in Varfell, Humphry remained in Penzance, lodging with a family friend who had a well-stocked library. This suited Davy who was a dreamy boy, showing no aptitude for science except in creating fireworks to amuse his sisters. He studied classics at the grammar school that now bears his name, then went on to Truro Grammar School. His only discernible talent as a youth was for storytelling and he developed a love for poetry, shooting and fishing, and a passion for all the wonders of nature which stayed with him all his life. The first glimmerings of an interest in science did not emerge until he was sixteen. Due to a downturn in the family fortunes following his father's death, he was apprenticed to Mr Bingham Borlase, an apothecary and surgeon, whose premises still stand at the top of New Street, narrowing the road past the market house. It was not until he was nineteen that he read his first works on the current state of chemistry.

Chemistry had lagged behind other sciences such as physics and medicine in the speed of its development. Its terminology was still stuck in the language of the seventeenth century or even of alchemy, with such vague concepts as: 'phlogiston', a mysterious substance said to be released during combustion; 'luminiferised aether', a supposed medium for the propagation of light; and 'caloric', the undiscovered medium by which heat was transferred.

Davy was able to prove that none of these actually existed. With the help of his friend Gregory Watt, son of mechanical pioneer James Watt, Davy started carrying out basic experiments in his spare time. Although devoted to the indefinable joys of poetry, he was from the start a most thorough and disciplined scientist. He was painstaking in his work, and additionally gifted with a tremendous imagination to put his experiments into context, to draw accurate inferences from them, and to envision the broader picture.

Davy caught the eye of Davies Gilbert, local MP and member of the Royal Society, and was introduced by him to Dr Thomas Beddoes of Bristol, a physician interested in the medicinal qualities of gases. Davy wrote up some of his experiments on the respiration of carbon dioxide and at the age of twenty presented his findings to Beddoes, who published them. Beddoes was setting up his own laboratory, the Pneumatic Institution in Clifton, Bristol, and invited Davy to join him there as its superintendent. It was just the opportunity he needed. With Beddoes' help he was able to pursue his early experiments, and in particular with nitrous oxide (laughing gas).

His experiments with gases included, among other methods, testing it first on animals and then on humans, often with himself as a guinea pig. It was a hazardous procedure, as he discovered when he tried inhaling carbon monoxide: 'I seemed to be sinking into annihilation, and had just power enough to drop the mouthpiece from my unclosed lips...'

Nitrous oxide was very different and its effects were so amusing that he and his colleagues became almost addicted to the other-worldly effects it produced. Davy perceived that it might have more useful applications than reducing rooms full of scientists to attacks of the giggles. Thanks to him, nitrous oxide was developed into medicine's first true anaesthetic.

One happy coincidence of his life in Bristol was that Beddoes was friendly with one of Davy's literary heroes, Samuel Taylor Coleridge, and through him

Davy met Coleridge, Wordsworth, Southey and other poets who inspired his own work. Davy remained friends with Coleridge in particular all his life.

He turned from gases to the novel effects produced by early voltaic electricity, and its potential ability to separate natural compounds into their respective elements. Both his ground-breaking work and his lively and pleasing personality brought him to the attention of the wider scientific community. At the prodigious age of twenty-two he was appointed assistant lecturer in chemistry and assistant editor of the famous journal at the Royal Institution. His first lectures gained excited reviews 'from the sparkling intelligence of his eye, his animated manner, and the "tout ensemble", we have no doubt of his attaining distinguished excellence'.

And so he did. Through the success of his lectures he became well-known and highly paid, though he was not tempted to exchange the glamour of the lecture stage for the rigour of the laboratory. His experiments helped to bring in a new forensic era to the science of chemistry. With the use of electricity he was able to isolate and describe for the first time such common elements as sodium, potassium and chlorine. He not only discovered but gave names to barium, boron, strontium, calcium and magnesium. He was knighted in 1812, and was held in such high general regard that Napoleon granted him free passage to cross France in wartime on his way to Naples, allowing him to visit Paris on the way.

A new era began the following year when, after being temporarily partially blinded by an explosion in the laboratory, he agreed to take on a young bookbinder who had been pestering him for a post. Davy warned his young assistant, Michael Faraday, that 'science is a harsh mistress, and in a pecuniary point of view poorly rewarding to those who devoted themselves to her service'. This was not strictly true, as Davy had been paid, for example, 500 guineas for a short series of lectures in Dublin. Michael Faraday has been ungraciously described by some scientists as Davy's greatest discovery, and he went on to bring electromagnetism and electrolysis to the world of science and, more recognisably for laymen, invented the electric motor with its thousands of applications.

In 1815, Davy was contacted by Revd Dr Gray, a member of a society set up to seek a solution to the coal mine explosions that had recently caused the death of ninety-two men and boys in Gateshead. Davy went to see John Buddle, head of the Wallsend colliery, to look at the practical nature of the problem, unknown in his inert local tin mines.

He immersed himself in the study of the nature of fire-damp (methane), the temperatures needed to ignite it, the apertures through which it could pass. The solution lay in the latter, and Davy experimented in passing methane through a series of fine metal gauzes. Eventually he found a gauze that allowed methane to burn on the inside of a cylinder without igniting the outside air. He refined the design, an air-tight lamp except for a covering of gauze containing a precisely calculated 576 apertures per square inch, with the inert exhaust gases expelled at the top. When the methane entered through the gauze at the lower end of the cylinder it glowed brightly but did not explode.

It was a beautiful solution, and when John Buddle tried it out in a coal mine,

> It is impossible for me to express my feelings at the time when I first suspended the lamp in the mine and saw it red hot ... I said to those around me, 'We have at last subdued this monster'.

He wrote to Davy,

> Instead of creeping inch by inch with a candle, as is usual, along the galleries of a mine suspected to contain fire-damp, we walk firmly in with the safe-lamps and with the utmost confidence prove the actual state of the mine ... it is of the utmost importance, not only to the great cause of humanity and to the mining interest of the country, but also to the commercial and manufacturing interest of the United Kingdom; for I am convinced that by the happy invention of the safe-lamp large proportions of the coal mines of the empire will be rendered available which otherwise might have remained inaccessible ... I cannot conclude without expressing my highest admiration for those talents which have developed the properties and controlled the power of one of the most dangerous elements which human enterprise has hitherto had to encounter.

Buddle urged Davy to patent his invention without delay, but Davy replied, 'My good friend I never thought of such a thing; my sole object was to serve the cause of humanity, and if I have succeeded I am amply rewarded in the gratifying reflection of having done so'.

It was a generous gesture. The future of the whole Industrial Revolution depended on a plentiful supply of coal, and his invention made mining possible, as Buddle had said, in places where it would previously have been lethal. Davy's work was most often confined to the test-tube and original experiments that few could understand, but the Davy lamp was something everyone could recognise, a material object that saved unknown numbers of lives. His fame, and the reverence in which he is still held in Cornwall, still relates mostly to that productive fortnight's work. It was fitting that when a statue was erected in Penzance in his honour in 1872, he holds his most famous invention in his right hand as he gazes down Market Jew Street.

Davy became president of the Royal Society. He lobbied in vain for a Natural History Museum, which did not materialise until long after his death, and he was a founder member of the Zoological Society and wrote the prospectus for the first London Zoo. He and Faraday began experiments that led to the invention of electric lighting. He also spent a long time at the Admiralty's request on solving the problem of corrosion of the copper sheeting beneath its warships, during which Davy unexpectedly came upon the possibility of desalinating seawater by means of electrolysis.

Despite his fame, Davy remained devoted to his family, his mother and sisters and his native West Cornwall which he revisited whenever he could.

In his declining years Davy spent his time travelling, fishing and writing a fanciful book on the pleasures of angling – *Salmonia* – and writing reams of poetry which sadly, even to those with a high tolerance for the Lake District Poets, never achieved anything like their quality. He died and was buried in Geneva in 1829.

His memory is celebrated not only in his statue but in Humphry Davy School, a pub in Alverton Street, and an annual Humphry Davy lecture held in Penzance. Sadly the whole-day holiday for the pupils of his old school on 17 December, his birthday, for which he left provision in his will, has long fallen foul of local education bureaucracy.

28

Expansion

It was as if Penzance had held its breath during the Napoleonic wars and upon victory suddenly inhaled, inflating its community like a balloon. The opening up of European markets for fish and tin breathed new life into these industries, but the whole spectrum of the town's activities and wealth improved. Up with this went its pride and self-confidence, an urge to improve every aspect of the town's life, and the money to make such dreams a reality.

The harbour was one of the drivers of the town's success. It was always a mixed blessing and curse, a reliable source of the corporation's income, but due to the ferocity of the occasional storm a continual drain on its resources, needing constant repair and occasional rebuilding.

The first stone pier was probably built in the early fifteenth century and was first recorded in 1512, a stone wall no longer than the medieval quay that still exists in Newlyn. The battery was added along with a protective wall leading to the quay in 1740. As Penzance did not have an enclosed harbour, the quay was the only point of protection and cargo transfer, so as it became busier it was always congested and in need of more space.

The inner pier was rebuilt in 1745, and greatly extended in 1764 to a planned length of 170 feet at a more protective north-easterly angle, although the money ran out after only 113 feet. The specifications were,

> To extend from the corner of the house now in possession of Jane Jeffery to the limit of the rock beyond the Gap commonly called the Grebe, and from thence towards the north-east for 170 feet, so as to gain 5 or 6 feet of water more than is at the present pier head, to be in height 27 feet, in breadth at the base 40 feet, to batter [taper] towards the top about 5 feet.

The remaining 57 feet were not added until 1776. In 1812, another 150 feet were added on in the same direction with a fine stone-built lighthouse at the pier's head.

A little way up the hill from the harbour, the long frustration between the growing community of Penzance and the church town of Madron continued to simmer. Since 1789, the chapel of St Mary had kept separate registers of Penzance baptisms and burials despite protests from Madron. In 1806, Valentine Le Grice became the chapel's curate and tried to circumvent the Marriage Act of 1754 so that Penzance people could marry in their own town, but the authorities insisted that marriages had to take place where the parish banns were called. However, the writing was on the wall for Madron. In 1824, Le Grice wrote to the corporation complaining that his chapel was in poor condition and far too small for the increasing congregation, and went to the length of offering £1,000 towards the cost of rebuilding it. Such developments, however, had to wait a little longer.

The modern town was taking shape. Alverton Street and Market Jew Street were both widened by the demolition of older buildings and the cutting down of two fine ash trees standing in front of where the current post office now stands, much to the anger of the Tonkin family who still held the manorial rights of Alverton. The bullock market and the pigs that were often tethered to the conveniently placed market cross were removed from the present Greenmarket, making it far more attractive for genteel folk. The livestock markets moved to what was waste land at the top of Causewayhead to remain there as the cattle and pig markets until they were turned into car parks. The central streets were cleaned by 'scavengers' and lit by oil lamps. Visitors were coming to the town on a regular basis, not many, but swelled by those who had been denied by war the pleasure of wintering on the continent. Penzance was 'discovered' on many occasions and praised for the mildness of its winter climate rather than its summer beaches. Wealthy invalids came to explore the 'new Montpellier' and even sea bathing from bathing machines began on the shores of the current harbour and the Western Green.

It was a period of transition. Since the days of the Stuarts, Cornwall had been of little interest to the country at large except as a possible seat of invasion. Penzance life had not significantly changed in the last 100 years, the simple parochial round of mining, fishing, farming, feast days and holidays, church, small houses and cottages with large families, scares from foreign shipping, plague, and bad harvests. It was still an inward-looking community for whom the affairs of the outside world had more often been a threat rather than a blessing, preferring to be left alone in its conservative ways to continue life as it had always been. But the outside world was forcing itself in. The last regular speakers of Cornish had finally died out and change was in the air.

Agriculture was in need of new ideas. During the war the pressure to feed the embattled country forced farmers to break in fields higher up on the hills, some of which had not been cultivated since the Iron Age. After the war a combination of poor summers and the restored imports of food led to a calamitous slump in prices and a crisis in local agriculture.

According to Davies Gilbert's survey, farmers were experiencing

A total inability to pay the rents ... a like inability to pay the taxes ... an inability in farmers in general to pay their tradesmens' bills, a total dereliction of all speculative improvements, and an abandonment of lands which they have lately brought into cultivation from a state of waste.

However, the first local demonstrations of the threshing machine took place in Penzance's Greenmarket in 1809, and the Penzance Agricultural Society had been formed to encourage not only new ideas but to modify old attitudes. Cornwall's mildness in better years allowed the growing of early crops, far in advance of those further to the east, but this was of local advantage only while no means of marketing or distribution was available.

In contrast to the fields, the fishing ports were doing good business. During the war the catches of pilchards had not slackened. Some of the cured fish was sent away to markets in Bristol and London, though when the market was glutted or salt was very short much of the catch had been ground into fertiliser at a considerable loss. When the European markets opened again in Italy and Spain the fishery enjoyed unprecedented prosperity.

But it was mining that made the greatest contribution to the increased wealth of the town. In 1800, Cornwall's mines numbered no more than around 75. By 1837, this had soared to 200 mines employing up to 30,000 men. Output increased from 2,500 tons of tin in 1800 to 4,100 in 1837; and copper increased even more dramatically from 5,000 tons to 12,000 tons in the same period. Sadly, much of this wealth only stayed in Cornwall long enough for it to be transferred to the 'up country' bank accounts of the lucky adventurers and investors. Not much of that was ever returned to the county but financed the building of fine houses and terraces in more fashionable parts of Britain, and little thought was given to the condition of the miners themselves.

An exception was the adventurer who wrote to his agent in contented terms in 1797,

I observe the very considerable remittance you have made my bankers of £1,530 7s 8d, considerable indeed! Which prompts me to make a little offering to those poor wretches the tinners to whom in a great measure Cornish landholders owe their affluence. You mentioned to me some time ago what a number of miserable poor creatures there were in and about the neighbourhood, without covering, shoes, stockings, and blankets etc.

However, there were limits: 'I should be glad therefore if you would dispose of twenty guineas from me among the wives and children.'

In the 1800 census Penzance had a population of 3,382, but in thirty years this would almost double.

Penzance's first bank was established in 1797 by John Batten, twelve times mayor of the town, with William Carne and Richard Oxnam, known originally just as the 'Penzance Bank'. Henry Boase, another mayor, joined the partnership in 1810 when the name was changed to Batten, Carne & Boase. A rival soon arose funded by the Bolitho family who had acquired the lucrative smelting works at Chyandour, The Commercial – later Bolitho's Bank – which eventually moved into Market Jew Street where Barclay's now stands; and a third, the Union Bank instigated by the Dennis family, set up in Chapel Street in 1810.

To some the surrounding hardship went almost unnoticed. The blithe and clearly susceptible Dr Paris' *Guide to Mount's Bay* in 1816, waxes almost poetical in his description of the market and those who attended it:

The market, for goodness, variety and cheapness of its commodities is certainly not to be equalled by any other in Great Britain. To the great quantity of salt usually mixed with the food of the hog is to be attributed the delicacy and richness of the pork, whilst owing to the rich pasturage the heifer beef is superior, beyond all comparison, to the Scotch. During the winter the market is filled with the greatest variety of wildfowl, as woodcock, snipe etc, which may be purchased for a few pence. Every variety of fish in season is offered for sale every day by the Newlyn fish-women, whose delicate complexions and the vivacity and brilliancy of whose jet-black eyes, darting their rays from beneath the shade of large beaver hats, fascinate the traveller...

The poor were not entirely forgotten. Each parish was responsible for its own poor and maintained poorhouses for the destitute. Penzance provided almshouses in Market Jew Street and a combined workhouse together with other parishes, in the South Folly by the Western Green. This was later moved to St Clare Street, on the site of the present hospital. The mayor had discretion to make small ad hoc payments to those who petitioned him, and many are recorded in the accounts: 5s to a poor woman whose husband had 'met with a misfortune by part of a house falling on him'; £1 to a poor woman delivered of triplets; £1 to two men whose houses had burned down; and £1 to two women whose husbands had been drowned 'off the pier head'.

The duties of a mayor were many and onerous. Pool's *History of Penzance* contains a lengthy extract from the mayor's (Henry Boase) diary of 1816/17. Among its entries,

Held a meeting of the Corporation who resolved to erect a capstan on the pier if it can be done for £25, a light if for £10, and to pave 50 feet in length with moor stones; also agreed to tax butter and salt-fish a penny a basket...

Rescorla's application for a beer license refused. Notices to prevent nuisances in the market place ordered to be put up, and two wheelbarrows for scavengers ordered...

Ordered removal of Ann Pender, a pauper, to Scilly, and suspended it on certificate of her illness...

Attended the market with constables and serjeant, enforcing the new toll of 1d per basket on butter and fish. Succeeded in part...

Hearing of John Newton, who promised to pay all expenses to which he is legally liable in the matter of Peggy Warren...

Occupied from 3 to 5 o'clock examining Mrs Crosswell's servants as to attempts to set fire to the house in which she lodges, strong circumstances of suspicion against the youngest waiting maid but not enough to warrant legal proceedings...

Many applications from paupers, some referred to the town works, some to the vestry, some relieved from my own purse. Application for a warrant from the servant girl of Mr Alexander Marrack against Webb, a carpenter, for assault and attempt to commit rape, recommended them to make it up...

A great storm and extraordinary high tide last night and this morning did great damage to the quay, shipping, boats, houses and sea fences, perhaps £500 at least...

Surveying the quay and found a great breach ... Twelve of the Corporation met and resolved to request Mr Richards to direct the propping up of the breach of the quay with oak timber to secure it till the weather permits further repair...

Granted leave to James Williams, a blind ballad singer, to hawk his papers today on condition of his departing quietly tomorrow...

Another humanitarian enterprise began in 1809 when those busy Penzance gentlefolk, Valentine Le Grice, Thomas Giddy and Dr John Bingham Borlase, to whom Humphry Davy had been apprenticed, formed the Penzance Public Dispensary and Humane Society. They helped to fund its operations in providing medical assistance and advice to the poor. It started beside the almshouses in Market Jew Street than moved down to Chapel Street.

Almost unnoticed in 1803 was the placement of one of Britain's first purpose-built lifeboats on a sandy bank near the present railway station. Losses at sea had been heavy, as reported in the *Royal Cornwall Gazette*,

... It being dark and blowing strong a transport with troops from Buenisaries ran ashore under old (Hal) Zephron Cliff, 40 or 50 men and children drowned...

In the gales of Thursday and Friday nights last two vessels were thrown shore at the [Loe] Bar. The first was a Spanish polacre; we are sorry to say every soul on board perished...

[HM frigate *Anson*] became embayed...rode in a most tremendous sea and as heavy a gale as was ever experienced. 4.00 am cable parted. 8.00am foretop sail cut and ship run ashore on the sand. Now commenced a most heart-rending scene to some hundreds of spectators who exerted themselves to the utmost at the imminent risk to their lives to save those of their drowning fellow men.

Though so close to shore, the captain and around 150 men were lost from the *Anson* in 1807, which inspired one of the watchers, Henry Trengrouse of Helston, to devise the breeches buoy lifesaving rocket apparatus.

The Penzance lifeboat was not at first a success. It was of a design more common on the east coast, and the local mariners treated it with suspicion, preferring to carry out rescues in their own vessels as before. The next lifeboat did not arrive until 1826, and that was wrecked itself a year later.

All around Britain a new spirit of enlightenment, of humanity and democracy was gaining ground. In 1830 a new Whig government came to power, determined to stamp out as much as possible of the graft and corruption in local and national government. Against enormous opposition it passed the Reform Act of 1832, dissolving many of the country's 'pocket' boroughs, which were previously perquisites of certain landed families. Cornwall was rich in these, sending forty-four members to parliament from such constituencies as East and West Looe, Grampound and Mitchell. These were reduced to fourteen, though, despite the efforts of Davies Gilbert, Penzance was still not one of them.

Having succeeded with Parliament, the government turned its attention to the boroughs. Most of these, like Penzance, were governed by a small self-perpetuating clique of influential men who selected each other for offices as aldermen and mayors, and in which the ordinary townsmen had no vote and no say whatever.

The government appointed municipal corporation commissioners to examine the administration of existing boroughs and reported on Penzance in 1833. They found its administration generally fair and honest compared with many, though they had their criticisms:

The town is not watched, unless occasionally when depredations have been frequent. In general the town is peaceable ... The town is not well supplied with water, though there are some pipes laid down and the corporation have works proceeding ... the soil of the town is sold and the proceeds added to the highway rate.

There are 22 licensed public houses; the number was formerly greater. The number of licensed beer shops is seven, formerly nine; they are stated to be prejudicial to the morals of the town.

The annual revenues of the Corporation are £2,093 13s, of which the quay duties are £1,410 and the Market tolls £530 ... The sum of £1,300 was borrowed for the purpose of procuring a site for a new market, which project has not been carried into effect as yet, owing to a disinclination of the inhabitants to bear any portion of the expense.

The town is said to be fast increasing, both in extent and prosperity. Many houses are being erected. The occupations of the inhabitants are very miscellaneous. The shops are numerous and good and the markets tolerable.

The Corporation and the inhabitants at large are not upon good terms. A general opinion appears to prevail that the very considerable funds of the Corporation ought to be rendered more subservient to public purposes...

The names of the final members of the old corporation were listed, their homes, occupations and, tellingly, their relationships, as in the Battens father and son, the Carne brothers, the Vibert cousins, and the Giddy brothers plus Davies Gilbert, their cousin.

On 31 December 1835, the old corporation of Penzance, as set up in James I's Charter of 1614, was officially dissolved. A new, young queen was soon to ascend the throne. A fresh wind blew throughout the land, and Penzance stood poised to take its greatest leap forward into the future.

29

'Ye Gods, Is This Penzance!'

To ordinary Penzance folk, who, like Thomas Giddy, constitutionally disliked innovation in any form, the events of the first few years of Victoria's reign must have been bewildering.

The old order of the corporation was gone. In the place of the former assistants and aldermen were eighteen elected councillors, also known as aldermen, who would run the town's business. It was not altogether surprising that only five of the previous administration were elected to be among them. Class does not die out so easily and soon a patronising rhyme was circulating in the town:

> Five bankers, two lawyers, and one auctioneer
> A doctor, a hatter, a man of veneer,
> Lloyds agent, a grocer, a dealer of wine
> A seller of goods in the drapery line
> A vendor of hardware, a burner of lime,
> By trickery and canvas, by desert or by chance
> Comprise the new Council of the town of Penzance.

They could not complain about the new corporation's industry. The harbour area was almost immediately extended with further work on the quay, and a new road and high protecting wall was created beside the Dolphin Inn.

Above it, in one of the old corporation's last bequests, the money had finally been raised to carry out Le Grice's wishes and rebuild the chapel of St Mary. Rebuilding was somewhat of an inadequate term. The lovely chapel with its low profile and dramatic spire had stood since 1672, welcoming all who approached by sea and standing tall in all depictions of the town. Its replacement was designed from the first as a far grander affair, suitable when the day finally came to take its place as mother church of the parish of Penzance.

That day was still much more than a generation away, but a likeness of the old chapel was engraved for posterity and it was then carefully taken down. On 17 August 1832, the foundation stone of the new chapel was laid. It was designed by Charles Hutchens, a self-taught and successful architect from St Buryan. He created a Gothic building on a different scale altogether. Due to its situation on the side of the hill and enormously tall in appearance, it confidently dominated the peninsula when seen from either side. The first service was held there in November 1835 and, shortly before being disbanded, the old corporation were therefore able to admire from the pews they had reserved for themselves their final conception.

Its appearance naturally led to dismay at Madron, especially when it was relicensed for marriages. Madron's vicar pleaded that it should be used as such only during the summer months, but only succeeded in securing the marriage fees for the rest of his incumbency.

One of the first preoccupations of the new council was the replacement of the old market house. As the municipal commissioners had pointed out, a sum had already been borrowed and set aside for this. The old market house was in poor repair and no longer big enough for the burgeoning trade of the town. A competition to design the new building had been held by the old corporation. However, they did not like the look of the original winner and opted instead for the second choice, designed by H. J. Whitling of London. The new corporation decided that this design was too expensive and instead accepted a third choice by William Harris of Bristol, despite Whitling's lawsuit for the breach of contract, which cost them £300. It was opened with great ceremony on 28 June 1838, the day of Queen Victoria's Coronation.

The economy of design and the continued use of Mr Daniell's old 'three-cornered site' in the middle of town resulted in a rather cramped interior, divided as it was into a market house on the west side and the town's guildhall on the east. On the outside it embodied all the self-regarding grandeur of the Victorian age, a tall pseudo-classical statement of pride and pomp. Pevsner referred to it as a 'dignified structure on an awkwardly narrow site', but William Bottrell dismissed it as an 'insipid, silly-looking structure', and it still divides opinion today.

By then, Market Jew Street was taking over from Chapel Street as the town's primary thoroughfare and trading centre. By cutting into the slope on its north side it was possible to form a raised terrace, which was paved with granite moor-stone sets and accessed by a series of turning steps down to road level. It was the age of the future rather than the past and local rumour says that the bulk of the excellent stone used for its construction was pillaged from the ruins of Chun Castle's ramparts. Whatever its origins, it was an inspirational design, as much a part of Penzance's townscape as any of its buildings.

The council turned its attention to persuading the increasing number of holiday visitors, who came to view the town but often passed on again, to stay in the town. It therefore conceived the promenade, built in 1844, a suitable place for gentlefolk to walk on without getting their clothes dirty and an excellent platform on which visitors and local worthies alike could parade in dignity. This involved building up the beach of the Western Green with a solid wall whose height created a risk of flooding behind it, though the building of Marine Terrace helped stem the flow of storm water to its occasional cost. Soon after it was built, it was covered with poor-quality tarmac, which ironically did make women's dresses dirty for years until their complaints were finally heard and the surface was paved.

The most incessant demands still came from the harbour. This was an index of its success, but despite a small wharf near the Battery Rocks, and a substantially larger one built by the gas company for its own coal deliveries, there was simply not enough room for all the work the harbour undertook. These included exports of ingots of tin and hogsheads of fish; imports of coal and timber, salt and limestone; the coastal transport of people and things; the weekly ferries to the Isles of Scilly; and the town's own fishing fleet, all jostling impatiently for space on the single quay and surrounding sheds. Some shipping traders were in the habit of avoiding the crush and the harbour dues by grounding at Chyandour and Lariggan, either side of the borough's boundaries, to unload directly into carts at low tide. This was often hazardous for the vessels if the wind turned, as well as a drain on council funds. The council began to agitate for a capital sum with which to create a properly enclosed harbour, and obtained parliamentary permission in 1840, despite the dry remark of J. J. Boase who debated the point of 'trying to create a Liverpool when there was no Manchester in the background'.

The original scheme was for a very large harbour with a new quay extending southwards from Chyandour to meet an extended south quay. This was unfortunately too ambitious and expensive. But, in 1845, the council managed to raise £15,000 in private loans and laid the foundation stone of the North (later the Albert) Pier. This jutted out from where the railway station was destined to stand, again in a direction straight towards the south quay. It was three years and another £8,000 before the project was completed, enclosing a harbour of 21 acres including plenty of quay space, berths, wharves, a dry dock, safe moorings, and a harbour protected from all but a certain quarter of a south-easterly wind (which still occasionally sneaks into it). However, what it couldn't provide was all-tide access, and even the shelter of the pier head was not accessible at very low tide. Several dangerous incidents occurred when ships tried to run for shelter at low water. The council put the hat round once again and raised another £9,000 to extend the South Quay another 300 feet further. This extension took a right turn, matching the angle of the medieval pier, to reach as much deep water as possible. The old stone lighthouse was taken down and replaced by a fine new cast-iron column manufactured in Copperhouse, Hayle.

What was really needed for the safety of the busy maritime traffic was an all-tide harbour of refuge, which sadly even the new extension could not provide. The obvious place for this was not Penzance at all but Newlyn, but relationships between Penzance and Newlyn had never been easy. Penzance's fashionable commercial centre was far higher up the social scale than Newlyn's working-class village community, permanently reeking of fish, and the prospect of sharing port facilities with their downmarket neighbour was rejected outright. Newlyn had put forward proposals as early as 1797 for a bigger harbour to supplement its old quay, but Penzance sent a deputation to parliament to oppose it, which was successful. Another attempt was made in 1811, but that too was quashed by opposition from Penzance. Many more ships and lives were to be lost before Newlyn finally got its way.

A significant and potentially transformational development was missed when instead of developing Newlyn; the council presented a petition to the admiralty for the construction of a massive breakwater, beginning at Penlee Point and extending for a mile north-east in the direction of Porthleven. It was designed to 'afford a thoroughly safe anchorage with ample accommodation and depth of water for a very large fleet of the Navy or mercantile marine'. With this, Penzance and Mount's Bay could have presented a serious alternative to Falmouth and Plymouth, an ideal refuge in Gwavas Lake for transatlantic merchantmen without the need to pass the Lizard, a facility for discharging, transhipping from larger vessels to smaller ones, docks, storage facilities, all the bustle and commerce of a major port. But this time the funds were not forthcoming. (A similar concept, Firstport, was revived in the 1990s, this time with the advantage of the rail link, but met a similar lack of support.)

In 1832, a most unwelcome visitor entered Mount's Bay, a sudden and devastating outbreak of cholera. This raged through the poorer parts of Penzance and Newlyn, taking the lives of sixty-six in Penzance and eighty-eight in Newlyn. Mousehole closed its village to all outsiders, Newlyn people especially, and escaped the plague, though this caused lasting bad blood between the villages. A small field was enclosed at Paul as a separate cemetery for the Newlyn casualties.

In 1848, the Public Health Act was passed, and the first survey on the sanitary condition of Penzance was carried out the following year. Mr George T. Clark, the superintending inspector, was not wholly critical in his report, but did not mince his words where necessary. He noted the increase in population, from 6,500 in 1832 to 8,578 in 1841 and reckoned it at around 9,500 in 1848, with 1,739 houses inhabited and 199 uninhabited or, significantly, in the process of being built.

He commended the gasworks, built in 1830, which replaced the public oil lamps of old and lit the town's main streets, but commented that the lights were 'very inefficient, and cut off altogether on moonlit nights'. The paving and cleanliness of the streets pleased him, but he observed that this was limited to the main thoroughfares only while the side streets and alleys were full of rubbish and so wet as to be impassable in winter. He continued, saying,

Public nuisances are tolerably numerous. The most considerable are the slaughter-houses, of which there are 14 in town and 9 in one street [this was surely Bread Street, which runs behind and to the north of Market Jew Street. It continued to house several slaughterhouses until after the Second World War and the coming of refrigeration]. In several of the larger squares and courts are open dung-heaps and cesspools, and a filthy depot for scavengers' dirt within the harbour, fed by a drop from the cliff, very foul and offensive. The vegetable or green-market held at the cross and the fish-market in front of the Guildhall [where Humphry Davy's statue now stands] are both serious pests to passers-by. Other commodities are also sold at stalls in the narrow street about the Guildhall, which matter the Corporation are about instantly to amend.

First, however, the corporation had to persuade the Newlyn women fish-sellers, who had no intention of paying the extra market dues, to take their trade under cover.

A new and commodious covered room has recently been opened as a poultry and fish market, but the fish-women decline taking possession of it and still expose their fish for sale in front of the town hall...

If Mr Clark seems a little over-fastidious about the basic necessities and commerce of the town, he strikes a more serious note when contemplating the working-class quarters:

Dysentery prevails in the lower part of the town and in certain parts of the higher town remarkable for their filth and want of drainage. It is impossible in words to convey an adequate idea of the filth of the older and more densely peopled quarter of the town near the quay, in which the cholera prevailed formerly. Its position moreover is naturally in all probability one of the most beautiful positions upon a bay proverbial for its salubrity and beauty. It would be difficult to find a spot so foul in which life is so seriously affected, or which it would cost so little to make pure.

There were twenty-three official public houses, one more than in 1832, and the beerhouses had increased from seven to nineteen. There were also 'eight low lodging-houses in various parts of the town; the persons frequenting them are dirty and objectionable, requiring the surveillance of the police'.

Mr Clark's main concern centred on fresh water and drainage. He states baldly that 'there are no sewers in Penzance and no house drainage.' For their water supplies he identifies six public pumps and fifty-three private wells and pumps, although, to the council's embarrassment, on the wet January day when he tested them four of the six public pumps were either out of action or dry. There were also six open shoots, but the overall evidence was that, especially in the summer, the supply of water was a serious issue. Many of the population had to go some distance to find it, and in a hot summer water-carts collected water from Lariggan stream and sold it for a farthing or halfpenny per pitcher. Unsurprisingly, '... the poor economise its use as much as possible, at the expense of cleanliness and health.'

The method of supply of water for fire-fighting by the town's two fire engines was entirely unique: 'During a fire the water from the reservoir is let loose to run down the streets and dammed up by sand-bags opposite the fire. This process is very inconvenient to the inhabitants.'

The council undertook the challenge. They installed three major cast-iron sewage outfalls, at Chyandour, the Battery Rocks and Lariggan and proceeded slowly to connect the town dwellings to them. As for fresh water, they constructed a new reservoir at Boscathnoe, west of Heamoor, and installed more public wells, underground leats and shoots to make it more accessible.

Nothing seemed beyond the town's enterprise and finance. This was partly due to the increased local prosperity, but funding was partly predicated on the expectation of the new business the coming of the railway would bring.

Richard Trevithick had demonstrated a perfectly viable steam locomotive as long ago as 1804 at Penydarren Ironworks in South Wales in response to a wager. It successfully carried 10 tons of ore (plus around 70 hangers-on) for 10 miles with no trouble except to the track itself. Having won his bet, Trevithick typically lost interest, so it was left to George Stephenson, who had seen another demonstration of Trevithick's locomotive at Gateshead, to continue to experiment with it at the nearby Killingworth Colliery. The early development of rail locomotives was aimed solely at freight transport, at first over short distances. Cornwall's first was from Hayle to Gwennap's rich tin fields. The train had to be drawn up Angarrack Hill by cable and needed the assistance of ropes in one or two places, but it worked well. It showed what a revolution railways could be, as opposed to horses, mules and carts in shifting tons of ore and waste. Stephenson and his son pressed on with their own designs, basing the track width on the arbitrary measurement of one of the wagons at Killingworth, a gauge of 4 foot 8½ inches, founding the Stockton & Darlington Railway in 1825 and the Liverpool–Manchester in 1830.

In 1833, the Great Western Railway was formed and had the good fortune to appoint a genius, Isambard Kingdom Brunel, as its chief engineer. Brunel started from scratch and decided instead on a gauge of just over 7 feet as most suitable in terms of stability and capacity. By 1849, the GWR had reached from London to Plymouth, where it naturally paused. In the meantime, the little Cornwall Railway had successfully created a narrow-gauge line from Penzance to Truro. Two mighty challenges remained, the crossing of the Tamar and the passage of the hills and valleys of north Cornwall requiring thirty-four new viaducts, a daunting engineering feat that took another ten years to achieve. West Cornwall could hardly wait. Its longings were voiced in dubiously poetical terms by Richard Edmonds, secretary of the Cornwall Archaeological Association:

> When Eastern Cornwall shall have made
> The rail she now requires
> And iron roads connect Mount's Bay
> With all Brittania's shires
> Then will this bay again become
> As in the days of yore
> The greatest port in all the land
> For foreign trade and store...

In 1859 his wishes finally came true. A continuous line, albeit with a change at Truro on to the then ubiquitous broad gauge, stretched from Penzance, over Brunel's Royal Albert Bridge, to Brunel-designed Paddington. Broad gauge finally gave way in 1892 after a long legal battle to Stephenson's more cramped narrow gauge, to our eternal loss.

It was a breakthrough in every sense. At a stroke it transformed the town from a remote and obscure dealer in tin and fish to part of the mainstream of Britain's commercial life. For the first time it offered a viable alternative to sea transport as a means of bringing its goods to market, which enabled growers to consider cultivating a far greater variety of produce. The early crops of vegetables encouraged by Penwith's mild climate suddenly gave them a huge advantage, supplying Covent Garden and the Midland markets virtually unopposed for several spring weeks. The sale of early spring flowers months before those from eastern nurseries became available then followed. This market was seized upon by Augustus Smith, tenant and governor of the Isles of Scilly, whose produce was several weeks earlier still. Fish could now be exported to Britain as well as Spain and Italy, not just salted fish in barrels but fresh fish packed in ice destined for Billingsgate. It became practical to transport livestock, anything from day-old chicks to pedigree cattle to circus elephants. In return, the essential supplies of coal, timber, salt, limestone, grain, tools, wine, and fashionable clothes could be ordered one day and arrive the next.

For local people who could afford it, the country was suddenly wide open for travel. Even visiting other parts of Cornwall had been a laborious exercise, so there was an almost child-like thrill in climbing into a railway carriage, however basic, and getting out *somewhere else.*

The converse was even more dramatic. Travellers to Cornwall had become more numerous as its greater comforts encouraged them, particularly well-off gentlefolk looking for a mild winter climate and students of its antiquities and countryside. Suddenly it was open to anyone who could afford the fare. What an adventure, to travel all the way to the end of the line, the romantic Cornwall of Arthur, to stay in one of Penzance's new hotels, to parade along the prom, to take excursions to scenic and historic locations like St Michael's Mount and Land's End, or hail an obliging boatman for a trip around the bay. Local people were suddenly in demand for such tasks as catering, cooking, taxiing, and guiding. They were paid in ready money and tips, so much easier than the hard labour to which they were accustomed. For the first time they experienced up-country 'foreigners' in bulk, and either did or did not adjust to the strangeness of being considered quaint, curious, amusing, in their rural ways and accents.

On the promenade, the Queen's Hotel was already rising to meet the railway tourists' needs and to dominate the promenade. Designed by borough surveyor John Matthews, it was an instant success and had to be extended within ten years of opening.

There was one final major piece of the jigsaw required to match Penzance with its now sky-high aspirations. The guildhall of the market house, splendid as it was, was much too small for the uses and cultural assemblies the townspeople were demanding. In 1862 a plan was prepared for,

A handsome edifice consisting of two wings connected by a central building, one wing to be devoted to the Geological Society, the other wing to serve the dual purpose of Guildhall and County Court, with the Police Station and cells, Council Chamber and committee rooms attached, and the central buildings to be managed by a public company and comprise a large public hall, news room, and other such buildings as may be deemed useful.

Also to be included were the meeting rooms of the local schools board and facilities for a masonic hall.

Some vacant glebe land on Alverton Street, although slightly detached from the town centre, had the space for such a project and was earmarked for the new building. The plans were again drawn up by John Matthews and the foundation stone was laid on 27 April 1864. Three years later, after many funding problems, a relieved mayor Francis Boase officially opened the Public Buildings with great pomp and ceremony. Matthews had created a somewhat severe design in undecorated granite. The top step of its imposing entrance was a monstrous granite slab, 17 feet 8 inches long, and in the forecourt another fine piece of granite work had pride of place, an elegant fountain whose shallow bowl, 12 feet in diameter, was carved from a single piece of stone (now to be seen in St Anthony's Gardens). Its main assembly room was christened after the town's patron saint, St John's Hall, a name which transferred by custom to include the whole building.

It had the desired effect as far as the western press were concerned: 'With hearty working, much personal liberality, and a genuine local patriotism all pulling cordially together, things are done which make the county ring with the praises of Penzance'.

The mayor, aldermen and councillors could sit back for a moment and bask in the warmth of general congratulations.

30

Guides

The first guidebook, *A Guide to the Mount's Bay*, had been published by Dr Paris (at first anonymously as 'A Physician') in 1824, and it was followed by J. S. Courtney's *Guide to Penzance* in 1845. Courtney's Penzance coincided with the building of the north pier and was just in time to celebrate the new 'esplanade'.

In his elegantly written guide, Courtney takes us by the hand and leads us along the pretty Eastern Green, separated from the sea by only a 'stripe of green turf', though shortly destined to carry the first wooden viaduct of the railway, then past the smoky smelting works and tanneries at Chyandour. He proceeds up Market Jew Street, pointing out the extended balcony of the Star Inn beneath which Humphry Davy used to while away time telling stories to his friends, and mourns that no memorial had yet been erected to mark his birthplace. He celebrates the notable architecture of the town already in place, the terraces of North and South Parade, Regent Terrace and Square, Wellington Terrace, Clarence Street and Place, Cornwall Terrace, Morrab Terrace and Place, St Mary's Terrace, St Michael's Terrace and down to Penrose Terrace. 'The other streets are inhabited by the labouring classes', he states in kindly contradiction of Mr Clark's survey just three years later, 'and although they possess nothing very attractive to the stranger, he will look in vain for those squalid habitations so often seen in larger towns'. He pauses to admire the grand market house and its shining dome, occupied in 1845 by the Penwith Natural History Society and open to visitors on Tuesdays, Thursday and Saturdays, the market days.

Courtney meets the celebrated Newlyn women fish-sellers, but warns us that while their strength and hardiness in carrying the huge weight of their wares is to be admired, the 'delicate complexions and jet-black eyes darting their rays' that bewitched Dr Paris are something of an exaggeration. He then passes down Chapel Street. He forebears to comment on one of its most unique properties, the astonishingly gaudy and eccentric Egyptian House recently built by John Lavin, mineralogist and Egyptologist, but notes with approval the large Wesleyan chapel and praises the new chapel (church) of St Mary at length. In the heart of the town he visits the library, next to South Parade, and the Geological Museum in North Parade, both destined soon to be moved into the public buildings. Going up Clarence Street he passes the heavily decorated doorway of the Baptist church of 1836, and lavishes his praises on the rather plain church of St Paul in Clarence Street, privately sponsored by Revd Henry Batten, a supporter of the High Church Oxford movement.

Courtney is no bigot and shares information on all the other places of worship in the town, dedicated to many and various worshippers. These included the Congregational Dissenters in Market Jew Street, the Weslyan Methodists in St Clare Street, the Weslyan Association in Queen Street, the Primitive Methodists in Mount Street, and the Bethel chapel for sailors near the quay. The Catholic church in Rosevean Road is mentioned, including the proposed extension which sadly has yet to take place. A Friends meeting house is operating in Causewayhead (North Street), as is the Jews' synagogue in New Street.

This last one had been set up in 1807. The Jewish community was very small, but it was supported by the famous Asher Laemle ben Eleazar, better known as the distiller Lemon Hart, whose rum business was so successful that he became the official supplier to the British Navy. His distillery was handily nearby at the top of Jennings Street. By Courtney's day the synagogue was well established and Penzance was the focus of Jews in West Cornwall, the next nearest community being at Penryn. It had also gained its own Jewish cemetery, a triangle of enclosed land tucked in behind Leskinnick Terrace on what was then the eastern limit of the town, known for a while as Jerusalem Terrace.

Insightful and beautifully written as Courtney's account is, it cannot compare with *Half a Century of Penzance 1825–1875*, faithfully written from his original notes and added to by his daughter, Louise. This contains far more rich and thorough details than can be reproduced here and is essential reading for any serious student of Victorian Penzance. These are a few of her insights:

On the left hand was Neddy Betty's Lane [present Albert Street]. At the corner was the remains of Betty's Inn, kept at one time by Edward Betty from whence came the name. At this house the Corporation in former times occasionally refreshed themselves.

Dick Rostrum, one of the oddities of the town... sometimes turned the tables on those who played jokes on him. When asked by two gentlemen who took him each by the arm whether he was a rogue or a fool he replied 'I believe I'm betwixt the two' – this gave rise to the saying 'Betwixt and between', says Dick Rostrum.

The shop of Mr Molyneaux, draper, was the first instance in Penzance when the lower part of a house was taken away leaving the upper part standing. It was successfully done by Messrs James and Edward Harvey, the immense weight being kept up by large girders supported by iron pillars ... the result was the finest shop in the west.

The manor of Connerton included nearly the whole of West Penwith ... every butcher in Penzance used to pay annually at Christmas to the bailiff of Connerton a marrow-bone or one shilling.

In the yard over the stables was the Penzance Theatre; of course there was rather a flavour of the stables but in other respects it was tolerably suitable for its purpose. I remember once seeing an American negro perform 'Othello' at this place.

The church-yard was a favourite spot for old sailors, etc., from the quay. In the autumn of 1825 when the first steam-boat came into Penzance I stood with many others in the church-yard watching its approach ... The church bell was not used for calling people to worship, that was done by the town crier Mr Sampson Reynolds who was also the Clerk. He went through the streets every Sunday ringing his bell as he walked.

On the corner of Chapel Street and Voundervour Lane, originally the only carriage road from Penzance to Newlyn, was one large house, believed to be haunted by the ghost of Mrs Baines, who was condemned to spin black wool into white.

In a field where the Queens Hotel now stands was held in 1829 the last wrestling match on a large scale in Penzance.

Rosevean Road was laid out for the purpose of making a carriage drive to the Rev Canon Rogers' property at Lescudjack Castle, which was to have been covered with villas and a very pretty plan was sketched out for it. But it never came to the desired end.

There is a survey of the street markets, which featured among others dozens of shoemakers, fisherwomen, dyers, curriers (of shoe leather), sellers of earthenware, hessian, butter and eggs, 'train' oil, grass seed, and 'it seemed that everyone who had goods to sell availed himself of this opportunity'. The crowded scene was occasionally enlivened by 'a pack of mules laden with copper ore, threading their way through the crowd and sometimes being a little restive'. Many pubs are mentioned, some still in place: the Globe; the Star; the London Inn; the Turk's Head; and others long gone like the Shoulder of Mutton and the Duke of Cumberland. Shopkeepers included drapers, chemists, shoemakers, druggists and grocers (a common combination), booksellers, and others including N. J. Hall's grocery in the Greenmarket, which continued virtually unchanged until after the Second World War.

Courtney's portrait of the town and its people had been anticipated seven years earlier in 1838 by a far more detailed and scientific survey carried out by the Statistical Society of London, later the Royal Statistical Society. It seems that it chose Madron parish and Penzance at random and commissioned Penzance solicitor and historian Richard Edmonds to provide them with an accurate portrait of the social structure of the district.

Edmonds is conscious of the Cornish proclivity for independence at best, quarrel and division at worst, which led to the large number of religious and other institutions. This applied particularly to Nonconformist worship, where the general pattern seemed to be a coming together of like-minded individuals followed at some inevitable point by a split into one or more 'daughter' institutions, often reaching out further and further into the countryside.

He collated the average Sunday congregation attendance numbers. The relative importance of the parish church of Madron with its average weekly congregation of just 150 compares with the regular attendance of 750–850 at St Mary's chapel of ease. These worshippers came and went cheek-by-jowl with the 900–1,000 who attended the adjacent Chapel Street Methodist chapel (though it was St Marys, not the Methodists which gave the street its name). The Jews and the Society of Friends (Quakers) had influence out of all proportion to their membership, which put together amounted to only around thirty, (though there had been another Friends meeting house in Marazion from 1688, still in regular use). The Catholic church's attendance was stated to be no more than forty, though this is doubtful. Meanwhile out in the fields, a faithful average of thirty-five souls received the Word in Tregavarah. Soon to be added (in 1842) was the Wesley Rock chapel in Heamoor, which features as the base of its pulpit a rock on which Wesley was reputed to stand while preaching in open ground nearby.

It was an age of many societies. It seemed to be a mark of civilisation to be enrolled in at least one of these, and they carried out many of the social functions that would later be taken on by government. One of the largest, despite the burgeoning numbers of pubs and beer houses, was the Temperance Society, later the Total Abstinence Society, which reckoned its active membership at 2,100. Methodism had inspired most of its membership, but even in faithful and devout Methodist communities there was some backsliding. In Nonconformist Newlyn, for example, the women and girls employed in cleaning and packing the pilchard catches were granted a glass of brandy every six hours to keep them going. Canny pubs ensured that they had a more discreet back entrance in addition to their front doors.

A number of charities were listed. Principal among them was the Penzance Public Dispensary on the site of the later hospital, which existed

> To offer medical and surgical assistance to those who are not able to procure it; to rescue the poor from Smallpox by encouraging vaccination; to endeavour to effect the recovery of persons in cases of suspended respiration; to impart necessities and comforts as well as the funds will admit.

It was open to all, except those already on the list of parish paupers or domestic servants whose health was presumably the responsibility of their employers. Four other charities attended the sick and infirm: the Humane Society, men who visited the sick at home; the Indigent Sick Society, women who did the same; the Penzance Dorcas Society, named after a provider of clothing to widows in the Acts of the Apostles, who distributed clothing to the poor of the town; and the Mount's Bay Ladies Dorcas Society who did the same in the countryside.

Edmonds counted no fewer than fifty 'schools' in Penzance, though most of these were dames' schools with half a dozen pupils or fewer. Of proper schools there were three: the grammar or classical school which Humphry Davy had attended, with just fifteen boys; the National School in Chapel Street, sponsored by the Church of England, with 225 boys and 150 girls; and the Free School at Chyandour supported by the Bolitho family, with the unique statistic of sixty girls and just six boys. Children in the outlying parts fared worse, tutored only in the basics until they could start work in the fields or the mines. Male literacy in Madron Parish at that time was reckoned at 73 per cent and 51 per cent for females.

By far the largest number of societies were those set up by the entrepreneurial class for their own protection in times of trouble, the Friendly Societies. There were twenty of these in Penzance alone, ranging from basic insurance arrangers for the well-off to some with more philanthropic aspirations, especially for women. Apart from the First Benevolent Female Society, the Female Tee-Total club and the Good Samaritans they were all exclusive to some extent, excluding the over-forties or fifties, and not open to 'soldiers, sailors, fishermen, tinners, livery servants or bailiffs'. The working classes were welcomed only in the improving, if short-lived, Penzance Institution for Providing Useful Knowledge and the Mechanics Institution. Also present in the town, though not included in the survey, were the Freemasons and other related lodges like the Forresters and Oddfellows.

Among the wealth of miscellaneous information in Edmonds' survey was the average number of children per family – 4.6; the highest and lowest temperatures in the last twenty years – 84 degrees and 19 degrees, respectively – with special mention of the heavy fall of snow that persisted for a fortnight in 1823; the number of registered ships – eighty-three; the earliest crops produced so far – a legendary smallholder having sown, grown, produced and sold his entire crop of new potatoes by 1 April; and the landlords' standard requirements to tenant farmers for fertilising their fields, with prescribed quantities of sea-sand, seaweed and ashes (to neutralise their acidity), stable dung and fishmeal.

It was a comprehensive study of the elements of the town, except for the working classes. What made the rapid expansion of Penzance and the creation of so many grand buildings and projects possible was the plentiful supply of cheap labour. Shortly before Edmonds' survey the country had been roused by the injustice of the Tolpuddle martyrs, sentenced to seven years transportation for meeting together in their mutual interest, a nascent Trade Union. The working-class Cornish were, however, instinctively wedded to free enterprise almost as much as their employers, and unionisation never took hold in Cornwall. This left them technically independent but vulnerable to every kind of exploitation, poverty, overcrowding, squalor, disease and crime.

Little was recorded by travellers or official surveys of the lives of ordinary working people, their culture, their pastimes, their sense of humour, their social network or their superstitions. Fortunately, William Bottrell, son of a well-to-do farming family of Raftra, St Levan, had picked up and remembered many colourful stories told around the kitchen fire in his childhood, especially by his grandmother, Mary Vingoe. Though he went to grammar school and was educated in the classics, he never forgot the folk tales he learned in his youth. Later in life he mixed with local tinners, whom he found to be full of 'intelligence, mother-wit, and memories from which I am able to garner an ample harvest'.

Bottrell revealed in his *Hearthside Stories* a whole rich world of local tales: stories of giants and piskeys; the Spriggans, Buccas and Knockers who haunted the dark corners of the mines; witches; mermaids and fairies; ghosts and the houses they haunted; the dreaded shades of Jan Tregeagle and Wild Harris by whom the countryside was still 'walked' at night; the Black Huntsman; the tale of Duffy and the Devil; and many more, most of which would have been well-known to local people.

There were other cultural traditions. There were the feast days with their selection of country sports and mystery plays. At Christmas, Mummers Plays took place in the pubs and squares, along with the related local custom of guise dancing. This consisted mainly of roving from pub to pub in outrageous clothes, often cross-dressed, made up often in black-face, singing, dancing and playing the fool, a brotherhood presumably not open to members of the Total Abstinence Society. (The word guise was short for 'disguise' and also gave rise to the slang word 'geezers'.)

Christianity, and especially Methodism, turned a grim countenance towards anything resembling revelry and put a stop to many of these and other annual celebrations. A vicar of Helston used to pay from his own pocket to take the churchwardens and the choir out of town each Helston Furry Day so that they would not have to witness its innocent celebration of spring.

For many years nothing could succeed in extinguishing Penzance's greatest annual festivity. This was recorded by Courtney, William Borlase and Dr Paris among others. This was Dr Paris' account of 1824:

The most singular custom is perhaps the celebration of the Eve of St John The Baptist, our town saint, which falls on Midsummer Eve and that of the Eve of St Peter, patron of fishermen.

No sooner does the tardy sun sink into the western ocean than the young and old of both sexes, animated by the genius of the night, assemble in the town and different villages of the bay with lighted torches. Tar barrels having been erected on tall poles in the market-place, on the pier and in other conspicuous spots, are soon urged into a state of vivid combustion, shedding an appalling glare on every surrounding object, and when multiplied by numerous reflections in the waves produce at a distant view a spectacle so singular and novel as to defy the powers of description, while the stranger who issues forth to gain a closer view of the festivities of the town may well imagine himself suddenly transported to the regions of the Furies and infernal Gods ... while the shrieks of the female spectators and the triumphant yells of the torch-bearers, with their hair streaming in the wind and their flamboys whirling with inconceivable velocity are realities not calculated to dispel the illusion.

No sooner are the torches burnt out than the numerous inhabitants engaged in the frolic, pouring forth from the quay and its neighbourhood, form a long string, and hand in hand run furiously through every street vociferating 'An eye! An eye! An eye!' At length they suddenly stop and the two last of the string, elevating their clasped hands, form an eye to this vast needle, through which the thread of the populace runs. And thus they continue to repeat the game until weariness dissolves the union, which rarely happens before midnight.

On the following day festivities of a very different character enliven the bay, and the spectator can hardly be induced to believe that the same actors are engaged in both dramas. At about four or five o clock in the afternoon the country people, dressed in their best apparel pour into Penzance from neighbouring villages for the purpose of performing an aquatic divertisement. At this hour the quay and pier are crowded with holiday-makers where a number of vessels, many of which are provided with music for the occasion, lie in readiness to receive them. In a short time the embarkation is completed and the sea continues for many hours to present a moving picture of the most animating description.

Courtney adds that on Midsummer Eve,

Fireworks of every description are set off without intermission and a continued series of flight and chase continues for many hours, it being a principal part of the sport to steal as quietly as possible amongst a crowd and disperse them by the unexpected report of a cracker ... although accidents have sometimes happened it seldom occurs that any are seriously hurt or that quarrels take place.

He also adds that all this takes place 'in spite of his Worship the Mayor', as the mayor 'always causes a proclamation to be made against these proceedings, which is however entirely disregarded'. A former mayor, Henry Boase, had firmly decided in 1817 to 'prevent the mischief of the Midsummer Bonfires by making an arranged and orderly exhibition on some proper ground out of the town.' But this had been gleefully ignored in the usual way.

Part of the proceedings was the election of a mock mayor. This traditional reversal of roles goes back to the Roman *Bacchanalia* and was once common in many parts of Cornwall. One year the mock mayor's procession in Penryn was met by the actual mayor and constables who, considering that matters had got out of hand, proposed to lock up the mischief makers in the town gaol to cool down. However, the crowd was with the revellers, and it was the mayor and constables who spent the rest of the night in the cells. As Courtney records, there was considerable official opposition to this rowdy occasion that Borlase called *Goluan*, meaning 'The Feast of John', and many serious attempts were made to stamp it out.

A later writer, Edgar Rees from Penzance, recalled some more elaborate variations. To the sound of the band of the local rifle volunteers an elaborate set-piece of fireworks was lit, while in the Greenmarket,

The Mock Mayor might often be seen surrounded by a number of youngsters, each holding a lighted hand-rocket above his head, the sparks falling about him giving the impression he was standing in the middle of a fountain of fire.

By then the fire brigade was standing by, and at midnight attached a hose to a hydrant 'and a stream of water dowsed the fires as well as baptising several of the fiery youngsters'.

The town's celebrations were considerably more demure during the royal visit in the summer of 1846. Queen Victoria, Prince Albert and some of their four children had undertaken a cruise on the royal yacht, and after visiting Falmouth sailed into Mount's Bay. There is a brass plaque in the form of Victoria's foot to mark where she landed on the Mount. The party sailed from there over to Penzance where they moored by mistake at the end of the incomplete North Pier instead of the completed section which had been made ready for them, as the Prince discovered when he stepped ashore. The mistake was quickly rectified and the pier was named the Albert Pier in commemoration of the visit.

There was another unexpected consequence of their stay. On their way around the Lizard Prince Albert decided to go ashore in Kynance Cove, and was introduced by the boatman to the Lizard's unique coloured serpentine stone. This had been worked into souvenirs on a small scale on the Lizard for many years, and a Penzance resident called Drew had started a similar business in Penzance. This had been so successful that a Penzance consortium decided to build a factory to supply souvenir-hungry tourists and also to make larger and more ornate pieces in the Classical style. In 1840 they acquired the derelict buildings of the defunct Wherry Mine. Prince Albert had been so entranced by the existence of such an exotic 'Cornish marble' that he arranged for the Queen to accompany him to Wherrytown to see it. This led to orders for mantelpieces and other large items for Osborne House, the elegant royal retreat under construction in the Isle of Wight.

With royal patronage the business took off in earnest and with the inclusion of some London businessmen, The London & Penzance Serpentine Co. was founded in 1851 with offices in Pall Mall, from which their products caused a small sensation at the Great Exhibition. Soon afterwards, a rival company was set up at Poltesco Cove on the Lizard itself, and The Lizard Serpentine Co. also opened London offices on The Strand. However, the demand soon worked out the Lizard's limited quarries and the vogue for serpentine declined, leading to the closure of the factories in 1865, although the souvenir trade continued to prosper in Penzance for many years, and still does in the Lizard village.

31

High Noon

In 1872, Mr Courtney's wish finally came true and a fine statue of Sir Humphry Davy was erected, mounted on a huge pedestal of Lamorna granite in front of the market house to dominate the main street and greet all visitors to the town. He looked down on a town whose aspirations had almost all been fulfilled. As well as its mainstays of tin and copper, fishing and farming, it was home to a large variety of enterprises. A later commentator writing in *The Cornishman* noted,

> It is hardly possible for anyone to be in the town many hours without being struck with the thriving aspect of the place. The number of shops, stores and warehouses seems quite out of proportion to the size of the place, and the doors of banks and the Post office are constantly on the swing. Down on the quays steamers, ships and a multitude of smaller craft may be seen loading and unloading, some engaged in foreign and others in the coasting trade; fishermen are busy overhauling their boats in preparation for the spring mackerel fishery; trains with passengers or merchandise are constantly arriving or departing; and numerous buses from morning to night ply their remunerative calling between the town and the neighbouring population, and on the Great Market Day (Thursday) thousands of people intent on spending and buying pour in from the surrounding districts.

Among the many local trades the correspondent noted were: the smelting works at Chyandour, still in full swing; an ice works at Gulval, and also a factory for producing novel fizzy drinks; rope making in several locations, including a stretch in the later Alverton Estate still called The Ropewalk and another one at the rear of Tolver Road; flour mills, now powered by steam finally replacing the old monopoly of the Tolcarne water mill, in Gulval and at the premises by the station still known as Branwell's Mill; next to that the gasworks with the distinctive odour that many older Penzance people can still recall; Holman's iron foundry and two other smaller foundries; sawmills and timber merchants in Wherrytown, Coinagehall Street and Victoria Square; five tanners and leather merchants; three coach-builders and a cart and wagon maker; four furniture makers; a nursery garden at Rosevale in Alexandra Road; eight basket-makers; a brickworks near Marazion; China clay works at Towednack and Leswidden near St Just (the latter inspiring serious proposals for an extension of the railway line to St Just, which only failed because the two rival consortia could not agree); quarries at Lamorna, Castallack, Penlee Point and Sheffield (the last so called because of the former coal miners who were brought down from Yorkshire to work it); and the numerous bakehouses, butchers, greengrocers, dairies and other shops. This saw many professions benefit from such a boom, including bankers, printers, house-builders with all their individual skills, house-agents, agricultural merchants, and naturally, in litigious Cornwall, an increasing number of solicitors.

Together with the industries came a huge demand for housing and a second expansion of the built-up area. To the east the hillside disappeared under an intensive development of 'artisans' dwellings', an area known anecdotally as the 'Battlefields' (according to some stories because of quarrels between rival builders, though it may be of far older origin), comprising streets dedicated to well-known saints such as St Mary, St Michael, St Francis and St Phillip, and more obscure ones such as St Dominic, St Henry and St Warren, plus Gwavas Street, presumably named when they had run out of saints.

To the north, the vacant land between Bread Street and Taroveor Road, mostly belonging to the Tonkin family, hosted a mixture of higher and lower middle-class terraces parallel to Causewayhead: High Street, with another Methodist chapel, Belgravia Street, St James Street, Albert Terrace (at the top of which is a private garden overlooked by one of the many reproductions of St John's holy head), Alma Terrace and Place (named like English streets everywhere after battles in the Crimean war) and the former stone quarry of Victoria Square, overlooked by a pretty Gothic-style cottage, once the house of the quarry foreman.

To the west a new road was conceived by John Matthews, architect of the public buildings, to 'square off' the western limits of the town and unite Alverton with the end of the promenade. It was built in 1865 and named after the new Princess of Wales, Alexandra.

There followed further infilling of the open land between Alverton Street and the seafront. The area known as Morrab fields was once owned by the Tremenheeres but later split into smaller lots. On the eastern side a brewer, Samuel Pidwell, had built Morrab House (now Morrab library) in 1841, a fine Georgian villa with a large garden. The land was purchased by the town corporation in 1889 and laid out as a public park and subtropical garden. The gardens became one of the great attractions of Penzance and were visited by many botanists and horticulturalists, amazed to find what exotic plants, shrubs and trees could be grown outdoors in Mount's Bay's climate.

The west side of Morrab fields was acquired by the mill owner J. R. Branwell who built Penlee House on it, surrounded by 15 acres of parkland. Between the two, Morrab Road burst through to make a way from Clarence Street straight down to the promenade, demolishing three or four houses in North Parade on its way and splitting it into two. Trewithen Road and Hawkins Road, letting into Alexandra Road, completed the development of the area with large family houses for the more prosperous.

Another long-held wish was fulfilled in 1871, not with a bang but an administrative whimper when the last formalities were completed to confirm on the church of St Mary the status it had assumed unofficially for so long, to be the parish church of the parish of Penzance.

The last ties with the parish of Madron were cut, though the vast and gloomy parish union workhouse on the moors above the village continued to dominate the skyline and the imagination of all those close to the breadline in the surrounding communities for years to come. The parishes themselves were changing their allegiance, as the diocese of Exeter was finally acknowledged to be too long and rural and too numerous in population to be managed centrally, and the new diocese of Truro was formed in 1876. In the same year a new sub-parish was created to serve the increased population of the east of Penzance with the creation of St John's church above Trewartha Terrace, in which the bell of the old St Mary's chapel still rests. Yet another Methodist chapel also appeared – the United Methodist Free church in Parade Street. William Booth came to Penzance on two occasions and set up a Salvation Army hostel in 1881.

Humanitarian services also grew. The Penzance Dispensary was extended in 1876 by the addition of an eight-bed infirmary, the forerunner of the later West Cornwall Hospital.

At the other end of town a new lifeboat house was built of Lamorna granite at the bottom of Jennings Street. The Royal National Institution for the Preservation of Life from Shipwreck, later the RNLI, had been formed in 1824 and Penzance's false start in this initiative was overcome mainly due to the efforts of town mayor and Lloyds' agent Richard Pearce. A series of temporary lifeboat houses had been used, and in 1865 a new lifeboat, the *Alexandra* was greeted with a formal reception, taken in procession down the new Alexandra Road followed by a cross-section of the great and the good, in the following order: St Buryan Artillery Band; coastguards, Royal Naval reserve and pensioners; the lifeboat *Alexandra* and crew; St Buryan Artillery; Penzance Brass Band; the First Duke of Cornwall's Rifles; Oddfellows with their regalia; Morvah Band; Members of the Wesleyan; Provident Society; Foresters in full costume; Penzance Drum and Fife Band; the Danish Standard (Alexandra was the former Princess of Denmark); the British Standard and Ensign; the town arms, sergeants-at-mace, town clerk and clerk of the peace; the mayor and justices; the corporation, clergy, magistrates and officers of HM Customs; Towednack Band; Trinity men (forty-five craftsmen involved in building the new lighthouse on the Wolf Rock); the Newmill Band and the police.

These arranged themselves together with a huge crowd on the promenade, 'not one of whom budged during a brief but pitiless shower', and the boat was duly christened by the Lady Mayoress.

Soon her replacement the *Richard Lewis*, named after the secretary of the RNLI, was performing great feats of heroism, as when she went to the assistance of the barque *North Britain* wrecked near the Mount in a terrible storm in 1868. Despite being totally capsized the lifeboat was righted, re-launched and succeeded in saving eight lives from the wreck shortly before it broke up, a rescue which earned the station five of the RNLI's coveted silver medals. These were presented in St John's Hall, pleasingly by Richard Lewis himself.

Penzance's first official guide for tourists was published in 1876. It is still an excellent piece of work, on a different scale of aspiration and scholarship than any subsequent guide. It contained a history of the borough by Mr George Millett, 'topographical and ichthyological studies' by Mr Thomas Cornish, and an antiquarian section by Mr William Borlase. There were many other learned contributions including a complete survey of Penwith's botany, together with more practical pages on train times, cab fares, advertisements for hotels, hats, sewing machines, baking powder, pianos, Mr Drew's serpentine souvenirs, and a fair number of Mr George Millett's other printed works. A sense of pride and satisfaction rings through its pages. Within the golden half-mile radius of the borough all was well. However, outside the bounds there were the first signs that West Cornwall had reached its apogee and was beginning to decline.

32

Holding On

In the 1861 census the population of Cornwall reached 369,390, a figure it would not surpass until 1971. The first crisis came in the copper mines. As the rest of the world learnt to exploit its mineral resources, very often with technology learned and perfected in Cornwall, more abundant and accessible deposits were found. In the next ten years the production of copper in Cornwall, once two-thirds of the entire world's supply, fell by 50 per cent. Many mines which had been working close to their margins or trying to keep going through an unprofitable period cut their losses and closed down. Once closed, the waters rose in their galleries, roofs fell in, machinery and sheds rotted, and it took more than a small upward fluctuation to save them. Adventurers lost their money and thousands of miners facing starvation followed the engineering equipment to the new mining fields over the sea. Some were drawn to the Australian gold rush, but there were many other parts of the globe into which they could stick a pin: South Africa; South America in the footsteps of Trevithick; Mexico; California; and Canada, so many areas of dramatic growth as opposed to the slow depression at home.

The trickle of miners away from Cornwall became a flood, while the families waited behind, subsisting any way they could while waiting for money to arrive by the post. Many miners were simply never heard of again once the trains had taken them up the line to the seaports. Some were injured or killed, some prospected in vain, others found consolation in new families and forgot those at home. But it was not all bad news. Others were free for the first time from the oppression of the mine owners and their paltry wages, and earned sums they had never dreamed of. Experience in the hard-rock mines of Cornwall fitted them for almost any task and they became supervisors, consultants, mine captains, sought-after and respected for the first time.

But back at home villages emptied, pubs and churches grew quiet, mine yards disappeared under bushes and weeds and sadness fell on the land. The blow fell hardest in the copper-rich east, but in West Penwith even great and venerable mines like Ding Dong shut down and flooded. The price of tin did not fall to the same extent as copper, and the stronger tin mines enjoyed another twenty years of good business, though due to mechanisation the number of employees and labourers fell considerably. Adding to the hazards of mining was the rock drill, which made light work of the stone but threw up a deadly dust which soaked into the lungs. The China clay works were an alternative for some but miners were a proud clan and most preferred to listen to the calls of 'Cousin Jack' elsewhere in the world encouraging them to leave Cornwall and join in the bonanza.

The fishing fleets had enjoyed a surge of boatbuilding and success, but this too began to fade. This was partly due to the failure of the pilchard fishery. Shoals of pilchards had arrived regularly if unpredictably every autumn, a brief but highly profitable cash crop, but towards the end of the century they changed their habits. The pilchard fishery came to a stuttering end, but never again would the huge shoals of millions of fish darken the seas in Mount's Bay or St Ives.

Another paradoxical problem for fishermen was the coming of the railway. This had been a boon to begin with as the market for fresh fish expanded, but after a while other fishing fleets, especially those depending on the North Sea herring fishery, took notice of the abundant Cornish fishing grounds and realised that they too could catch fish and send them off to market by train from Penzance. Cornish fishermen had never had to face serious competition before, and did not like it.

There were other aggravating factors. Many east coast boats were steam powered, able to put to sea when they wished and steam in any direction they liked, whereas the home fleet was still made up of sailing boats. There was also a religious issue. Methodist Cornish fleets did not put to sea on the Sabbath, while their rivals had no such scruples. This meant that the visitors landed several days' worth of fish unopposed on a Monday morning and spoiled the market for the rest of the week. Matters soon came to a head in Newlyn.

Though less than a mile apart, Newlyn and Penzance were different worlds. Penzance had always done its best to stymie Newlyn's ambitions and it was not until the fishing boat *Jane* was lost off Penzance quay, within sight of the horrified population, that the call for a proper harbour of refuge in Mount's Bay was finally heard. Newlyn's south quay had been built and work began on the north arm to enclose a fine harbour of 40 acres. In 1894 it was officially opened by Penzance's mayor in a gesture of reconciliation, admitting in his speech that relationships had not always been ideal but offering the 'right hand of friendship' for the future.

Two years later in 1896, the tension between the Newlyn men and the 'Yorkies' – actually mostly from Lowestoft in Suffolk – rose to such an extent that on Monday 18 May, as they were landing the Sunday catch, around sixteen of the Lowestoft boats were set upon by a large and furious crowd of local men and their fish were thrown into the harbour. The following day the police arrived and skirmishes ensued (though the only recorded casualty was an Inspector Matthews who was hit on the head by a fish-box), and the matter was reported to the authorities. It was a long time since Cornish rebellions had troubled Parliament, and with something of an overreaction Parliament sent down a special train containing a regiment of 350 Royal Berkshires, who marched into Newlyn in their red uniforms amid jeers of derision. On the next day a group of youths from Penzance, together with some 'Yorkies' who had moved their boats there, clashed with the Newlyn fishermen on Newlyn Green and the troops had to form a cordon to keep them apart. To add to the farce of the situation a naval ship gloriously named HMS *Ferret* arrived in the bay to assist, followed later by two more naval gunboats, while Porthleven and even St Ives fishermen sailed around to Newlyn in solidarity with the Newlyn men. As the situation gradually simmered down, Penzance Corporation offered the Lowestoft fleet landing facilities in their own harbour, which they filled from side to side. The right hand of friendship appeared to be back in its pocket and relationships between Penzance and Newlyn deteriorated further.

However, there was one completely unexpected development that favoured Newlyn more than its neighbour. Sitting in the Union Hotel one morning in January 1884 was a young itinerant artist called Stanhope Forbes, who wrote to his mother to say he was looking for 'a more picturesque place than Manaccan' and was about to explore Porthleven, 'unless I prefer a place called Newlyn, within a mile of this town.'

He did, and he was not the first. Walter Langley and several others were already there and by the end of that year *The Cornishman* reported twenty-seven full-time artists in residence. They came to Mount's Bay in a roundabout way, having mostly been influenced in Paris by the new fashion for natural scenes and ordinary working people, preferably outside *en plein air*. Many of them headed for Brittany, and on returning to England realised that their native country had its own 'Brittany'. They sought out the most characteristic working fishing ports and soon settled on St Ives and Newlyn. Surprisingly, the chemistry between the artists, most of whom enjoyed private means, and the tough fishermen worked well. The artists treated the fishing community with due respect and the fishermen appreciated the accuracy and sympathy of their portraits, as well as the few pence they or their hard-working families could earn by just 'sitting'.

Penzance had already had an art school for some time, firstly in Voundervour Lane and then in a quirky building at the top of Morrab Road designed by the famous Sivanus Trevail, extended in 1888 with a 'twin' building as an art museum, later the public library. It provided one of the few home-grown artists to rival the outside invasion – Harold Harvey. Harvey was born in North Parade and attended the Penzance Art School under the tuition of Norman Garstin, before spending two years completing his education in Paris. He came back to Cornwall to stay, though he deserted Penzance for Newlyn. In 1894, the philanthropist John Passmore Edwards funded the building of Newlyn's own gallery in New Road which he dedicated to the 'Cornish Wonder', the portraitist John Opie. Most of the 'school's' early works were painted in and around Newlyn, but later Forbes and others ventured into Penzance, portraying Market Jew Street and the railway station among other subjects.

Building in Penzance had never stopped and the fashion had turned to terraces of large granite family houses for the middle class. To the east, Penzance spilled over the hill beneath Lescudjack Castle with Chyandour Terrace looking over the horse-drawn traffic and the smoky railway line to the sea. Rising up the hill, wrapping around the old town limits of Penrose and Trewartha Terraces and the Battlefields, came plainer bulkier dwellings such as Lanoweth Road, Thornberry Terrace, Penare Road, Lescudjack Road, Barwis Hill, Castle Road, etc.

Leading north from Taroveor Road were more substantial terraces like Tolver Road and Place, some built beside Coombe Road on the Tremenheere Estate, as in Tremenheere Road and Pendarves Road. Local architect Oliver Caldwell, who had designed many grand and even eccentric individual buildings around the town, including the highly decorated brick-faced shop premises opposite the bottom of Causewayhead, is ironically celebrated in one of its plainer streets, Caldwells Road.

To the south-west, Penzance's most favoured quarter, several small pretty terraces were built in the area known as Redinnick behind the Promenade, and the more sizable and ambitious Mennaye Road arose opposite the open Mennaye Fields.

Even more Methodist churches sprang up, one hosting the Methodist New Connection on a corner of Mennaye Road, and the more ambitious Richmond Methodist church in Tolver Place, described in Peter Law's exemplary 'Review of the Architecture of Penzance' in Pool's *History of Penzance*, as a fine example of Arts and Crafts Gothic.

The Education Act of 1870 required local boards to make provision for all the children in their area, and the Education Act of 1880 made attendance compulsory, at least to the age of eleven and later twelve. This was of particular benefit to the country children who had often been put to work as soon as they were able with the minimum of education. Elementary schools were built in various convenient parts of the town, mostly named after saints, and others were formed by converting large private houses. Anxious to avoid these, several private schools were founded for the children of gentlefolk, again often in large, elegant houses. One of the earliest was the Penzance Church of England High School for Girls that began in Clarence House, later the home of St Erbyn's School, and then moved to Trewithen House a little further west where it was renamed the School of St Clare.

Penzance gained one more claim to fame. At some point in 1879, Messrs Gilbert and Sullivan rejected the reputed working title of 'The Robbers of Redruth' in preference for something equally sonorous. *The Pirates of Penzance* (or *The Slave of Duty*) opened on New Year's Eve in New York and proceeded to entrance both England and America as their former triumphs had done. It may not have been the dignified entrance into public consciousness that the corporation would have wished for, but the connection stuck and the town eventually embraced it in many ways. On both sides of the Atlantic, 'Penzance' became a familiar word, though few knew any more about it than its utterly mythical band of bold buccaneers who continue to represent the town on stages round the world.

33

The Early Twentieth Century

Visual portrayals of Penzance and its surrounds no longer depended on engravings or the work of local artists. Popular photography had revealed the town in sepia portraits and postcards showing sedate streets, tidy buildings, various kinds of horse transport, the busy harbour, the wide-open seafront, Market Jew Street and Humphry Davy's statue, designed to tell a story of Penzance's attractions and success.

Side by side with the photographic evidence came the initiatives taken by later generations to record the lives of their forebears while they were still alive to tell them. Living memory was not restricted to one generation but held oral details of many earlier eras, recorded in family bibles or passed down from one generation to the next. Fascination with the past was nothing new. The Natural History and Antiquarian Society of Penzance had been formed as early as 1845 and received (and published) distinguished reports on ancient sites and discoveries as well as thorough scientific explorations of the area's flora and fauna, though little detail of contemporary lives. J. S. Courtney's notes had included several personal glimpses, for example,

> About the middle of the north side of Market Jew Street lived three maiden sisters named Read. They were attendants at church and at such times the eldest always came out first, then the second-born and lastly the youngest. In this order they walked to church and in the same order they returned. The arrangement of their tea-table was also very peculiar, each sister having a separate tea-pot.

Or the itinerant knife-grinder,

> He was ambitious of having a very long name painted on his machine to announce his trade. When I enquired what it meant the man said he

didn't know but it was the longest word that could be found – the word was 'Honorifacabilitudinatas'. He was also a corn doctor, and one of his patients informed me, a very skilled operator.

Or the redoubtable Mrs Gudgeon who kept a fine house in Alverton, who 'used to express herself strongly about educating servants. "Bother your education! Bye and bye the servants behind your chairs will be correcting your grammar!"'

Meanwhile, the foreground was changing as the century turned. In a thrilling incident in 1898, a Daimler, making the first motor journey from John o' Groats to Land's End at an average speed of 10 mph, entered Market Jew Street:

As we reached the town and commenced the long ascent our ride became a triumphal procession. The elevated footways as well as the roads were crowded with sightseers. Every window had its occupants and a perfect roar of applause greeted us as we progressed ... with all the available police force of the town engaged in keeping a narrow way for our progress.

Or, as *The Cornishman* put it,

Great excitement prevailed as the machine hove in sight and proceeded very swiftly and easily up Market Jew Street. A stop was made for a few minutes outside the Western Hotel and admiring crowds endeavoured to sniff as much ill smell of benzoline and hear as much whirring of the works as time allowed them.

There had been a strange emptying of roads since the arrival of the railways, filled only by the popularity of the bicycle. The last turnpikes became county roads in 1885. The early requirement for motor vehicles was to carry a crew of three, two aboard and one walking ahead with a red flag or at night a red lantern, but this had been lifted and the roads were open for all. With motor cars came garages, many of them former blacksmiths, cycle shops, stables and coach-builders. Penzance's first adventurers in the garage trade were foundry owners Holmans, and S. R. Taylor & Sons, engineers.

From 1904, all motor cars had to be registered with their registration numbers and letters of origin displayed on them. Cornwall was delegated the letters 'AF', then 'RL' and in the late 1920s 'CV'. In 1904, just 100 were registered in Cornwall and AF 500 was not reached until 1910 (a Wolseley Siddeley belonging to Maj. Hugh Bateman, for his private use and also in his official duties as chief constable of Cornwall). Motor buses followed, the first sponsored by the entrepreneurial GWR to add another strand to its railway services. Many local roads were still rough muddy lanes through which they could not pass. Their first service ran from Penzance to Marazion. West of Penzance many tracks and lanes were deeply rutted by heavy steam 'traction' engines pulling even heavier land trains of wagons to deliver coal to the mines and carry the ore back to the harbour. The track to Newlyn originally ran next to the sea, but it had been washed away many times, and was eventually replaced further inland by the present New Road. The impact of road traffic was less instant and dramatic than that of the railways and local cars were still relatively few until the 1930s.

On Coombe Road, the old Penzance Grammar School, which had moved over the years from one location to another (including the market house) and had closed down twice, came to rest as the County School for Boys in 1909, and three years later was accompanied on the other side of its playing fields by the Girls' County School, accessed from St Clare Street.

Other emblems of modern life were appearing. The telegraph arrived on its raised poles around 1890, and by 1912 Penzance was lit no longer by the faithful gasworks but by electricity. In 1900, Corpus Christi Fair included a 'biograph' entertainment presented by Professor Anderton of Anderton & Rowland on his new projector, attracting a large crowd. Soon, music halls were being adapted to show moving pictures. One of them, the Victoria Hall Music Hall in Causewayhead, later the Savoy Cinema, began showing films in 1912 and has been showing films ever since, reputedly the longest continuously running cinema in England.

Another entertainment of a more physical kind was rugby football. Penzance had put together a team as early as 1870, playing twenty-a-side until 1876, including thirteen forwards, which made it little different from the hurling of old. They played first in the grounds of Poltair House on the road to Madron and in various other locations around the town. It suited Penzance men very well, and they were Cornwall champions in 1896 and 1897. Penzance RFC provided Barrie Bennetts for the Cornwall team that won the national County Championship in 1908, and also for the England team in the 1908 Olympic Games. From 1894 onwards Newlyn created its own team, playing on a sloping field at St Golder. They were not of Penzance's standards but were reputed as a hard team and 'good singers', often preceding a game with some rousing Methodist hymns. Relationships with their near neighbour were well represented by a minute in their rulebook: 'We accept no player or committeeman from Penzance'.

The original railway station, unkindly described at the time as 'a large dog's house of the nastiest and draughtiest kind' had been rebuilt in 1880 and in 1904 hosted the first arrival of the Cornish Riviera Express, the 'Riv'. This sped daily through southern England without stopping until it came to Plymouth and then served local stations down to Penzance, taking a mere seven hours for the journey and arriving more often than not on time.

From 1904 onwards the price of tin rose to such an extent that some western mines were worth reopening, while the replacement of steam with electric power allowed a huge saving in both coal and manpower. The price fluctuated until the outbreak of the First World War but output continued to rise. However, miners continued to drain out of Cornwall, along with others determined to seek new lives overseas. By 1911, there were around 7,000 miners left in Cornwall from the tens of thousands in the bustling crowds the older people still remembered. Danger still stalked the mines, and in 1894 miners in Wheal Owles at St Just inadvertently broke through to the defunct Wheal Drea workings nearby. Wheal Drea was flooded with seawater that rushed into Wheal Owles, drowning nineteen men and a boy.

The harbour, with or without its complement of Lowestoft fishermen, continued to prosper. A new road had snaked around the wharves in 1881, completed pragmatically by a swing bridge allowing access into the Abbey Basin and dry dock. It was constructed from an adapted railway turntable, and named after five times mayor of Penzance and former MP, Charles Ross. The floating dock with its lock gates had been enclosed in 1884. Steamers continued to carry goods unsuitable for the railway, and a steamer service had been established to the Isles of Scilly, to the relief of those who had previously had to rely on a sailing journey which could take anything from a few hours to as much as two days.

Among the more relaxed visitors to Penzance was the naturalist and chronicler W. H. Hudson. He was less than impressed with the town:

The town itself interested me as little as any country town I have seen. Streets narrow, some narrower still, some straight, some very crooked with houses on either side all more or less mean or commonplace in their appearance.

However, Hudson was as keen a student of the human animal as any other and the market-day crowd came in for more favourable comment:

> Not only was this the healthiest-looking crowd I had ever seen in a town, without a sickly or degraded face in it, but it was undoubtedly the most cheerful and at the same time the most sober. It was a new and curious experience to find myself in a considerable gathering of rustics who had succeeded in getting through their day so pleasantly without the aid of intoxicants.

Hudson's account of the inevitable tourist pilgrimage to Land's End is a classic, noting how the spirits of those in the packed coaches gradually declined as they near the famed spot:

> ... the bright eager look that expected so much ... increasing as they advance over that rude moorland country ... fading out of the various faces at the end, to that blank look ... 'Is this the Land's End? Is this all?'

The population of Penzance was falling. In the 1811 census it was 4,022. Ninety years later it had reduced to 3,088, and still further by 1911. But then came the First World War, which changed everything. Its greedy consumption of men sucked away fishermen for the Royal Naval Reserve and miners for the army, causing serious shortages and rising prices. The great boom was over and wartime austerity took its place. A. L. Rowse described the local scene in the village of his childhood as it slowly emptied of men and led to the night scares, the lack of police, the terror of strangers and tramps, the gradual neglect of formerly cared for places and buildings and even the important question of who was to kill the Christmas fowl.

The war broke out in time to cancel any celebrations of Penzance borough's tercentenary, but in commemoration the Bolitho gardens were laid out on the seafront between Lariggan and Newlyn.

A naval base was established in Penzance, mainly escorting convoys to France but also using fishing boats to survey shipping. A new terror was abroad off Mount's Bay to replace the privateers and xebecs of the past, German submarines who preyed successfully on merchant ships. Army units came to Penzance for training, and a prisoner of war camp was established at Chyandour. Anti-German feeling rose and rose, as D. H. Lawrence discovered when he moved to Zennor with his German wife and was accused of signalling to enemy submarines after dark.

The most visible innovation in Mount's Bay was the Newlyn Air Station. Using the reliably calm sea conditions of Gwavas Lake, a shore base and landing stage for seaplanes was set up below the workings of Penlee Quarry on the road to Mousehole, which had started operations around 1900. From there a detachment of the RFC and later the newly formed 235 Squadron of the Royal Air Force flew Short Type 184 and 240 seaplanes on missions all around the western approaches. Some of these were for reconnaissance but they were armed and on the lookout for submarines, carrying depth charges as well as small bombs. A short concrete jetty was built for the tenders that served them, often mistaken now for a quarry pier.

Looking in the other direction there was an even more spectacular sight. An airship base was set up on the Lizard at Bonython and Mullion and the giant dirigibles also went hunting submarines with some success.

More and more men left the area as conscription took the place of the carefree volunteering spirit in which the war had started. Most of them were to return, but Penzance added its tally to the roll of honour taken from every town and village, over 200 dead and uncounted wounded, including names from almost every local family. All classes combined in death, and Penzance's losses included men of every station, from Lt William Torquill McLeod Bolitho, killed in action in France, to the four sons of Mrs Rowe of St Henry Street: Charlie, killed by shrapnel in a naval engagement; Bertie, a merchant seaman drowned when his ship SS *Coath* was torpedoed; Sidney, killed in action with the Royal Worcestershire Regiment in France in 1917; and Fred, who came home but died of his wounds in 1919. By the worst twist of fate, many others who did come home succumbed to the influenza epidemic shortly afterwards.

34

The Hungry Years

West Cornwall emerged from the war in a much grimmer mood, and tried to recover life as it had been before. The fishing fleet was reconstituted and benefited at first from the rested fishing grounds and the demand from the English market, but prices gradually fell back and competition from French and Belgian boats increased.

Mining – what was left of it – had also revived, the price of tin reaching new heights due to war's demands. However, the mines had suffered from the insistent demand coupled with the ever-decreasing number of available men. This meant that all efforts were dedicated to increase production from existing lodes, which meant no one was prospecting for new deposits, as the old mining saying went, 'Picking the eyes out of the mine'. Between 1920 and 1921 the price of tin dropped from £400 a ton to £140. It was the last straw for all but a few, and those miners not able to follow the previous exodus abroad suffered terribly from the depression. The dole did not even feed families adequately and only soup kitchens and other charitable acts kept them from starvation.

St Just suffered yet another blow. On 20 October 1919 the shift was coming up in the Levant Mine when the iron strap securing the 'man engine' broke at the top. A man engine was a series of vertical beams with small projections on which a man could stand and a series of fixed platforms on the sides, so that when the beam rose and fell the miner could step on and off and rise, level by level. Around 100 men were on the engine when it collapsed and fell into the depths, and thirty-one were crushed to death. Penwith's north coast was no stranger to funerals, but this was the greatest disaster in the area's history. The lower levels of Levant were never reopened. A relief fund was soon subscribed, although this led to further resentment. The funds were held in a trust administered by prominent local businessmen, from whom those in need had to beg for every necessity and prove their need for as much as a pair of shoes to the trustees' satisfaction.

The war had begun to fracture the rigid social class system, and the drastic effects of unemployment caused a sullen revolt against society's inequalities. It was not in the nature of the Cornish to strike and few joined in the General Strike, but the relationship between master and man was never the same. Neither was the relationship between men and women. Having lobbied with great bravery but little success through the pre-war years, women were finally given voting powers (for the over-thirties in 1918, and full equality in 1928). In the absence of men they had undertaken all kinds of roles previously thought un-ladylike, working in factories, driving buses, undertaking all kinds of manual labour, earning their own money and enjoying some independence. When the men returned they were reluctant to go back into the kitchen and fulfil the ideal of the Victorian wife.

As the 1920s turned into the '30s the nationwide need for relief from the general gloom helped to revive the tourist trade. This had ceased almost completely during the war, and those who could afford it returned with pleasure to the seaside. However, apart from such pockets of gaiety, there was little to be cheerful about. The coastal trade into Penzance harbour shrank away and the fishing fleet was surviving on scraps. A telling statistic is the record of the lifeboat, which had by now moved to – and taken its name from – its 1912 boathouse at Penlee Point. It recorded no more than eight missions from 1930 to 1939. By an irony of fate the Newlyn fishing fleet survived only by returning the compliments of 1896 and sailing en masse every autumn to the North Sea to work its fishing grounds alongside the Lowestoft boats.

Administrative life went on. In 1934 the government decided to reduce the number of individual boroughs by means of amalgamation into larger ones. In terms of West Cornwall this caused the old rivals of Camborne and Redruth to be forced into unwilling union, St Ives to join with Lelant and Carbis Bay, and Hayle to lose its urban status altogether. As for Penzance, the old half-mile radius granted by King James I was finally to be extinguished and extended in every direction except the sea. Included in the borough of Penzance were Mousehole, Newlyn, Paul village, Sheffield, Heamoor, and much of Gulval. Penzance's ambitions to swallow Madron and Marazion were not realised, but its area of control rose from 438 to 3,155 acres, and its population from 11,342 in 1931 to an estimated 19,340 by 1939. The electoral wards doubled from two to four, its aldermen increased from six to eight and its councillors from eighteen to twenty-four.

Part of the remit handed down to them by central government was the provision of housing. At the close of war the people had been promised 'Homes Fit for Heroes', a promise signally unfulfilled. It was determined now to make up the deficiency and start a huge initiative in housebuilding, destroying the slums and raising housing standards. Penzance's first council houses were a development of twenty workmen's cottages at The Weethes back in 1916, but they started work on the large Penalverne estate in 1933. In 1936, they paid a Mr Daniel a small sum in compensation for being prevented from planting his customary crop of cabbages in Treneere Fields, for which they had bigger ideas. They also took the initiative with what they considered their own slums, and demolished much of Jennings Street, many small streets and courts around the harbour, Windsor Place, part of St Clare Street in the north part of town, and less explicably the whole length of Camberwell Street, which ran parallel to Adelaide Street and Mount Street.

'In Penzance practically all houses are either reasonably good, or utterly bad,' noted the borough surveyor Capt. Frank Latham, and with the destruction of its obvious slum areas, he was satisfied.

At the same time as the cottages around the harbour and Coinagehall Street were falling, Capt. Latham had more than one reason to be satisfied. In 1935, in a celebration of King George V's Silver Jubilee, the Jubilee Pool, built to his design, was standing in all its white glory on the Battery Rocks. Designed with soft curves to divert the power of the waves and a fanciful gull-like shape, it was a classic Art-Deco lido, which has delighted swimmers and photographers and has been one of the town's favourite pictorial emblems ever since.

However, not everyone was pleased. In 1922, Penzance's war memorial had been built, a stark, dignified column standing in solemn isolation on the rocks where Penzance was born. The intrusion into this picture of a lido full of frolicking half-naked visitors caused a great deal of shock and adverse comment.

However, this controversy was nothing compared to what was about to happen in Newlyn. Penzance people did not generally go to Newlyn, and so the official visit by the medical officer of health in 1935 was something of a leap into the unknown. Most Newlyn houses had neither water nor sewage of their own. For water they were still visiting one of the village's many shoots, and their sewage arrangements consisted of a family Elsan bucket, emptied nightly after dark 'over cliff'. Following his inspection, the medical officer, Richard Lawry, concluded that under current standards most of Newlyn was unfit for human habitation and baldly recommended that the village should be largely demolished and rebuilt.

Penzance Council did not object to this but took it even further, drawing up plans for a futuristic arrangement of large blocks of flats, surrounded by green space and served by wide roadways. To compensate for the loss of housing, they undertook to identify a suitable piece of open space nearby to lay out a new estate of council houses. In the offices of the county surveyor in Bodmin the ideal site was identified, a group of eight fields between the neighbouring farms of Trewarveneth and Gwavas. However, the planners discounted one obvious problem, that the fields were around 350 feet higher than the village. The plans were drawn and the first of the demolition orders was issued.

A shock ran through Newlyn as the occupants realised their fate. They knew where their real slums were and had no objection to their destruction, but the new plans made no distinction between them and decent, well-built family houses. To achieve the utopian scheme of the planners and clear the sites they would all have to go, good and bad alike. Newlyn rose in furious protest. The Newlyn riots had happened only forty years earlier and they scented another piece of mischief on behalf of their unbeloved neighbour.

Protests of working men and women of a fishing village would usually have carried little weight with the authorities. However, Newlyn was also home to the colony of working artists who had chosen the village precisely for its picturesque collection of cottages and courts. These were led by Geoffery Garnier and Phyllis, the daughter of artist Thomas Gotch, who had briefly married a French count and was styled the Marquise de Verdieres. They instigated a media campaign, bringing down journalists, photographers and even Pathé News to tell the story of a simple village's battle for its homes against the heartless bureaucrats of Penzance.

The press lapped it up with articles and photo features comparing the pretty little streets of the Fradgan to the characterless houses rising on the hill at Gwavas Estate. Embattled, Penzance Council kept a chilly silence on the subject and proceeded with their scheme.

Eventually, after making no progress, the Newlyn committee came up with the inspired idea of sending a petition to parliament in a uniquely Newlyn way, by taking a fishing boat up the Thames and mooring it outside the House of Commons. On 22 October 1937, Cecil Richards' boat, the *Rosebud*, sailed up the Thames to a phenomenal reception – the banks and bridges filled with people, with a small flotilla of boats which carried press photographers in their wake.

The minister of housing could hardly rescind his own legislation, and after letting the fuss die down he 'spared' around 100 houses, and gave Penzance's scheme his blessing. The scheme involved the demolition of not just houses and streets but 6¼ acres of Newlyn, to be followed in due course by a similar scheme in Mousehole. However, the nation was thoroughly aroused by the voyage of the *Rosebud*. Penzance Council were under unfriendly press scrutiny and could no longer send their demolition gangs to get on with the job without a fight. Newlyn householders brought in innumerable legal disputes, delaying the scheme to a slow struggle. Large parts of southern and central Newlyn had already fallen, and the rest seemed doomed to the same fate.

However, by late 1937, there were many more factors to consider than the fate of a Cornish fishing village. Despite the horrors and still fresh losses of the First World War, events in Europe were leading inexorably to another global conflict.

35

War and Peace

As ever in wartime, Cornwall was on the front line, England's vulnerable heel into which foreign troops might chance a raid at any time. The hundreds of miles of beaches and coves were an invitation to landing craft, parachutists, gliders, or the landing of spies and saboteurs. Measures were taken to try to form a cordon of defences around the whole coastline. Gun emplacements were built, some in existing historical locations, many more by the placing small concrete bunkers, quickly dubbed pillboxes, in strategic locations. Henry VIII's Pendennis Castle became Cornwall's command centre. An anti-aircraft battery was set up in Penzance, inevitably on the Battery Rocks. Barbed wire sprang up everywhere. On the beaches sea defences, which included the erection of metal pole frameworks designed to discourage aircraft landings (many of these still exist deep in the sands of Marazion and Long Rock beaches and occasionally re-emerge after a storm). At Porthcurno unemployed miners found work as huge tunnels were hewed out of the rock to protect the crucial headquarters of the transatlantic cables. Cornwall took on the appearance of an armed camp.

Once again normal life was laid aside. Conscription returned, the young men left, the older men turned out for the Home Guard, strangers arrived, and anxiety grew. This time, fear was felt not solely on behalf of the men who marched away but for those left behind, as the Home Front became a terrifying reality. No bombs were dropped in Cornwall until June 1940, but the raids came further and further west as France fell and airfields across the Channel became available. Bombing was not always coherent or deliberate but Cornwall lay across the flightpath from northern France to the prime targets in South Wales or Liverpool. If for any reason any aircraft failed to bomb there they often jettisoned their bombs at random or chose any civilian target they could find on the way back.

In July, a clutch of mines was dropped outside Newlyn Harbour, claiming the *Royalo*, a Grimsby trawler-cum-minesweeper, off Penzance in September. Penzance remained unscathed until the early morning of 2 October 1940 when several bombs fell in the station area, demolishing Hosking's garage, damaging several houses and smashing windows in many more. A combined high explosive incendiary bomb came through the roof of a house in Lanoweth Road, through two occupied bedrooms, out of the bedroom window and into the road, where it failed to explode. Schoolchildren gathered around it for a photograph, but it had fortunately been moved away later as a Royal Engineer attempted to defuse it. The bomb exploded, killing him instantly and damaging a large number of nearby buildings.

The sight of burnt and ruined houses with the rafters open to the skies, broken glass, rubble, and the smell of smoke, shattered stone, slate and clay became all too familiar.

On 7 November the war came to Penzance in earnest. A tremendous hail of up to sixty bombs were dropped in the central area, destroying Belair House in Alverton, killing three people and seriously injuring a further sixteen. One dropped just outside the Union Hotel next to some petrol tanks. Like many others it did not explode but remained a cause of evacuation and disruption until it was made safe. Penzance had been blooded by enemy action for the first time since 1648, but there was plenty more to come.

In 1941 there was a series of incidents, some of them random and bizarre. Four bombs fell in Newlyn in January, all dropped too low to explode, and were taken to Sandy Cove for defusing. One of these (emptied of explosives) subsequently ended up in the Fisherman's Arms as a souvenir. A bomb clipped the roof of Richmond chapel, snapping off the granite crucifix, which was then mounted on a plinth in the grounds where it still stands. Bombs destroyed Heamoor Scout Hall and blew the apples off all the nearby trees. Tregavarah chapel, another less than crucial target, was totally destroyed. Paul was bombed, cracking some of the church's stained glass, and even more glass was shattered when a bomb fell in Trewidden gardens. Near Heamoor, a local woman ran to a Beaufort fighter that had crash landed to care for the injured crew, one of whom she subsequently married. In Redruth, a bomb fell into the band room, fortunately empty, and a cornet was later found embedded in the masonry at the top of the clock tower.

But it was no laughing matter. There were three raids in June 1941 alone, the most serious demolishing most of Alma Place and another bomb in the middle of St James' Street, damaging over 300 houses. Nine people died and twenty-six were injured, seven of them seriously. Even Land's End Hotel was bombed, killing one and injuring seventeen. Outlying farms were hit and their livestock joined the casualty lists.

Many more raids occurred in 1942, the most serious in September when explosives and incendiaries destroyed buildings including a brewery in the heart of the town, as well as parts of the Greenmarket, North Parade, and virtually obliterated Union Street.

However, the most painful raid, remembered with the greatest bitterness, happened one fine morning on 28 August 1942 when two Focke-Wulf fighter bombers took off from Caen and made what was known as a 'tip-and-run' raid on West Cornwall. They went first to St Ives where they hit the gasworks, a legitimate target, but then went on a killing spree, bombing a house where a woman returning home with her shopping was killed outside her front door, strafing Porthmeor beach which was packed with people, then following the A30 towards Penzance. At Ludgvan Leaze they hit a vicar's car, killed a postman on a bicycle, shot up a crowded bus injuring two children, then turned towards Marazion where they strafed several women who were putting out their washing, badly injuring two of them. No action in the whole war aroused such anti-German feeling in West Penwith as that morning's work.

The Union Street raid was the last serious assault on West Cornwall. Allied air superiority ensured that bombing raids in the west were restricted to the 'tip-and-run' kind or died out altogether. It had been a period of unbearable tension. The German forces had been poised for invasion. The night air was filled with the sound of enemy aircraft overhead, mostly returning from other raids but without warning raining death and destruction below. There were the distant sounds of other nearby raids, and the glow in the night of another Cornish town burning.

As the tide of the war turned, the focus was on the Fal and the Helford Estuary where British and American invading forces were massing. Something that brightened many of Penzance's population was the American camp at Trengwainton, waiting for D-Day.

There were fringe benefits for some. After razing parts of southern Newlyn to the ground and building two of their idealistic bocks of flats,

Penzance Council had been forced to cease work. Shortly before the war they were questioned by the emergency authorities with a regard to refugees. Did they happen to have any vacant property available? Having evicted around 1,000 people in order to fill Gwavas Estate, they had to reluctantly admit they had half a village of empty property, but added that the houses were officially unfit for human habitation. The authorities pondered this and decided that although not fit for humans they might be good enough for foreigners. They demanded that the council install the water and drainage they had formerly denied was possible, and open the houses up for occupation by Belgian refugees. When Newlyn residents came down the hill from Gwavas to look at their old condemned cottages, they found them full of 'Belgiques', which lowered their opinion of the authorities even further. At the end of the war, with so many houses destroyed, the impetus to demolish acres of Newlyn disappeared, and Mousehole was never touched at all. Most of the condemned cottages still stand, now protected with conservation orders by the authorities that had once tried to destroy them, and the *Rosebud* is commemorated in many places in the village.

Though Penzance was denuded of people, new ones arrived to bring a different flavour to the area. Evacuees from London and the Midlands flooded into the town. The bombing had ceased in the west but the Blitz continued in the cities, later in the South East with the addition of flying bombs and rockets. Children arrived at Penzance station with their gas masks and nametags to take potluck with a local family. For some it was a miserable experience: they were homesick and treated as a necessary nuisance by their hosts and picked on for their 'foreign' accents at school, but for others it was almost magical. Many had never been out of the city before, had never seen the sea or even a cow.

Local people too had to adjust. One prominent Penzance house 'had two boys about twelve and ten. Granny used to make them change into clean white shirts every evening and wait at table.' Despite protests from her more enlightened daughter-in-law, Granny persisted, saying, 'We do a great deal for them and they can do a certain amount for us.' Ironically one of these evacuees later became head waiter in a London hotel. While all those who could returned home, it inspired in most a lifelong love for Cornwall and the people who had shown them such kindness.

More exotic to the conservative west were the land girls. Though they were hardworking they were considered outrageous by the Victorian older generation – rooming together in houses with no chaperones, smoking, dancing to the gramophone, consorting with servicemen and wearing trousers; the future had arrived with a breath of fresh air. Many land girls never went back to their smoky cities but married local men and became part of the community.

Also integrating in a similar way were foreigners brought in to help work the mines. German prisoners of war were beyond the pale, but there was a camp of interned Italians on the north coast who were given a good degree of freedom. Fuelled by romantic images from the local cinemas – there were now three in Penzance and one in Newlyn – they exerted a considerable appeal, and many of them, as well as Poles and other refugees, came to stay and added their unfamiliar surnames to the local rolls.

As in every war, local shipping had taken a beating. U-boats roamed in packs with often only the track of a running torpedo to give warning of their presence. In 1944, a small squadron of fast German E-boats, similar to those which had made such a devastating raid on American forces off Slapton Sands, slipped across the channel in the night and lay in wait under the cliffs near Porthcurno. A convoy of mainly slow colliers was rounding Land's End and the E-boats fell on them, sinking most of the convoy with great loss of life. Shipwrecked sailors were regularly brought into Penzance and Newlyn, while empty lifeboats, wreckage and other grim reminders of losses at sea came ashore all around the peninsula. A group of boys swimming off Newlyn Green were warned off just in time as they tried to bring ashore an unfamiliar floating object, which was in fact a German mine.

Mount's Bay's most famous maritime casualty did not appear until after the war, in April 1947. Two tugs towing the battleship HMS *Warspite* to its final destination at the breakers' yards of the Clyde met severe weather off the bay, preventing the passage of Land's End. The battleship broke its tow and started drifting towards the shore, making a landfall at Prussia Cove. Its passage crew of eight were rescued with great difficulty by the Penlee lifeboat, and when she was refloated she was thought too fragile to travel any further. Instead she was beached on the sands adjacent to St Michael's Mount, to be demolished bit by bit over the next few years. In the last stages dynamite was used and the sound of the explosions joined the regular lunchtime blasting from Penlee Quarry as it echoed around the bay.

In West Cornwall the euphoria of victory quickly wore off and the long hangover of the 1940s and '50s began. The servicemen came home with their demob suits to a grey and austere town. Local industries had limped through the war but the shortage of labour, materials and markets proved fatal to many of them in the peace. The industrial heyday of Penzance had passed, never to return.

Much of the country was shattered and official help was directed at the cities, with little except basic safety and tidying up reserved for the provinces. Rationing had been borne with forbearance as part of the cost of war, but it did not stop when the guns fell silent. Hunger was a constant companion – it was not easy feeding families on personal weekly rations of a few ounces each of butter, tea, cheese, jam, lard, and one fresh egg. There were restrictions on many household items like soap and clothing, and for the children 12 ounces of sweets per month. The joy of peace was dampened by the poor summer of 1946, which decimated the harvest and added bread to the ration book, and the legendary winter of 1947, with its prolonged Arctic conditions that destroyed potato stores, added them also. In towns and villages a flourishing black market in eggs, milk, meat and fish – especially in Newlyn – struck many deals around back doors after dark. For the better-off, petrol rationing made the cars they had bought in the 1930s manufacturing boom almost useless. Rationing continued until as late as 1954.

Not everyone suffered alike. The wartime blockade that restricted Britain to its own home-grown resources had put farmers on the front line and they prospered as never before. Fishing recovered slowly after the war and the much reduced Newlyn fleet no longer decamped to the east for months on end. Of the warren of mines in West Cornwall, only Geevor remained in operation. Tin prices had been sky-high and demand extreme but it came too late to save the rest, and post-war imports soon put prices back down. The men whose efforts had so recently been crucial to their country's survival felt unwanted, many of them unemployed some returning from the sapping experience of prisoner of war camps. Nostalgia for that period is felt by few who lived through it.

The corporation of the enlarged borough did what they could to relieve the gloom. In 1949 they built the town's third large housing estate,

Alverton, on both sides of the road on the west of the town. It was the most attractive of the three – well landscaped, sparing as many trees as possible – and remained very popular. The corporation had also acquired Penlee House and gardens on behalf of the townspeople as a memorial to the war. The 1,000-year-old market cross was brought to rest outside, and a beautifully concealed and peaceful garden of remembrance was laid out in the walled former kitchen garden. Penlee Park joined Morrab Gardens as a place of protected green space and refreshment.

In an unlikely gesture of peace and reconciliation the neighbouring rugby clubs, which had closed during the war, overcame their fierce rivalry and were amalgamated – not without some initial friction – into Penzance & Newlyn RFC, the Pirates.

Two factors saved Penzance from absolute misery. One was its status as the market centre of West Penwith. People from all over the peninsula still flocked there, especially on the Thursday market days and Saturdays to buy, sell, meet and socialise. They went to Penzance to go to the cinema, and to the Pavillion Theatre on the promenade to see the Penzance Players or the repertory performances in the summer season. The young gathered to see and to be seen on the promenade in their single-sex gaggles on a Sunday evening, or to swim in the reopened Jubilee Pool, or to dance at the Winter Gardens at the bottom of Alexandra Road on its dancefloor of 'sprung Canadian maple'. Others came to attend the Orchestral and Choral societies' more sedate entertainments in St John's Hall. Money did not go very far but much of what there was ended up in Penzance.

The other factor was the longing of the workers in the revived factories of the north and the Midlands for a holiday by the sea. This had formerly been satisfied by a day out in Scarborough or Skegness, but when many of the factories closed for an annual fortnight's maintenance, the lure of West Cornwall, just a train ride away, brought a river and then a flood of families, from Yorkshire and Lanacashire in particular.

Their pockets did not usually stretch to Penzance's range of 'proper' hotels so they sought guesthouses instead. These could not nearly cope with the demand and, scenting an opportunity, an instant regiment of amateur caterers seized their chance to profit from the windfall. Large houses, especially the Edwardian terraces nearest to the railway station, converted for a few summer weeks to B&Bs, putting out signs offering bed and breakfast, optional evening meal, running hot and cold water and other delights. The instant landladies were reasonably strict, banning smoking, drinking, noise, any whiff of immorality, and a number of other rules usually pinned to the bedroom walls, and heartlessly turned out their guests during the day whatever the weather.

Other Cornish towns touched by the GWR went over to the tourist trade 100 per cent, and St Ives, Newquay, Looe, Falmouth, Perranporth, etc. virtually reinvented themselves, adding to the harvest of their accommodation with cafés, souvenir shops, ice cream, beachware, pleasure boats, anything to take the visitors' fancy.

Penzance, however, remained uncomfortably equivocal. Victorian dignity still set the tone of the town, and the good burghers who ran it were unwilling to allow it to sink to the vulgarity they perceived in other places. The town opted to benefit from mass tourism as much as it could, but also in a way to try to ignore it. The main streets provided little for their new clientele and it was left to the seafront to provide a warmer welcome. In some ways they missed the best of the bonanza, but they avoided the fate of other more popular resorts, which went from summer crowds to a desperate ghost town winter existence.

36

'Modern' Times

The flavour of the peninsula slowly changed. Some of the more enterprising visitors baulked at the idea of taking their families back to their blackened, crowded, northern industrial streets and turned from customer to host, running guesthouses and souvenir shops of their own. They often railed against what they perceived as the slow pace of the local authorities in exploiting the tourist boom to the full. There was a mild clash of cultures, but the local authorities had a longer view and brought in planning restrictions on businesses and random housebuilding just in time to save the prettiest areas from unthinking overdevelopment.

As the 1950s progressed, a second wave of tourists appeared. With the end of fuel rationing and cheaper cars, a more affluent class of visitors arrived to complement the railway tourists, extending the summer season and bringing with them demands for higher standards from their accommodation. Penzance adapted well to these, but had not long (or completely) left the days of the horse and cart. Traffic became a serious issue for the first time, as did parking.

Some measures were taken to respond to the problem. Causewayhead gave up the struggle to accommodate holiday traffic clashing with delivery vans for the shops, and became the town's first one-way street. A great novelty were the traffic lights that appeared at the crossroads by the railway station. A few car parks were set up, but nowhere near enough to solve the problem. Schemes were considered for diverting the traffic to allow the bulk of it through to its inevitable destination, Land's End. One scheme involved a kind of inner bypass, along the Wharf Road, up Abbey Slip, smashing through historic lower Chapel Street and other historic southern streets to join the promenade further to the west. Like other bizarre schemes of the time, for example the decision to site a nuclear power station at Zennor (passed by the local council in the 1960s), it fortunately came to nothing. A route around the northern boundary of the town had been envisioned and protected from other development since the 1930s, but its time was yet to come.

On 7 March 1962 the roadways of the town were further disrupted by a familiar foe. On the evening of Ash Wednesday a dreadful storm brought the fateful combination of a high spring tide and a south-easterly gale to bear on the seafront. By the next day large parts of the promenade, Wherrytown, Newlyn Green and the Tolcarne area of Newlyn were a shambles of boulders, rubble and gigantic craters. Local schools were closed and the children went down to the seafront to help with the clear up. The surface of the promenade had to be completely rebuilt. The reconstruction included new anti-flooding walls, which saved some of the streets behind from their regular inundation.

Five years later, on 18 March, the seafront was again closed, but for a dramatically different reason. On a fine, calm morning the super tanker *Torrey Canyon*, carrying a full load of oil from Kuwait en route to Milford Haven, rose over the southern horizon, and to the astonishment of local boatmen fishing off the Seven Stones Reef, came directly towards them and ploughed into the Pollard Rock at full speed. Immediately, its load of 120,000 tons of crude oil began to pour into the sea. It was the first calamitous oil spill of its kind in British waters and there were no contingency plans to cope with it. The oil slick spread, mercifully sparing the Isles of Scilly just a few miles away, but westward, thickening and widening until it embraced both coasts of West Penwith. West Cornwall's beaches weren't strangers to oil pollution, usually in small quantities of congealed tar, but this came inches thick, subduing the waves, of a consistency of brown custard, and a smell that pervaded every street, house and field of the peninsula.

The first thought was for the forthcoming holiday season. The spill was national news, and holiday cancellations poured in. The response by the government was to send in the RAF and bomb the wreck with napalm, hoping to burn off as much oil as possible. After some less than impressive target practice some fires were started, but quickly went out. The only other weapon to hand for the authorities was raw detergent to clean it off the beaches and rocks, and emulsify it so that it sank at sea. Thousands of gallons of undiluted detergent were poured onto the sands, only for the next tide to bring in another blanket of stinking sludge, but there was no alternative and the detergent continued to flow.

The eventual damage to the environment owed almost as much to the detergent as to the oil, as the entire ecosystem of beaches and rock pools died and the tidal zone was destroyed. Some pollution occurred at greater depths that affected crustaceans and the shellfish market collapsed. But most visible and heartbreaking of all was the effect of the oil on seabirds. The gulls went largely unscathed but diving birds like gannets and cormorants, and in particular swimming divers like guillemots, razorbills, puffins and grebes died in their thousands. The Mousehole Wild Bird Hospital, founded as a small bird infirmary by sisters Phyllis and Dorothy Eglesias, was in the eye of the storm, trying to cope with oil-soaked birds which were brought up its steps in bags and boxes every few minutes. The volunteers did their best, including the necessary mass culling of the worst cases whose pain could only be imagined, but only a tiny percentage of rescued birds rescued ever returned to the sea.

Penzance and Newlyn began to resemble their wartime appearance, with road blocks, army lorries and depots, all marked TC (*Torrey Canyon*), and even a detachment of American servicemen for the final touch. The oil moved on to cause further distress in Brittany and beyond. Town mayors turned out on windy beaches on both sides of the Channel to demonstrate the cleanliness of their beaches by taking a brief dip in front of a press corps, and the news that Cornwall was open for business went around, saving most of the season.

Socially, Penzance was changing with the times. Although the democratic fellowship of the war had broken down many of the class barriers, Penzance's affairs were still mainly run by established local families with familiar names, businessmen and landowners, doctors and other professionals. The 1944 'Butler' Education Act had enshrined the right of secondary education for all children up to the age of fifteen, and this raised the aspiration of local children to possibilities outside their own communities, particularly into higher education. The act brought its own divisions, as children were separated by the notorious eleven-plus exam which directed them either into high quality and well-resourced grammar schools, or into poorly resourced and overcrowded secondary modern schools. The boys' and girls' county schools changed into grammar schools, while the main secondary modern facilities were offered at Lescudjack School on the Princess May recreation ground, and later at Mount's Bay School at Heamoor. The Boys' Grammar School was renamed after Sir Humphry Davy in 1960 and retained the name when it and the other Penzance secondary schools joined the comprehensive system in 1980.

The 1960s brought a concentration on youth, teenagers who had spending power for the first time and created a revolution in fashion and popular music. Other cultures flourished too. The attraction of the far west for artists had spread to lovers of the wider arts, and musicians, actors, sculptors, poets, and authors had trickled into the area. Less focussed members of alternative cultures came along too, successively known as bohemians, Beatniks and hippies. They were happy to hang out in relaxed clumps in the summer months to the suspicion and annoyance of local holiday traders, who were convinced that their untidy appearance and louche lifestyle would put off the more upright families they depended upon. In St Ives in particular, the local populace declared war on them, banned them from local pubs and drove them off the beaches, in one case with guard dogs. It was a cultural clash, but the area came to accept its 'arty' image as a positive attraction, and even in Penzance art galleries and arts centres opened and flourished. The unique Minack Cliff Theatre at Porthcurno, created by the redoubtable Rowena Cade, became more accessible and popular and instituted a long summer season attracting thousands of visitors.

The local cinemas had suffered as all cinemas had with the onset of television. The 1936 Art-Deco Ritz in Queen Street became a bingo hall, the charming Gaiety Cinema approached by a bridge over the stream in Newlyn became a faux-medieval Meadery. The Regal in Morrab Place was demolished and the site was unconscionably used for the construction of the disproportionate tax office, Penlowarth, which towered above its historic neighbours and was once voted Britain's seventh ugliest building. Only the Savoy in Causewayhead survived to see cinemas' fortunes revive.

Musically, the Winter Gardens tucked away at the bottom of Alexandra Road had moved with the times, abandoning the genteel atmosphere of such joys as the foxtrot and the 'ladies' excuse-me' for up-and-coming bands like Status Quo, Jethro Tull, and the locally formed Queen, and later hosted cutting-edge punk bands like the Damned, the Sex Pistols and the Ramones.

Employment in traditional industries was declining fast. Non-holiday related employment remained available at Penlee Quarry, Holman's Dry Dock, various small industries at Long Rock, Penzance Laundry, the growing West Cornwall Hospital, schools, shops and local authorities. Fishing, farming and mining were shedding jobs continuously and were ceasing for the first time to underpin the area's basic economy. Mechanisation of farms with tractors, combine harvesters, milking machines and many innovative devices made the majority of farm labourers redundant. Seasonal activities like flower picking and cauliflower cutting came to rely on casual labour, of which there was a great deal available, and the former labourers' cottages were left empty. The countryside began to fall silent, the long companionship of numerous farmworkers disappearing, replaced by a single man on a tractor. West Cornwall's less productive fields, every one of which had had to be cultivated if necessary by manual labour during the war years, fell into neglect. Young people moved into towns and old ones retired, leaving a strange void in the landscape.

Fortunately, planning regulations ensured that this void was not completely filled by unsightly holiday developments such as chalet and caravan camps, though many individual battles were fought between landowners and local planners. There were winners and losers. The beautifully stark north coast road from St Ives to St Just was assailed by various plans for chalets, motels, housing estates and even a helicopter training base, but all were fought off by local artists like Patrick Heron and public figures like John Betjeman, well connected with the national press. The south coast had a more mixed outcome. Praa Sands became a large holiday caravan destination, and Penzance's Eastern Green, J. S. Courtney's 'stripe of green turf', was betrayed by a concoction of intensive holiday caravans, later 'converted' to chalets, to which industrial developments and supermarkets were later added.

Property was relatively cheap, especially by 'up-country' standards. As well as the farm cottages, many fishermen's damp granite dwellings were happily abandoned by their occupants in favour of cleaner, warmer modern homes with up-to-date facilities. Almost no one locally wanted to buy such things and it was left to newcomers to perceive the charm and comforts that could be applied with the help of a little money. Hippies and other alternative families moved into the countryside, and many of the pretty harbour cottages were purchased and renovated to become second homes or to join in the novel business of self-catering holidays.

Traffic became a curse of monumental proportions. In 1968 Penzance took the brave step of abandoning almost half its harbour capacity and filling it in as a large car park. It was not a great loss as the inner harbour was largely unused by then. The odorous gasworks had closed and so had most of the warehouses near the station, and the high level of silt had left it unnavigable during most stages of the tide. It was not a pretty scheme and not without controversy, but it did relieve some of Penzance's inner congestion. Equally unattractive was the bare polluted plot left when the gasworks site was cleared. A succession of development schemes were mooted by a succession of distant property development companies, but the bleak site, filled only with buddleia, remained in their property banks and none of them wanted to risk investing in Penzance. For a while it was earmarked for Penzance's first supermarket, but it took until the twenty-first century for the Wharfside Shopping Centre to be completed. In pictorial terms the harbourside still fails to provide anything by way of charm or beauty.

The outer harbour gradually turned over to providing marina facilities, though they were restricted by being tidal. None of the various schemes for an all-tide marina came to pass, despite numerous surveys and reports. The main commercial operations centred on the dry dock and the regular sailings of passenger and freight vessels to the Isles of Scilly. These had been carried out by a succession of sturdy ferries, a pleasant enough voyage in fair weather but made considerably less comfortable by the shallow berth in St Mary's harbour which dictated a maximum draught of 3 m, not enough to prevent a very lively movement in the open Atlantic waters. An alternative air service had been provided at St Just airport by picturesque de Havilland Rapide biplanes, but in 1964 a far more modern option appeared at Eastern Green, Britain's first civil passenger helicopter service. This was owned by BEA (British European Airways), then sold to British International Helicopters. The sound and sight of the Sikorsky helicopters became familiar over the bay.

In 1974, local government underwent another major convulsion. The Charter Penzance had received in 1614 had lasted for 320 years, but the enlarged borough was considered redundant after only forty. Once more amalgamation into larger authorities was the aim, something that had some support, though arguments raged about how the existing disparate and often quarrelsome bodies could peacefully coalesce. The new western body was to include Penzance Borough, St Ives Borough, St Just Urban District Council, and West Penwith Rural District Council. Any suggestions that Penzance should swallow up the rest as it had done in 1934 or that the new body should bear Penzance's name were quashed from the outset, and a compromise was eventually reached with the name of Penwith District Council, one of just six local authorities in Cornwall plus the county council. The existence of Penzance's ancient town council was in doubt for a while as it would have little future influence or authority, but it survived to continue its unbroken line from 1614, as did the local parish councils. The new district council set up its offices in the former buildings of the West Cornwall School for Girls at St Clare, including the historic York House, complete – so excited local rumour had it – with a nuclear fallout shelter. The former junior block became the local fire station. The council set to work on its new responsibilities.

These had changed little in the interim. Out on the A30, for example, things were as bad as ever. The summer queues into Penzance stretched beyond Crowlas, and back into Marazion. Those visiting Cornwall by car needed considerable stamina. The road wound through the centre of all the towns on its way through Cornwall after the long, motorway-free trail down from the Midlands and the north. A car journey from Lancashire could easily take thirteen hours and was relatively unrelieved by petrol stations, cafés or toilets. Cornwall's first bypass appeared at Redruth, though others were slow to follow. Penwith finally attended to its own needs as late as 1987, completing the bypass route scheduled in the 1930s around the town after a spirited public enquiry.

Other works of public utility were clamouring for attention. One had been solved in 1961 by the provision of a large dam at Drift, beside the road to Sancreed. Inevitably, its footprint inundated a pretty valley, a farmhouse and some cottages, but it succeeded Boscathnoe Reservoir in securing Penzance and district's increasing water needs. Updating its equally demanding sewage requirements took a good deal longer. The three main outfalls, plus one in Newlyn, still drained the town perfectly well, but although the sewage was released on an outgoing tide it often ended up back on the beach with disgusting results. This was well known to local people who were never tempted to swim on the beaches beneath the Promenade or along Newlyn Green or Eastern Green, but as standards of public health grew and tourists made the unwelcome discovery for themselves, a better solution was demanded.

The local water board had been taken over by South West Water in 1973, and their suggested solution was to amalgamate all the outfalls into one single system and discharge the sewage further out into the bay, but this was strongly rejected. The 'Pipeline' controversy rumbled on without resolution for twenty years, but eventually South West Water devised a scheme to pump treated sewage across the peninsula into St Ives Bay. This naturally pleased everyone around Mount's Bay but merely moved the problem and the controversy a few miles to the north. However, that was what they did in 1996, though complaints, especially from the north coast surfing community, still roll in.

Surfing had become another useful addition to West Cornwall's holiday attractions. Sennen Cove, where once seine boats had deposited millions of pilchards, was 'discovered' as one of the finest surfing locations in the country. Marazion also benefitted when the wind was favourable. From simple bodyboarding to all the complexity of today's sport, surfing grew into a sizable business employing many local people.

In response to the holiday crowds, lifesaving became a priority. Several tricky beaches with changeable sandbanks took an almost annual toll of drowning, and among the tasks undertaken by the new district council was the provision of summer lifeguards. Penlee Lifeboat, joined for a few years by a small RNLI station on St Michael's Mount, policed the wider bay with its increasing number of pleasure boats, and the RNAS station at Culdrose provided helicopter assistance. Tragically, neither service was able to save the coaster *Union Star* when it suffered engine failure and was driven towards the cliffs to the west of Lamorna Cove in December 1981 in a colossal southerly storm. Its complement of eight, including the captain's two step-daughters, perished and so, to the shock and grief of the whole community and the country, did the eight volunteer crew of the lifeboat *Solomon Browne*. In true lifeboat tradition, a volunteer replacement crew offered their services the next morning. Soon afterwards the lifeboat station moved from Penlee Point back to Newlyn, but there are many memorials to the lost crew in Mousehole where they had all lived, and their names are read out in an annual lifeboat service in Mousehole Harbour every summer.

In March 1985, another upsetting if less tragic incident occurred when a mentally unstable sixteen-year-old boy started a fire in St Mary's church, which caused considerable damage and destroyed many of its historic fittings. It was closed for two years for renovations to take place.

Rugby became another unlikely local employer, as the sport turned professional. Supported by the Pirates' president and chief benefactor Dick Evans, the club rose up the league tables, joined for a time at the Mennaye

Fields by a separate local club, Mount's Bay. Both teams travelled to the EDF championships at Twickenham in 2007 and both won their respective finals, though by then Dick Evans had decided to upgrade the Penzance and Newlyn RFC to the Cornish Pirates, and ironically neither cup bore the name of the teams' hometown.

Almost unnoticed in 1990, Geevor mine closed its gates, the last remnant of the trade that had sustained West Cornwall through the millennia. Eight years later, South Crofty at Camborne finally gave up the struggle too. The last working tin mine in Cornwall had gone. Geevor later opened as a mining museum, and the north coast tin fields became a World Heritage Site. Anyone wanting an insight into the conditions miners faced will find Geevor Museum a vivid and humbling experience.

One happy addition to the entertainment and celebration of Penzance was initiated in the post-boom days of the early 1990s. The old midsummer Golowan festival of fire and fun had been thoroughly discouraged in late Victorian times and had slowly dwindled to a complete stop by the First World War. Penzance's air of strict propriety gave way only for a couple of hours during the town's annual carnival, and other public celebrations seemed beneath its dignity.

In 1991, a group led by local residents Stephen Hall and Annamaria Murphy, including members of Kneehigh Theatre and Alverton School, closed Market Jew Street to traffic for a day to celebrate the Feast of St John, with the help of spectacular processions of giant images carried by the schoolchildren. Despite heavy rain it was a great success. From this one-day event Golowan grew each year until it became a ten-day festival, with a large variety of events. The traditional elements recorded by historians long before – the fireworks, the wild serpent dance, the mock mayor elections, the torchlit processions with the fearsome 'horse', Penglaz – were all revived. Golowan worked in tandem with the Acorn Arts Centre, converted from the Methodist chapel in Parade Street in 1969, which is still at the heart of the town's cultural life today.

The success of Golowan, and in particular its climax Mazey Day, inspired other Cornish towns to revive traditions of their own. With the exception of Heston's Furry (Flora) Day and Padstow's May Day, they had all disappeared, but soon Camborne was celebrating Richard Trevithick, Redruth was celebrating William Murdoch, Bodmin had revived its Bodmin Riding tradition and many others followed. In Penzance a midwinter festival,

Montol, rose again out of the history books, as well as the tradition of May Day horns and Easter's 'Allan Apples'. Golowan was treated cautiously to begin with by the local councils and even more so by the Methodist Church, but seeing its innocent success they all came around to its support and it has become one of the most eagerly awaited dates in Penzance's calendar.

37

A New Century

In the twenty-first century the urge for greater and greater centralisation infected Cornwall, with serious consequences for the more remote communities. Gradually the gravitational pull of Truro, with its county council buildings, its major hospital, its huge new college complex and its flourishing variety of offices and shops exerted a negative influence over towns like Penzance. Penzance's shopping centre had always been one of its strengths. It had usually satisfied the needs of its people, with the exception of the occasional pilgrimage to Falmouth, which for years hosted the county's only Marks & Spencer store. But supermarkets at Long Rock and Eastern Green captured much of the food shopping market and people became accustomed to drive to the shops, which worked to Truro's advantage. Many of Penzance's most prominent shop premises had been acquired by distant property companies who leased them in turn to chain stores who could outbid local businesses. The phenomenal growth of charity shops also took root. They, unlike other traders, paid little or no business rates and acquired most of their staff and their stock for free, which meant they could afford to pay higher rents than most local traders could afford. High Street shops, once in such great demand, began to close. Some, like the old clothing firm of Simpsons Bros, opted instead to shrink in size. Online shopping took its toll. Trading was always a matter of survival but as trade dropped and margins reduced it became more and more of a struggle.

The Wharfside Shopping Centre was a welcome addition to the main street, but the closure of large established shops like Woolworth's and Humphry Davy's old workplace, Peasegood's Chemists, deadened the centre of the town. The property companies preferred to keep their premises empty rather than to let them out at lower rents. While the central area became less and less attractive, the four arms of the original crossroads,

Lower Market Jew Street, Chapel Street, Alverton and Causewayhead, still hosted lively small local businesses, which managed to keep the interest of the town alive.

Local housing provision also changed for the worse. In the late twentieth century there was a viable pathway for local young families to climb on to the housing ladder and work their way up as income and family needs dictated. However, the disparity between local pockets and those of people moving in to live or to obtain a holiday home outbid what the low-paid locals could offer. The curse of empty second homes affected Penzance less than some of its surrounding villages, but the prospects of house ownership faded for many young people, who were forced instead into rented accommodation.

The pull of Truro and the constant urge of administrators at every level to centralise affected much more than the shops. Treliske Hospital had begun life at the end of a long windy field in Highertown, but building by building it filled the field, with specialisations in most disciplines. Since it provided all the essential services, administrative eyes focussed on West Cornwall Hospital and formulated plans to reduce its scope or close it for acute cases altogether.

Recognising the inhumane consequences such bureaucratic logic would cause, Penzance was stung into furious action. On 14 April 2002 a protest march took place, led by local MP Andrew George. It was a phenomenal success with a crowd estimated at 20,000 and the leaders reaching the hospital long before the rearguard had left Penlee Park, making Penzance and Penwith's reaction to the potential loss of its hospital abundantly clear. A series of compromises over the level of services began, and are still proceeding.

The most notorious centralisation was still to come. The government had made it known that in its opinion six local authorities, in fact the whole middle echelon of local government in a county like Cornwall, was a luxury the country could no longer afford. It proposed and pushed through, despite concerted protest, the concept of a unitary authority to undertake the administration of the whole county, situated inevitably in Truro. Cornwall Council was to represent a county 90 miles long, with town and rural districts which had nothing in common or even contrary interests. Penwith District Council had lasted just thirty-five years. Only the town and parish councils remained to represent specific local communities, though their remit was reduced still further. To add to the ensuing chaos, Cornwall Council's inauguration in 2009 coincided with a national economic collapse. Its funds were drastically cut, making an already overwhelming task virtually impossible to deliver. It passed on its cutbacks in sometimes inexplicable ways, closing public toilets and tourist information centres that were essential to Cornwall's sole remaining industry – tourism.

One of the schemes the unitary authority had inherited concerned Penzance directly. The former Penwith District Council had begun to make contingency plans for the replacement of *Scillonian III*, the ferry that had served the Isles of Scilly since 1977. When these plans were revealed in 2008 they had grown from a like-for-like replacement to a major new restructuring of the harbours at both ends of the crossing. The Penzance plans included a further extension of the quay, a large passengers' waiting hall, and an even larger freight depot placed to the immediate east of the Jubilee Pool, occupying part of the Battery Rocks. The scheme divided the town, with a majority demanding a less obtrusive solution. Cornwall Council opted to press on regardless with the assistance of a large EU grant. Relationships between the new authority and the Penzance protestors, which included the town council, deteriorated to an alarming extent. Other Penzance factions campaigned in the scheme's favour and it became a serious controversy, resolved only when the Minister of Transport threw out the scheme on grounds of cost, leaving a smouldering legacy and the worst possible start for a new authority. The subsequent closure of the Eastern Green heliport and its replacement with another supermarket did nothing to sweeten the air.

So the circle of history continues to roll. In 2014, Penzance celebrated 400 years as a Charter Town. The celebrations found it diminished in prosperity and influence, poorer in wages and employment, but still optimistic for its future.

Its greatest and longest-held wish remains unfulfilled: a harbour full of water at all states of the tide. This would no longer be needed for the use of privateers or merchantmen but for modern sailing yachts and the wealth they bring. Despite its length, so often extended, the pier head at low water still only dips its ankles in the sea. It needs the vision the Victorians had and the money they were able to find to make this dream come true.

Penzance is a substantial town, made independent and pragmatic by its very remoteness. It is accepting and tolerant now, free of the stiffness and snobbery of the past, with a healthy volunteering spirit that does not take itself too seriously. The west's economy did not attract many of Britain's immigrants from Asia or the Caribbean, but a number of Eastern Europeans have found a welcome in Penzance and added a further flavour to the richness of the mix. Many people have moved there and changed its nature but the town has gained far more than it has lost with the expectations outsiders bring.

Penzance has known warfare, rebellion, starvation, assault from sea, land, and air, and many fluctuations in its fortunes. Today nothing menaces its coast but the occasional storm and no one starves. The expansion of Penwith College, the leisure centre, sports facilities, bars, restaurants, galleries and even pop-up shops have all in their ways countered the downturn in its fortunes and it remains a most pleasing place for people to live. Despite all its changes, it retains an atmosphere, a character and a pride that is all its own.

Bibliography

Boggis, Revd R. J. E., *History of the Diocese of Exeter* (Exeter, 1922).

Boase, G. C., *Reminiscences of Penzance by a Native from* The Cornishman *1883/84* (Penzance Old Cornwall Society, 1976).

Borlase, William, *Observations on the Antiquities of Cornwall* (Bowyer & Nichols, 1769).

Bottrell, William, *Hearthside Stories of West Cornwall* (W. Cornish, 1870).

Carew, Richard, *The Survey of Cornwall* (Augustus Kelly, 1953).

Chope, E. Pearce, *Early Tours in Devon and Cornwall* (Exeter, 1918).

Coate, Mary, *Cornwall in the Great Civil War and Interregnum* (Truro: Bradford Barton, 1963).

Courtney, J. S., *A Guide to Penzance and its Neighbourhood* (London: E. Rowe, 1845).

Courtney, Louise, *Half a Century of Penzance* (Peter Dalwood, 1972).

Dearlove, Jenny (ed.), 'Eighteenth-Century Life in West Cornwall', Penwith Local History Group (2014).

Edmonds, Richard, *The Land's End District* (London: J. Russell Smith, 1862).

Garstin, Garstin, *The Owl's House* (1924).

Goskar, Tehmina, 'Alice de Lisle Paper' (2013).

Halliday, Frank, *A History of Cornwall* (Duckworth, 1958).

Hartley, Sir Harold, *Humphry Davy* (E. P. Publishing, 1966).

Hoyle, Susan (ed.), 'West Cornwall in the Twentieth Century', Penwith Local History Group (2007).

Jenkin, Hamiton, *The Cornish Miner* (David & Charles, 1927).

Jennings, Revd Henry, *Historical Notes on Madron, Morvah and Penzance* Saundry's (1936).

Lach-Szyrma, Revd W. S. A., *Short History of Penzance, St Michael's Mount and Land's End*.

Mattingly, Joanna, *Cornwall and the Coast, Mousehole and Newlyn*

(Phillimore, 2009).

Moorhouse, Geoffrey, *The Pilgrimage of Grace* (Phoenix, 2002).

Orme, Nicholas, *Cornwall and the Cross* (Phillimore, 2007).

Palmer, June (ed.), 'In and Around Penzance in Napoleonic Times' Penwith Local History Group (2014).

Paris, Dr, *A Guide to the Mount's Bay* (London: W. Phillips, 1824).

Pearce, Keith and Helen Fry, *The Lost Jews of Cornwall* (Redcliffe Press, 2000).

Penzance Natural History and Antiquarian Society Transactions.

Pool, P. S. A., *The History of the Town and Borough of Penzance* (Penzance Corporation, 1974).

Rees, Edgar, *Old Penzance* (Wordens, 1956).

Rowse, A. L., *A Cornish Childhood* (Jonathan Cape, 1942).

Royle, Trevor, *Civil War: The Wars of the Three Kingdoms* (Abacus, 2004).

Sagar-Fenton, Michael, *About St Michael's Mount* (Bossiney Books, 1999).

Sagar-Fenton, Michael, *Penlee Lifeboat – The First 200 Years of the Penlee Branch of the RNLI* (2005).

Sagar-Fenton, Michael, *The* Rosebud *and the Newlyn Clearances* (Truran, 2003).

Sagar-Fenton, Michael and Stuart B. Smith, *Serpentine* (Truran, 2005).

Schama, Simon, *A History of Britain* (BBC Publications, 2000).

Skidmore, Chris, *Edward VI: The Lost King of England* (Phoenix, 2002).

Stuart, John, *Revolt in the West* (Devon Books, 1987).

Thomas, John, *History of Mount's Bay* (Self-published, 1831).

Todd, Malcolm, *The South West to AD 1000* (Longman, 2007).

Tremenheere, Seymour Grieg, *The Tremenheeres* (Self-published, 1925).

Trevennen Jenkin, Ann, *Notes on the Prayer Book Rebellion of 1549* (Noonvares Press, 1999).

Vale, Edward, 'The Harveys of Hayle', *The Trevithick Society* (2009).

Various authors, *The Official Guide to Penzance* (Beare & Son, 1876).

Zeigler, Phillip, *The Black Death* (Sutton Publishing, 1969).

Index

Albert (North) Pier 161, 177

Alexandra Road 179–81, 210

Alverton, Manor of 27, 28, 33–5, 51, 83, 87, 103, 108, 111, 151

Alverton Street 67, 80, 142, 149, 151, 167, 180, 200, 218

Alward 26, 112

an Gof, Michael Joseph 51, 59

Bartinney 17

Basset, Sir Arthur 96, 100

Basset, Sir Francis 90, 93

Batten, John 153

Battery Rocks 12, 61, 108, 133, 160, 164, 196, 199, 219

Beddoes, Dr Thomas 146–7

Boase, Henry 140–1, 153–4, 176

Bodmin 36–9, 49, 53, 57, 91, 94, 197, 215

Body, William 54–5

Boleigh 10, 25

Bolitho Family 153, 173

Bolitho, Thomas 141

Borlase Family 103, 113, 117, 121, 128–9, 130, 141, 145, 155, 175–6, 182

Boscawen-Un 10

Bottrell, William 159, 174

Braganza, Catherine of 107

Branwell, Maria 142

Brunel, Isambard Kingdom 165

Burley, Richard 65, 69

Caer Bran 17

Carew, Richard 52, 66, 72–3, 74–5, 77, 78, 106

Carn Euny 19

Carne Family 157

Carne, William 153

Carlos de Amesquita, Don 65, 67

Carveth, John 109–111, 128, 141

Castle-an-Dinas 17

Castle Horneck 141

Causewayhead (North Street) 67, 71, 130, 151, 169, 179, 187, 190, 207, 210, 218

Chapel Street 12, 33, 67, 108, 118,

141, 142, 153, 155, 160, 169–70, 173, 207, 218

Chapel Street Methodist chapel 169, 172

Charles I 53, 88, 99, 132

Charles II 99, 101–2, 107

Charter of Incorporation 36, 68, 78–9, 80, 87, 212, 219

Chun Castle 17, 160

Chyandour 18, 80, 107–8, 153, 160–1, 164, 168, 173, 178, 186, 193

Chysauster 19–20, 24

Chywoone Hill 66–67

Connerton, Manor of 170

Courtney, J. S. 168–9, 171, 175–6, 188, 211

Courtney, Louise 169

Cromwell, Oliver 98, 100–1

Curtis, Thomas 126

Daniell, Alexander 88

Daniell, Richard 83, 88, 103, 111

Davy, Sir Humphry 144, 145–9, 155, 163, 168, 173, 178, 188, 210, 217

Defoe, Daniel 113

De Lisle, Alice 33–5, 36

De Lisle, Warin 33

De Pomeroy, Henry 45

Diodorus Siculus 15

Dolcoath Mine 137

Drake, Sir Francis 63, 64, 68–9

Duchy of Cornwall 36–8, 57, 100

Earl of Oxford 46, 48

Eastern Green 168, 211–13, 217, 219

Edmonds, Richard 163, 171–3

Edward II 33–4

Edward III 36, 38

Edward VI 54, 60

Egbert 25

Egyptian House, The 169

Elizabeth I 45, 61, 63, 78, 88

Exeter 21, 25, 27, 28–9, 53, 56–7, 58, 61, 89, 91–2, 94–5, 108

Fairfax, Sir Thomas 95

Falmouth 63, 65–6, 68, 93, 116, 143–4, 162, 177, 206, 217

Faraday, Michael 147, 149

Fiennes, Celia 105–5

Forbes, Stanhope 185–6

Geevor Mine 138, 204, 215

Giddy, Edward 119, 122

Giddy, Thomas 132, 143, 155, 157, 158

Gilbert, Davies 136, 146, 152, 156

Godolphin, Sir Francis 64–7, 69–70, 90, 93

Golowan Festival 175–7, 215–16

Goring, Lord 95

Greenmarket, The 151–2, 176, 201

Grenville, Sir Bevill 90, 91–5

Grenville, Sir John 98, 101

Grenville, Richard 93, 95, 98

Gulval 19, 27, 28, 87, 97, 178, 195

Halliday, Frank 117, 137–9

Harvey, Harold 186

Harveys of Hayle 135–8

Hayle 13, 23, 104, 161, 164, 195

Heamoor 164, 172, 195, 200, 209

Helston 36–7, 43, 55, 84, 97–8, 102–3, 117, 156, 174

Henrietta Maria 92

Henry IV 43, 46

Henry V 46

Henry VI 46

Henry VII 49–51

Henry VIII 51–7, 65, 83

Hopton, Ralph 91–6, 98, 100–1

Howard, Admiral Charles 64

Hudson, W. H. 191–2

Ictis 16

Ireland 8, 9, 10, 11–13, 14, 16, 24, 64–5, 114, 120

Isles of Scilly 5, 7, 69, 96, 98, 100, 105, 117, 160, 166, 191, 208, 212, 219

James I 78, 83, 157, 195

Jenkin, Hamilton 37

John, William 128
Jubilee Pool 12, 130, 196, 205, 219
Keigwin, Jenkin 65
Killigrew family 62, 85, 90, 101, 116
Land's End 9, 13, 50, 104–5, 113, 116, 118, 166, 189, 192, 201, 203, 207
Lariggan 80, 88, 160, 164, 192
Launceston 29, 30, 36, 56, 93–5
Le Grice, Valentine 141–4, 151, 155, 158
Leland, John 50–1, 61
Lescudjack Castle 17, 18–19, 26, 171, 186
Le Tyes, Henry 32–3, 59
Lizard, the 7, 9, 65, 69, 84–5, 97–8, 105, 116, 162, 177, 193
Ludgvan 17, 28, 72, 145, 201
Lyonesse 10
Maddern, William 87
Madron 13, 27, 31, 33, 44–5, 59–60, 108–9, 110–11, 121, 130, 143, 151, 159, 171–3, 180, 190, 195
Marazion 29, 34, 44, 46, 50, 61, 68, 71–2, 82–5, 89, 113, 118–19, 172, 179, 190, 195, 199, 201, 213–4
Market House 82, 84, 128–9, 142–3, 145
Market Jew Street 108, 142, 143, 149, 151–3, 154–5, 160, 162, 168–9, 186, 188–9, 215, 218
Mary I 60–1
Maton G. W. 126, 140
Matthews, John 166–79, 185
Mennaye 26, 187
Michael Joseph an Gof 48, 56
Minack Theatre 210
Mont St Michel 29, 46
Mousehole 11, 22, 31, 33–6, 80, 59–71, 74, 81, 85, 97, 108, 118, 162, 193, 195, 198, 202, 209, 214
Mullion 31, 98, 193
Nelson, Admiral Lord 143
Newlyn 13, 26, 34, 50, 51, 61–75, 89, 111, 118, 121–2, 131, 133, 150, 154, 161–3, 166, 170, 172, 184–6, 190, 192, 193, 195–8, 200–15
North Parade 141, 169, 180, 186, 201
Oxnam, Richard 141, 153
Padstow 13, 65, 215

Parade Street 142, 180, 215
Paris, Dr 123, 153–4, 159, 168, 175
Parliament 44, 60, 64, 82, 84, 89–92, 95, 97–8, 100–1, 156, 185, 198
Paul 27, 31, 33–4, 61, 65–7, 107, 162, 169, 195, 200
Pearce, Richard 181
Penlee House 186, 205
Penlee Lifeboat 203, 214
Penlee Park 31, 205, 218
Penlee Point 161, 179, 195, 214
Penlee Quarry 193, 204, 210
Penrose Terrace 168
Penryn 36, 56, 84, 115, 169, 176
Penzance Harbour 22, 195
Pilgrimage of Grace 53, 57, 59
Plague 40–5, 61, 64, 97, 131
Polkinghorne, Alderman Roger 86–8
Pool, Mr P. A. S. 102, 154, 187
Porthleven 118, 161, 185
Porthmeor 19, 201
Portreath 19, 201
Prayer Book Rebellion 68
Price, Sir Rose 141
Prison, Penzance 81, 113, 129
Promenade, the 88, 160, 166, 180–1, 187
Pytheas 15, 16, 50
Queen Street 169, 210
Queen's Hotel 166
Rawles, William 128–9
Read, John 128–9
Rees, Edgar 176
Richard III 47
Robert, Count of Mortain 28
Roscadghill 141
Rosevean Road 169, 171
Rotterdam Buildings 141, 142
St Anthony 26, 31, 32
St Aubyn, John 82, 90, 103, 113, 114
St Clare 45, 80, 154, 169, 187, 190, 196, 213
St Hilary 44
St Ives 50, 59, 89, 97, 104, 120–1, 184, 186, 195, 201, 206, 210, 212, 214
St John the Baptist 82, 175
St John's church 180
St John's Hall (Public Buildings) 167, 181, 205
St Just 13, 59, 74, 78, 102, 107, 121, 138, 179, 191, 193, 211–12

St Keverne, 48, 65, 98
St Mary's chapel (from 1672) 88, 105, 108, 110, 141, 171, 180
St Mary's church 31, 214
St Mary's Terrace 168
St Michael's Mount 11, 13, 16, 22, 29, 32, 33, 46, 48–9, 52, 58, 76, 84, 90, 93, 96, 100–1, 113, 133, 166, 203, 214
St Michael's Terrace 168
St Piran 24
Sancreed 17, 19, 107, 213
Sennen 29, 31, 49, 214
Ship & Castle (Union Hotel) 141, 143, 185, 200
Smuggling 115, 118–19, 122
South Folly 154
South Parade 142, 168–9
South Quay 12, 161, 185
Stanneries 30, 57, 84
Star Inn 168
Synagogue, the Penzance 169
Tolcarne Mill 111, 141
Tonkin, Alderman William 109
Tonkin, Thomas 128
Torrey Canyon, the 208–9
Tregavarah 172, 200
Tregeseal 10
Tremenheere Family 72, 107
Treneere Manor 141, 201
Trengwainton 141, 201
Trereife 111, 141–2
Trevithick, Richard 135–7, 164, 183, 215
Trewidden 141, 200
Truro 36–7, 53, 57, 83, 96, 140, 165, 180, 217–18
Victoria, Queen 158–9, 177, 180, 217–18
Voundervour Lane 170, 186
Warbeck, Perkin 48–9
Wellington Terrace 168
Wesley, Charles 120
Wesley, John 119–23
Wesley Rock Chapel 172
Western Green 12, 26, 68, 133, 151, 154, 160
Wherrytown 80, 127
Wherry Mine 126–7, 140
William of Worcester 50
York House 141, 213